CW01500528

I dedicate this book to my grandfather, Radivoj Todoreskov, who passed away before I had the chance to finish it. Nobody believed in me more than you did. My heart always sinks when I remember that you're gone.

You are irreplaceable, unforgettable and forever in my heart.

Digesting Femininities

Natalie Jovanovski

Digesting Femininities

The Feminist Politics of Contemporary
Food Culture

Natalie Jovanovski
Swinburne University of Technology
Melbourne, Victoria, Australia

ISBN 978-3-319-86510-2   ISBN 978-3-319-58925-1   (eBook)
DOI 10.1007/978-3-319-58925-1

This Palgrave Macmillan imprint is published by Springer Nature
The registered company is Springer International Publishing AG
The registered company address is: Gewerbestrasse 11, 6330 Cham, Switzerland

ACKNOWLEDGEMENTS

There are so many people to thank who supported me behind the scenes during the writing of this book. Firstly, I would like to thank the team at Palgrave Macmillan, and specifically Alexis Nelson and Kyra Saniewski, for giving me the opportunity to write this book and share it with the world.

I also send a big, warm thank you to everyone in my family and to all my friends for being a constant source of support during the often stressful writing and editing process. I'd like to especially thank my mother, Mira, and father, Slobodan, who selflessly loved and fed me when I suffered from writer's block, and to my best friend and brother, Miroslav, who kept me sane when I was at my most stressed. (He refused to read my manuscript because he's lazy, but I still love him.)

To my friends and colleagues, a big thank you for your love and patience. Especially to Melanie Thomas and Associate Professor Julie Stephens, who painstakingly read my draft and encouraged me to do my best throughout the process. Also, a big thanks to Maria Iuscu and Vicki Koukos who made me laugh and forget about my deadlines.

I would also like to thank the anonymous radical feminist activists and artists who regularly covered Melbourne in messages and slogans of sisterhood and inspiration, and for claiming the city as a space for women. Every little message and act of rebellion counted.

And last, but definitely not the least, I'd like to extend my greatest thanks to Dr. Meagan Tyler. Not only did she encourage me to get my book published, but she believed in me and showered me with ongoing kindness and support. I am forever thankful for all that she has done for me.

CONTENTS

CHAPTER 1

Digesting Femininities: Gendered Food Discourses and Body-Policing Narratives

The relationship women have with food, eating and their bodies is a topic of intense public interest, filling psychology journals and wallpapering magazine stands. Curiously, what is less often discussed by mainstream and academic sources are the cultural messages about food and eating that surround women, promoting confusing, and often conflicting, narratives that promise answers, but leave women with further questions. From the meteoric rise of celebrity cooks and their reclamation of all things domestic, to the stream of ever-changing diets reinforced by reality TV health experts, the gendered marketing of food is an undeniably powerful discourse that reflects tensions about how women relate to food in their everyday lives and, indeed, how they fall short of reaching certain ideals. But what happens when these rich narratives about food and eating, which dominate bookshelves and the world of television, emphatically promote messages about a woman's right to hedonism and indulgence with just a pinch of self-consciousness thrown in? Indeed, what does it mean when this form of oppressive gendered socialisation around food and eating is rebranded as a feminist pursuit? And what is the function of presenting femininity, and the sexist expectations that women face around food, eating and their bodies, as a veritable smorgasbord of marketable identities ready to be freely chosen? In this book, I address these questions by examining the way that gendered discourses on food and eating reinforce body-policing cultural narratives aimed at women. Specifically, I focus on how the advice given to women about food and eating in influential food discourses, such as diet books, cookbooks and iconic feminist texts, is founded upon

© The Author(s) 2017
N. Jovanovski, *Digesting Femininities*,
DOI 10.1007/978-3-319-58925-1_1

1

gender stereotypes that instantiate and normalise how women police their own bodies and the pleasure they receive from food. The way that women police their bodies and, indeed, objectify themselves, is intimately tied to notions of gender. Over the last four decades, feminist writers and scholars have problematised the practice of self-objectification, or the process of judging one's body as an object to be evaluated, and acknowledged the importance of locating and theorising the cultural origins of women's obsession with body-policing practices (Bartky 1990; Fredrickson et al. 1998; McKinley and Hyde 1996). This body of research has implicated the harmful role that fashion and beauty discourses play in the practice of self-objectification, and linked these practices to the development of 'disordered' eating (Ahern et al. 2011; Grogan 2008). Yet these approaches, while generating a significant and influential body of literature explaining, at least partially, where women's conflicted relationships with their bodies originate, have been largely body-centric, focusing on how the size and shape of the female body is depicted in the media and overlooking the power of other significant discourses in perpetuating harmful self-objectifying messages (Malson 2009, p. 135; Probyn 2008). Despite the strong association between women policing their bodies and simultaneously displaying 'disordered' eating behaviour (Tiggemann 2013), very few studies have addressed the role that gendered discourses on food and eating and previous feminist analyses of women's relationships to food, play in the reinforcement of women's body-policing narratives. In this book, I take up the task of examining these gendered discourses on food and eating, for the myriad of ways harmful body-conscious narratives are constructed and reproduced. Indeed, I argue that this culture is even permeated in popular texts informed by feminist understandings, where body-policing is reinforced as an individual responsibility rather than challenged at a broad cultural level. In essence, women are given seemingly different versions of femininity to digest in food discourses that may not always be as palatable as they seem.

Being critical of one's body, and imposing a rigid level of surveillance over it, is considered to be both normative and problematic behaviour for women in contemporary Western culture (Bartky 1990; Rodin et al. 1984; Wolf 1990). Despite an increase in public awareness over the dangers of extreme weight loss and yo-yo dieting, women are encouraged more than ever to strive for an ideal feminine aesthetic, a look often defined by a slim and sometimes athletic-looking body (Bordo 2004; Grogan 2008). While fashion, beauty and fitness discourses encourage women to adopt a leaner and supposedly healthier body weight through various dietary and surgical methods (Murray 2008), a growing medical and psychological consensus problematises women's perceived choices to engage in these behaviours (Orbach 2010). This conflicting mixture of views has, unsurprisingly, generated confusion among women regarding how to perceive their bodies, underlying the importance of understanding how body-policing narratives are culturally determined rather than simply individually mediated (Popa 2012).

Influential feminist writers, including Sandra Lee Bartky (1990), Susan Bordo (2004) and Susie Orbach (2010), have played a seminal role in understanding the cultural origins of why women police their bodies. They conceptualise women's dissatisfaction with, and surveillance over, their bodies as a sign of patriarchal oppression, an exaggerated expression of femininity, and as an inevitable result of the cultural objectification of the female body. Bartky (1990), for example, describes the objectification of the female body as a process where a woman's "sexual parts or sexual functions are separated out from the rest of her personality and reduced to the status of mere instruments or else regarded as if they were capable of representing her" (p. 26). One of the harmful features of the cultural objectification of women's bodies is the tendency to see one's body through a critical, outsider's perspective (Jack 1993). In psychological literature, this phenomenon is referred to as both self-objectification (Fredrickson et al. 1998) and objectified body-consciousness (McKinley and Hyde 1996). While self-objectifying attitudes and behaviours play a central role in the representation of women in popular culture (Bordo 2004; Jeffreys 2005; Piran and Cormier 2005), they have also been associated with a host of detrimental physical and psychological outcomes. One of these outcomes is a conflicted and sometimes disordered relationship with food (see Tiggemann 2013). In this book, the self-objectification, objectified body-consciousness or body-policing that women experience as part of their normative and yet problematic socialisation into femininity will be described through the interrelated use of the terms 'self-objectification,' 'body-consciousness,' 'self-policing' and 'body-policing.'

The self-policing quest for an ideal body is one that often compromises women's relationships with food and eating (Bordo 2004; Grogan 2008). Throughout the last two decades, both correlational and causative links have been found between self-objectifying attitudes and disordered eating behaviours in women (see Tiggemann 2013). Psychological researchers have identified these links in non-clinical samples of women (Vinkers et al. 2012), affecting women of all ages (Augustus-Horvath and Tylka 2009; Grippo and Hill 2008), ethnicities (Fitzsimmons-Craft and Bardone-Cone 2012; Hebl et al. 2004) and sexual orientations (Hill and Fischer 2008). One factor that occurs resoundingly across these studies is that self-objectifying behaviours are a part of mainstream Western culture, and not just confined to clinical samples of women (Tiggemann 2013). Generated by a host of socialisation practices and proscriptions to feminine beauty ideals, women are said to be taught that their self-surveillance practices are merely a normative part of being female (Bartky 1990). There has been a growing interest in feminist and psychological theory in the power of cultural discourses that promote a thin bodily aesthetic and disordered relationship with food (Bordo 2004; Grogan 2008; Harper and Tiggemann 2008). Psychological and feminist studies implicate fashion and beauty discourses for their construction of a poor body image in women (Prichard and Tiggemann 2012; Tiggemann et al. 2009; Wilson 2005; Young 2005). Some of these studies call for the diversification of representations of the female body in the media and address just one aspect of the body-policing society women live in, failing to identify the power of other and, perhaps, less obvious discourses in instantiating this harmful message (Malson 2009, p. 135; see Probyn 2008). In *Digesting Femininities*, I take up the task of filling the gap in the current literature by examining alternative cultural discourses for different ways that body-surveillance messages are normalised and perpetuated.

The choice to centre this project on food and eating-related discourses comes from the growing popularity of guidance-based, or 'self-help' content directed towards women in relation to food and the construction of gender more generally (Winch 2011). Currently, a thriving and profitable culture of food and eating has occupied Western media, branching off into multiple and seemingly disparate genres with neoliberal underpinnings (Miller 2007). This culture of food and eating has offered women new ways to connect to food in times where confusing messages about women's entitlement to consume has been paramount, be it through cooking (Greer 1999; Neuhaus 1999), nourishing the body via diet and exercise (Heyes 2006; Coleman 2010) or through understanding the political origins behind why women binge or restrict their food intake. The success of these discourses stems in part from the contradictions and complexities that surround women's relationships with food, contributing to a range of food femininities, or gendered ways of relating to food, for women to 'choose' from. While gendered narratives on food and eating remain popular among women, however, their failure to provide any coherent advice on how women should relate to food and eating has exacerbated the confusion that already defines women's relationships with food. Rather, these seemingly conflicting texts have both marketed and offered women a smorgasbord of food femininities to choose from, and left them with the paralysing task of being a responsible, knowledgeable and empowered consumer in a cultural landscape that produces often harmful and conflicting messages (Popa 2012).

It is this notion that popular food discourses are sites of gendered meaning and, potentially, the site of harmful gender norms that underpins this book. The concept of 'food femininities,' that is, the multiple versions of gender offered to women throughout cultural discourses about food and eating, will be used to describe the many different ways in which the authors of cookbooks, diet books and iconic feminist texts instantiate and reproduce harmful gender stereotypes by using food as a mouthpiece. Specifically, this book focuses on how these different food femininities, which frame discourses on food and eating, promote harmful self-objectifying attitudes in women, and how they are marketed to women in a variety of forms to make otherwise harmful gender norms seem more culturally palatable. While the term food femininities was originally used by Cairns et al. (2010) in their study on the gendering of foodie culture, where they identified the various ways in which people 'do' gender through their relationships with food, in this book, the term food femininities is used to focus on the oppressive or harmful gender stereotypes that define women's conflicted relationships with food and their bodies.

A feminist understanding of discourse, one that acknowledges the social construction of gender and the ways in which power and hegemony operate throughout language, is of central concern in this book (Haslanger 2002; Lazar 2004; Malson 2009; Weedon 1997). The analysis of food and eating-related discourses in this book is therefore informed by feminist understandings of discourse as a patriarchal tool. According to Lazar (2004), the term discourse can be understood as the "complex workings of power and ideology... [that] sustain[s] gendered social order" (p. 1). Writers devoted to using feminist ideas in their research associate the notion of gender as being reconstructed and perpetuated in language, and as something that takes shape through language in a multitude of ways. This is especially so for feminist writers who deal with women's conflicted relationships with food and their bodies (e.g., Burns and Gavey 2004; Malson 2009). The way gender is used in food and eating-related discourses aimed at women is, thus, important to understand.

One feature that distinguishes feminist understandings of discourse from other, non-feminist epistemological positions is the emphasis on patriarchy as a powerful driving force behind language (Bartky 1990). According to Speer (2005), language is "one of the primary means through which patriarchy and oppressive norms... instantiate and reproduce" (p. 7) gender inequalities, and this is often reflected in everyday talk or text. While a great deal of attention has been paid to cultural discourses that display and promote an emaciated body shape in women, such as fashion and beauty discourses (e.g., Prichard and Tiggemann 2012; Tiggemann et al. 2009; Wilson 2005; Young 2005), relatively little has been said about the way that food discourses operate through a gendered narrative to achieve a similar outcome. In this book, a feminist understanding of discourse, as a place where gender is positioned in a multitude of ways, is used to uncover how discussions of food ultimately centre women's anxieties about their bodies.

Understanding the power of language in perpetuating the social construction of gender and, indeed, the expectation that food discourses are a celebratory feature in women's lives is an important component of understanding how gender is constructed and reproduced in discussions of food and eating. Gender, in this book, is both a site in which patriarchal social structures demarcate the sexes and position women as a subordinate social class, and a way to market pseudo-feminist messages of empowerment (Baxter 2007; Lazar 2004; Speer 2005; Weedon 1997). Indeed, gender is a political phenomenon that operates discursively and often expresses itself through a multitude of seemingly distinct guises. These versions of gender can be malleable and, thus, subject to change through acts of resistance (Lazar 2004; Weedon 1997, p. 121). In this project, the discursive construction and perpetuation of gender is addressed through the various food femininities identified in the texts, that is, through the gendered ways that authors position women's relationships with food and their bodies. The multiple food femininities that I identify in this book indicate the multiple ways that gendered subordination is marketed to women in food discourses, offering what initially seems like a veritable smorgasbord of food femininities for women to 'choose' from. These stereotypes of women form the basis of the feminist critical discourse analysis that will be conducted on the data (see Chap. 2), where it is posited that multiple food femininities in gendered discourses on food and eating in diet books, cookbooks and iconic feminist texts result in the continued perpetuation and normalisation of body-policing practices in women.

DEVELOPMENT OF THE PROJECT

Digesting Femininities was originally conceived from my interest in the body-surveillance practices of women and the way in which this phenomenon has been reinforced and even normalised throughout popular cultural discourses as an unspoken feature of being female. Influenced by both feminist (Bartky 1990; Bordo 2004; Dworkin 1974) and psychological writers (e.g., Fredrickson et al. 1998; McKinley and Hyde 1996; Tiggemann 2013) who position self-objectification as a harmful gendered practice, I became increasingly interested in the way women are oppressed through everyday cultural messages found in the media, and the way in which the cultural perception of the 'oppressor' has shifted from being part of a male-supremacist culture (Dworkin 1974; MacKinnon 1989) to the internal state of women themselves in contemporary Western society (Bartky 1990; Rodin et al. 1984). As a young woman who is part of a contemporary Western society, I was particularly interested in the way mainstream cultural discourses promote the idea that femininity is an identity to be worked on rather than an oppressive feature of being female, and how they use certain gendered objects to convey this message (see Watkins 2006).

While studying the harmful influence of the media on women's normative fixation with policing their bodies, I noticed that an overwhelming number of feminist studies were focused on the notion that women's problems stemmed from the influence of emaciated supermodels and celebrities, and the lack of plus-sized examples of female beauty (Prichard and Tiggemann 2012; Tiggemann et al. 2009; Wilson 2005; Young 2005). These studies, while raising some important questions on the current status of women's relationships with their bodies, tended to position the female body as a fixed rather than a fluid cultural object, as being powerful enough to perpetuate harmful attitudes towards the body (Probyn 2008). While I noted the importance of these discussions, this literature left me wondering if other cultural discourses were also implicated in the Western woman's obsession with body surveillance. I aligned my argument with Elspeth Probyn's (2008) assertion on the current state of feminist research, where she states that, "it's hard to believe that 30 years of quite sophisticated theoretical and methodological debates within feminism are now reduced to complaints about the lack of images of 'plus-sized' women or to the outcry at the emaciated state of catwalk models" (p. 403). Indeed, looking beyond the superficial contours of the body in popular culture, and delving into the language that reinforces messages of body-anxiety in women, eventually became the primary focus of the book.

The direction that I decided to take was based, in part, on Helen Malson's (2009) assertion that a "bizarre" (p. 135) lack of academic research currently implicates discourses other than those of fashion and beauty to women's dissatisfaction with, and surveillance over, their bodies. Taking into account the significant body of psychological research making strong links between self-objectification practices and disordered eating behaviours among women (see Tiggemann 2013), I wanted to understand if popular discourses on food and eating played a role in perpetuating self-objectifying attitudes among women. Drawing on the feminist literature addressing women's relationships with food (Probyn 2000), feeding (Cairns et al. 2010) and eating (Orbach 2010), it became clear that women's relationships with food were just as significant as indicators of their gendered socialisation as were the messages about their bodies. I was curious to find out if the gendered way that food and eating were discussed in certain parts of mainstream Western culture played a part in furthering the gendered obsession with body-policing practices. The importance of food as both a symbol of women's subordination *and* resistance to gender stereotyping was impossible to ignore. As a result, the central question underpinning this book is as follows: How do discourses on food and eating employ gender stereotypes to construct and perpetuate a culture of body-policing attitudes among women?

To answer this question, the book became a feminist critique of gendered discourses on food and eating and, specifically, on the role of cookbooks, diet books and influential feminist texts in perpetuating a culture of body surveillance among women. Lazar's (2004) Feminist Critical Discourse Analysis was used as a way to analyse the primary source material, where food femininities were identified and scrutinised on the basis of what they really offered their female readers. Extending on radical feminist understandings of femininity, which positions women as a subordinate social class, this book used evidence of the gendered construction of food and eating and, specifically, on how different types of femininity (or food femininities) are offered to women that serve to instantiate and reproduce harmful body-policing narratives.

The choice of texts used in the book reflects the popularity of the authors and the influential status of their work (for a more nuanced discussion on the background of the texts studied, please refer to Chaps. 3, 4 and 5). Cookbooks and diet books were used, as data were based on their current popularity in contemporary Western culture (Orbach 2010). Both culinary and dietary books have been used by women as helpful guides, promising to quell anxieties about their eating behaviours and, simultaneously, reinforcing certain gender identities (Winch 2011). Cookbooks, in particular, have been associated with socialising women into feminine practices, such as domesticity and nurturing (Neuhaus 1999). The cookbooks selected for this book were written by female celebrities currently occupying the mainstream culinary arena (Mitchell 2010; Scholes 2011). These authors were examined for the expression of their food femininities, which they reinforced through various versions of food femininity for the female reader to choose from. Two international authors, Nigella Lawson and Tana Ramsay, were selected on the basis of their mainstream media exposure, with Lawson known worldwide for her sultry, yet domesticated, public persona (Hollows 2003), and Ramsay known for her television cooking shows in the UK and her well-publicised marriage to celebrity chef, Gordon Ramsay (Lawson 2011). The two Australian authors, Julie Goodwin and Poh Ling-Yeow, were selected for similar reasons, that is, their participation on the first series of *MasterChef Australia*, which has cemented their place in both magazine columns and television cooking programmes.

The decision to analyse diet books was based on similar reasoning. While diet culture has been steadily criticised by both mainstream and feminist sources over the last three decades, it is still backed by a lucrative and financially successful industry (Drew 2009; Orbach 2010). The role that diet books play in the contemporary arena has changed to include more self-empowering perspectives, with women being offered supposedly agentic (rather than victimised) versions of femininity relating to food and their bodies (Coleman 2010; Heyes 2006; Winch 2011). This cultural shift in the construction of women from passive victims to active agents of their lives has led to changes in the way diet books have been marketed to women. The four diet books analysed in this book were, thus, selected due to their widespread popularity and also the 'empowered' ways in which they were marketed to appeal to female audiences. Rather than focusing on the diets themselves, I was more interested in selecting books on the basis of the authors and the celebrity status they hold. The two international diet books, *Skinny Bitch* and *Skinny Bitch in the Kitch*, were chosen on the basis of their popularity amongst female celebrities, such as Victoria 'Posh Spice' Beckham (Moskin 2008; Rich 2007). The two Australian diet books, *Losing the Last Five Kilos* and *Crunch Time*

Cookbook, were chosen due to the popularity of their author, television fitness trainer Michelle Bridges, who has become a household name through her involvement in the Australian series of the weight-loss reality programme *The Biggest Loser*.

While diet books and cookbooks seemed like obvious discourses to study, as both sources—albeit distinctively—occupy an important place in women's cultural relationships with food and eating, the choice to analyse influential feminist texts as data was motivated by different factors. One factor was that in both academic literature on contemporary cookbooks and diet books and in the books themselves, feminist terminology is used to express the message. This overlap has been met with scepticism among some writers, including myself (Winch 2011). Rather than assuming that these sources have always misused feminist understandings of women's relationships with food and their bodies, I question whether influential feminist texts themselves contain elements of harmful gender practices that normalise body-policing practices in women. Two iconic feminists were used in the book, both known for their influential perspectives of women's disordered relationships with food and their bodies (Bordo 2004). Firstly, feminist psychotherapist Susie Orbach and the 2006 edition of her groundbreaking analysis *Fat is a Feminist Issue* are examined in this book. The second iconic feminist text under investigation is Naomi Wolf's seminal piece *The Beauty Myth*. Both of these texts are examined for the versions of food femininity they offer to women, and whether these gendered constructions reinforce a pervasive cultural attitude that positions women's relationships with food and eating from a body-policing perspective.

Overview

Chapter 2 looks at the way existing feminist literature has been dominated by research of the effects of the fashion and beauty industries on women's obsessive surveillance over their bodies. Specifically, a review of this literature will draw attention to the body-centrism dominating understandings of self-objectification and disordered eating, and the need to study alternative discourses for their potentially harmful contributions. Once this literature is reviewed, a rationale for focusing on food and eating-related discourses is provided, where feminist analyses of cookbooks, diet books and iconic feminist texts are discussed. Chapter 3, then, provides a defence for the study of food and eating-related discourses by describing the use-fulness of Lazar's (2004) Feminist Critical Discourse Analysis as a meth-odological framework. In this chapter, definitions of discourse, femininity and the emancipatory potential for analysing gendered discourses on food and eating will be discussed from a radical feminist perspective.

Chapter 4 offers an analysis of the body-policing culture constructed in best-selling diet books and diet cookbooks written by women. Two diet books and their corresponding diet cookbooks (e.g., Bridges 2010, 2011; Freedman and Barnouin 2005, 2007) are analysed, with a specific emphasis on the food femininities they promote. Drawing on analyses from Chap. 2, it is argued that body-policing narratives around food and eating will not only be dictated upon through culinary practices, but also perpetuated in the advice given to women about their health and eating behaviour. It is posited in this chapter that the versions of food femininity offered to women rely on an element of feminist terminology that posi-tions women as active subjects rather than passive objects. Post-feminist and liberal-individualist constructions of femininity are examined, with an emphasis on how confusing roles around food and eating create a nar-rative of self-objectification for women. It is concluded in this chapter that the influence of diet books on women's body-policing attitudes is mediated by both post-feminist and liberal-individualist versions of food femininity, meaning that they perpetuate an individualistic narrative of personal choice and agency from a depoliticised and supposedly empow-ering perspective.

Chapter 5 builds upon the arguments put forth in the previous chapter, where popular cookbooks written by female food celebrities are examined for their gendered promotion of body-policing practices among women. Two Australian (e.g., Goodwin 2011; Ling-Yeow 2010) and three interna-tional cookbooks (e.g., Lawson 2006; Ramsay 2009, 2010) will be exam-ined for the food femininities their authors promote. This chapter identifies two dominant versions of food femininity, one traditional (maternal food femininities) and one contemporary (hedonistic food femininities), and how the conflict between these two food narratives reveals an implicit mes-sage of self-objectification. It is posited in this chapter that in cookbooks, body-policing practices thrive in women's changing gender roles around food, which have clashed between the selfless, other-oriented stereotype of the traditional feeder (Greer 1999) and the promising, pleasure-oriented stereotype of the contemporary eater (Popa 2012). It is concluded that the food femininities constructed and perpetuated in cookbooks reflect elements of body-policing narratives that may be explained by the changing gender roles ascribed to women about food and cooking.

Having established that both diet books and cookbooks are founded upon harmful gender stereotypes that instantiate self-objectifying attitudes among women, Chap. 6 looks at the influence of iconic feminist texts in doing the same. In this chapter, Susie Orbach's *Fat is a Feminist Issue* and Naomi Wolf's *The Beauty Myth* are analysed for the food femininities they offer their female audience. Drawing on analyses from the previous two chapters, I argue in this chapter that even iconic feminist voices, which criticise gender and deconstruct women's conflicting relationships with food and their bodies, are also responsible for perpetuating body-policing narratives through their discussions of food and eating. It is concluded that iconic feminist voices present a politicisation of women's self-objectifying relationships with food, but rely on an individual woman to change her mindset. It is argued that this conflicting message has played a part in infiltrating current discourses on food and eating that use feminist terminology to create change.

Chapter 7 brings the three analyses together and acknowledges the similarities and differences between their messages. Drawing on analyses from the previous chapters, this chapter illustrates that all three genres, despite their seemingly disparate messages, reinforce a harmful narrative of body policing that can be viewed as a pathogenic or bulimic cultural consciousness of food and eating (Bordo 2004; Malson 2009; Popa 2012). I argue in this chapter that the patriarchal confines of gender reinforce women's relationships with food, which are reflected in their obsessive surveillance over their bodies, and that the fragmentation of food femininities further complicates the process as women are given the illusion of choice, despite their uniform reinforcement of body policing. This chapter also illustrates how women are offered supposedly resistant versions of food femininities and how these narratives mask the neoliberal intentions of these discourses, and how exposure to body-policing practices is framed as an inevitable part of being a female in contemporary Western culture. It is concluded that popular discourses on food and eating play a critical role in instantiating body-policing narratives among women, and that the investigation of how food and eating are constructed in popular culture indicates that radical social change belongs in challenging this culture, not the perceived choices individual women may make.

REFERENCES

Ahern, A. L., Bennett, K. M., & Hetherington, M. M. (2011). A qualitative exploration of young women's attitudes towards the thin ideal. *Journal of Health Psychology, 16*(1), 70–79.

Augustus-Horvath, C. L., & Tylka, T. L. (2009). A test and extension of objectification theory as it predicts disordered eating: Does women's age matter? *Journal of Counselling Psychology, 56*(2), 253–265.

Bartky, S. L. (1990). *Femininity and domination: Studies in the phenomenology of oppression.* New York: Routledge/Taylor & Francis Group.

Baxter, J. (2007). *Positioning gender in discourse: A feminist methodology.* Basingstoke: Palgrave Macmillan.

Bordo, S. (2004). *Unbearable weight: Feminism, Western culture, and the body.* Berkeley: University of California Press.

Bridges, M. (2010). *Crunch time cookbook: 100 knockout recipes for rapid weight loss.* Melbourne: Penguin Books.

Bridges, M. (2011). *Losing the last 5 kilos: Your kick-arse guide to looking and feeling fantastic.* Melbourne: Penguin Books.

Burns, M., & Gavey, N. (2004). 'Healthy weight' at what cost? 'Bulimia' and a discourse of weight control. *Journal of Health Psychology, 9*(4), 549–565.

Cairns, K., Johnston, J., & Baumann, S. (2010). Caring about food: Doing gender in the foodie kitchen. *Gender and Society, 24*(5), 591–615.

Coleman, R. (2010). Dieting temporalities: Interaction, agency and the measure of online weight watching. *Time Society, 19*(2), 265–285.

Drew, P. (2009). Dieting. In J. O'Brien (Ed.), *Encyclopaedia of gender and society* (Vol. 1). London: Sage.

Dworkin, A. (1974). *Woman hating: A radical look at sexuality.* New York: E. P. Dutton.

Fitzsimmons-Craft, E. B., & Bardone-Cone, A. M. (2012). Examining prospective mediation models of body surveillance, trait anxiety, and body dissatisfaction in African American and Caucasian college women. *Sex Roles, 67*(3–4), 187–200.

Fredrickson, B. L., Roberts, T.-A., Noll, S. M., Quinn, D. M., & Twenge, J. M. (1998). That swimsuit becomes you: Sex differences in self-objectification, restrained eating, and math performance. *Journal of Personality and Social Psychology, 75*(1), 269–284.

Freedman, R., & Barnouin, K. (2005). *Skinny bitch: A no-nonsense, tough-love guide for savvy girls who want to stop eating crap and start looking fabulous!* Philadelphia: Running Press.

Freedman, R., & Barnouin, K. (2007). *Skinny bitch in the kitch: Kick-ass recipes for hungry girls who want to stop cooking crap (and start looking hot!).* Philadelphia: Running Press.

Goodwin, J. (2011). *The heart of the home.* North Sydney: Random House.

Greer, G. (1999). *The whole woman*. London: Doubleday.

Grippo, K. P., & Hill, M. S. (2008). Self-objectification, habitual body monitoring, and body dissatisfaction in older European American women: Exploring age and feminism as moderators. *Body Image, 5*(2), 173–182.

Grogan, S. (2008). *Body image: Understanding body dissatisfaction in men, women, and children*. New York: Routledge.

Harper, B., & Tiggemann, M. (2008). The effect of thin ideal media images on women's self-objectification, mood, and body image. *Sex Roles, 58*, 649–657.

Haslanger, S. (2002). On being objective and being objectified. In L. M. Antony & C. E. Witt (Eds.), *A mind of one's own: Feminist essays on reason and objectivity*. Boulder: Westview Press.

Hebl, M. R., King, E. B., & Lin, J. (2004). The swimsuit becomes us all: Ethnicity, gender, and vulnerability to self-objectification. *Personality and Social Psychology Bulletin, 30*(10), 1322–1331.

Heyes, C. J. (2006). Foucault goes to weight watchers. *Hypatia, 21*(2), 126–149.

Hill, M. S., & Fischer, A. R. (2008). Examining objectification theory: Lesbian and heterosexual women's experiences with sexual- and self-objectification. *Counselling Psychologist, 36*(5), 745–776.

Hollows, J. (2003). Feeling like a domestic goddess: Postfeminism and cooking. *European Journal of Cultural Studies, 6*(2), 179–202.

Jack, D. C. (1993). *Silencing the self: Women and depression*. New York: Harper Perennial.

Jeffreys, S. (2005). *Beauty and misogyny: Harmful cultural practices in the west*. East Sussex: Routledge.

Lawson, N. (2006). *Feast: Food that celebrates life*. London: Chatto & Windus.

Lawson, J. (2011). Food legacies: Playing the culinary feminine. *Women and Performance: A Journal of Feminist Theory, 21*(3), 337–366.

Lazar, M. (2004). *Feminist critical discourse analysis: Gender, power and ideology in discourse*. New York: Palgrave Macmillan.

Ling-Yeow, P. (2010). *Poh's kitchen: My cooking adventures*. Sydney: Harper Collins Publishers.

MacKinnon, C. A. (1989). *Toward a feminist theory of the state*. Cambridge: Harvard University Press.

Malson, H. (2009). Appearing to disappear: Postmodern femininities and self-starved subjectivities. In H. Malson & M. Burns (Eds.), *Critical feminist approaches to eating dis/orders*. London: Routledge, Taylor and Francis Group.

McKinley, N. M., & Hyde, J. S. (1996). The objectified body consciousness scale development and validation. *Psychology of Women Quarterly, 20*(2), 181–215.

Miller, T. (2007). *Cultural citizenship cosmopolitanism, consumerism, and television in a neoliberal age*. Philadelphia: Temple University Press.

Mitchell, C. M. (2010). The rhetoric of celebrity cookbooks. *The Journal of Popular Culture, 43*(3), 524–539.

Moskin, J. (2008). *Still skinny, but now they can cook.* Retrieved from http://www. nytimes.com/2008/01/02/dining/02skin.html?pagewanted=all

Murray, S. (2008). *The 'fat' female body.* London: Palgrave Macmillan.

Neuhaus, J. (1999). The way to a man's heart: Gender roles, domestic ideology, and cookbooks in the 1950s. *Journal of Social History, 32*(3), 529–555.

Orbach, S. (2010). *Bodies.* London: Profile Books.

Piran, N., & Cormier, H. C. (2005). The social construction of women and disordered eating patterns. *Journal of Counselling Psychology, 52*(4), 549–558.

Popa, T. (2012). Eating disorders in a hyper-consumerist and post-feminist context. *Scientific Journal of Humanistic Studies, 4*(7), 162–166.

Prichard, I., & Tiggemann, M. (2012). The effect of simultaneous exercise and exposure to thin-ideal music videos on women's state self-objectification, mood and body satisfaction. *Sex Roles, 67*(3–4), 201–210.

Probyn, E. (2000). *Carnal appetites: FoodSexIdentities.* London: Routledge.

Probyn, E. (2008). IV. Silences behind the mantra: Critiquing feminist fat. *Feminism and Psychology, 18*(3), 401–404.

Ramsay, T. (2009). *Tana Ramsay's real family food.* Hammersmith: Harper Collins Publishers.

Ramsay, T. (2010). *Tana's kitchen secrets.* London: Mitchell Beazley.

Rich, M. (2007). *A diet book serves up a side order of attitude.* Retrieved from http://www.nytimes.com/2007/08/01/books/01skin.html?pagewanted=all

Rodin, J., Silberstein, L., & Striegel-Moore, R. (1984). Women and weight: A normative discontent. *Nebraska Symposium on Motivation, 32*, 267–307.

Scholes, L. (2011). A slave to the stove? The TV celebrity chef abandons the kitchen: Lifestyle TV, domesticity and gender. *Critical Quarterly, 53*(3), 44–59.

Speer, S. A. (2005). *Gender talk: Feminism, discourse and conversation analysis.* East Sussex: Routledge.

Tiggemann, M. (2013). Objectification theory: Of relevance for eating disorder researchers and clinicians. *Clinical Psychologist, 17*(2), 35–45.

Tiggemann, M., Polivy, J., & Hargreaves, D. (2009). The processing of thin ideals in fashion magazines: A source of social comparison or fantasy? *Journal of Social and Clinical Psychology, 28*(1), 73–93.

Vinkers, C. D. W., Evers, C., Adriaanse, M. A., & de Ridder, D. T. D. (2012). Body esteem and eating disorder symptomatology: The mediating role of appearance-motivated exercise in a non-clinical adult female sample. *Eating Behaviours, 13*(3), 214–218.

Watkins, H. (2006). Beauty queens, bulletin board and browser: Rescripting the refrigerator. *Gender, Place & Culture, 13*(2), 143–152.

Weedon, C. (1997). *Feminist practice and poststructuralist theory* (2nd ed.). Oxford: Blackwell Publishers.

Wilson, N. (2005). Vilifying former fatties: Media representations of weight loss surgery. *Feminist Media Studies, 5*(2), 252–255.

Winch, A. (2011). 'Your new smart-mouthed girlfriends': Postfeminist conduct books. *Journal of Gender Studies, 20*(4), 359–370.

Wolf, N. (1990). *The beauty myth: How images of beauty are used against women.* London: Vintage.

Young, M. (2005). One size fits all: Disrupting the commercialised, pathologised, fat female form. *Feminist Media Studies, 5*(2), 249–252.

CHAPTER 2

Beyond Body-Centrism: Making Food Discourses the Main Course of Feminist Analysis

In a contemporary Western context, it has become virtually impossible to flick through a magazine, watch a TV show or navigate the online world of social media without coming across some reference to why our bodies are imperfect and our food choices are wrong. In response to these ongoing cultural narratives, feminist and psychological researchers over the last four decades have focused their attention on the cultural narratives that reinforce messages of body-consciousness and surveillance in women and tried to understand how culture influences individual women's behaviour, especially around food and eating. While the existent literature on the strength of cultural discourses has been powerful in its politicisation of women's dysfunctional relationships with food and their bodies (Tiggemann 2013), especially in reference to the impact of fashion and beauty discourses, what is often overlooked is the potentially damaging way(s) that women are socialised to relate to food. To get a greater understanding of the significance of food discourses and their capacity to reproduce and perpetuate narratives of body anxiety in women, this chapter will examine how the feminist and psychological literature has discussed women's relationships with food and their perceptions of their bodies. This chapter will discuss how psychological and feminist researchers have constructed what I call a body-centric understanding of women's surveillance over their bodies, and how both approaches fail to acknowledge sufficiently the importance of influential food discourses in perpetuating these messages. I will also provide an overview of the various feminist approaches to the study of

© The Author(s) 2017
N. Jovanovski, *Digesting Femininities*,
DOI 10.1007/978-3-319-58925-1_2

food and eating, with a specific focus on the notion of dieting, cooking and eating disorders. In reviewing this literature, I point out that there is a major gap in the way that researchers have looked at food discourses thus far, and the potential of food discourses to perpetuate regressive narratives about the body to women.

BODY POLICING AS GENDERED SOCIALISATION

The idea of 'body policing' plays a central role to the arguments presented in this book, especially in reference to feminist discussions about women's cultural subordination, and to the notion that body policing is a central component of being socialised into womanhood. Despite being manifested in the attitudes and behaviours of the individual, it is useful to consider body-surveillance practices as symptoms of a pathogenic culture (Bordo 2004; see Malson 2009, pp. 135–138). The feminist literature indicates that body-policing practices in women can be traced back to a range of sociocultural factors, one factor being the cultural sexual objectification of the female body (Bartky 1990; Bordo 2004; Fredrickson and Roberts 1997; Harper and Tiggemann 2008; Jeffreys 2005; McKinley and Hyde 1996). Fredrickson and Roberts (1997, p. 174) describe 'sexual objectification' as "the experience of being treated as a body (or collection of body parts) valued predominantly for its use (or consumption by) others." As a harmful gendered phenomenon, sexual objectification is widely attributed to the patriarchal, or 'male supremacist', structure of culture, where women are said to be harmed through their treatment as sex objects and taught that their bodies are a constant work in progress (Bartky 1990; Bordo 2004; Dworkin 1974; Fredrickson and Roberts 1997; Jeffreys 2005; McKinley and Hyde 1996; MacKinnon 1989; Wolf 1990).

Radical feminist research is credited with first associating sexual objectification with male supremacy. In her radical feminist treatise *Woman Hating*, for example, Andrea Dworkin (1974) identifies the sexual objectification of women in cultural discourses, such as pornography and beauty magazines. Dworkin argues that these examples are evidence of women's subordinated cultural status, and that the more a woman is sexualised and viewed for her body parts rather than her personhood, the more she is dehumanised and treated as chattel. Radical feminist theorist Sheila Jeffreys (2005) echoes these sentiments in her book *Beauty and Misogyny*. She too perceives the sexual objectification of women as an important feature of male-supremacist cultural institutions, and conceptualises fashion and beauty practices as the cultural eroticisation of inequalities between the sexes. Being sexually objectified is seen as an unavoidable part of being female under systems of male domination and is, more or less, normalised in both mainstream cultural discourses and everyday social interactions (Bartky 1990). It is argued that one way women adjust to the unwanted sexual scrutiny of their bodies is by internalising the watchful gaze of patriarchy and subsequently acting on it by conforming to a host of weight-loss or cosmetic practices (Bordo 2004). Feminist and psychological studies, to differing degrees, use radical feminist understandings of sexual objectification to understand how women are subjectively harmed by the male gaze (de Vries and Peter 2013; Fredrickson and Roberts 1997; Fredrickson et al. 1998; McKinley and Hyde 1996). Instead of understanding body policing as a normative part of being female, writers such as Bartky (1990) and Bordo (2004) perceive objectification as a form of gendered psychological oppression. In her seminal text *Femininity and Domination*, Sandra Lee Bartky (1990) argues that, through the repeated objectification of their bodies, women internalise the male gaze and punitively judge their bodies in a futile effort to cope with the demands it sets for them. In a fitting personal example, Bartky (1990) demonstrates how the cultural sexual objectification of her own body led to her internalisation of the male gaze:

> It is a fine spring day, and with an utter lack of self-consciousness, I am bouncing down the street. Suddenly I hear men's voices. Catcalls and whistles fill the air. These noises are clearly sexual in intent and they are meant for me; they come from across the street. I freeze. As Sartre would say, I have been petrified by the gaze of the Other. My face flushes and my motions become stiff and self-conscious. The body which only a moment before I inhabited with such ease now floods my consciousness. I have been made into an object (p. 27).

Enacted in a street harassment context, Bartky's (1990, p. 27) example of being "made into an object" shows just how the external and unwanted sexual gaze of the Other is internalised to become part of one's own self-monitoring schema. Outside of a face-to-face context, however, the male gaze operates throughout popular cultural discourses to infiltrate body-policing norms in women, norms that have been linked to women's disordered relationships with food and eating (Bartky 1990; Bordo 2004). In this book, the surveillance women cast over their bodies, and the surveillance that social institutions and discourses cast over women's bodies, are referred to as self-objectification, body-consciousness, self-policing and body-policing narratives. Although these terms come from different psychological and feminist sources, their central message of body surveillance (and, in many cases, dissatisfaction) is considered to be of upmost importance in this book, and thus, used interchangeably. Although the terms self-policing and body policing may seem different, I argue against Cartesian dualist approaches that view the body and the self as two different entities. Rather, I perceive the policing of one's body as being inextricable from the policing of oneself.

Psychological and feminist researchers have, over the years, tried to understand why women police their bodies and how this may affect their eating behaviour. The psychological literature focusing on women's anxious relationships with their bodies and on their self-monitoring behaviours has also focused on their dysfunctional relationships with food and the development of eating disorders (Fitzsimmons-Craft and Bardone-Cone 2012; Kroon and Perez 2013; Monro and Huon 2006). A large part of this literature focuses on women's relationships with food and their bodies from a psychopathological or clinical perspective (Harper and Tiggemann 2008; Tiggemann 2013). The feminist literature, however, focuses strongly on sociocultural factors contributing to women's pathological relationships with food and their bodies, such as the influence of the fashion and beauty industries (Brown 2005; Wilson 2005; Wolf 1990). In this literature, the cultural discourse surrounding women is considered, but the focus of investigation remains body-centric, scrutinising discourses of the body at the expense of other, equally influential discourses. I argue that neither the feminist nor the psychological literature has adequately addressed the way food discourses instantiate and normalise body-policing narratives which are aimed at women.

Eating Disorders: Understanding Body Policing Through a Pathologising Lens

One of the greatest limitations of psychological literature understanding women's body-policing practices is the focus on intrapsychic experiences and, specifically, the tendency for individual women to monitor their bodies and their relationships with food. Indeed, many psychological researchers argue that women's body-surveillance practices and their subsequent dissatisfaction with their bodies are inextricably linked to their pathological relationships with food and eating (Diest and Perez 2013; Fitzsimmons-Craft and Bardone-Cone 2012; Monro and Huon 2006). Generally speaking, clinical researchers focus a great deal of attention on the notion of psychopathology and, specifically, the idea that disordered eating patterns arise due to reasons pertaining to the individual, paying little attention to the sociocultural backdrop from which these individuals reside. According to the current *Diagnostic and Statistical Manual of Mental Disorders* (DSM-5; American Psychological Association 2013), eating disorders are characterised by "a persistent disturbance of eating or eating-related behaviour" (p. 329), which impairs both social and occupational functioning. While estimates vary from source to source, it is suggested that prodromal eating disorders, or the period of time where initial symptoms are being presented, affect approximately 35–70% of the population and between 1% and 4% of women clinically (Hoyt and Ross 2003), with the majority of cases affecting women between the ages of 15 and 25. Anorexia and bulimia nervosa are typically the focus of investigation in this literature (Kaye et al. 2000). Anorexia nervosa is characterised by "an inexplicable fear of weight gain and unrelenting obsession with fatness" (Kaye et al. 2000, p. 299). Women with anorexic symptoms are said to exhibit higher-than-average rates of "perfectionism, conformity, obsessionality, constriction of affect and emotional expressiveness, and reduced social spontaneity" (p. 301). Bulimia nervosa, on the other hand, is described as a psychological disorder that involves "binge eating ... followed by either self-induced vomiting or some other means of compensation for the excess of food ingested" (p. 299). Unlike women experiencing anorexia, women with bulimia nervosa tend to "display ... impulse-control problems such as shoplifting and self-injurious behaviours" (p. 301). While both anorexia and bulimia are driven by a multitude of factors that detrimentally influence women's relationships with food and their surveillance of their bodies, psychological researchers largely focus on individual factors that contribute to psychopathology and, in some cases, inadvertently minimise the importance of sociocultural messages that may prompt, mimic or, to varying degrees, reinforce the symptoms of these disorders (Tiggemann 2013).

Over the course of four decades, many psychological researchers have argued that women who exhibit dysfunctional relationships with food and habitually scrutinise and police their bodies are driven by a range of individual factors that predispose them to eating disorder symptoms.

Perhaps contradictorily, the same researchers who question why women police their bodies and food intake also argue that women's body weight and shape must be monitored to ensure treatment efficacy (British Psychological Society 2004; Bruch 1973). Indeed, some researchers advocate for treatment methods that involve focusing on the individual factors driving the dysfunctional relationship with food (and the body), and design treatment plans catering to individuals (Alvarenga et al. 2014; Kaye et al. 2000).

In their article on the aetiological factors behind anorexia and bulimia nervosa, for example, Kaye et al. (2000) argue that women who clinically present with disordered relationships with food and their bodies should be subject to treatment methods that focus on modifying their maladaptive attitudes and behaviours, and place a strong emphasis on the weight and size of women's bodies during the recovery process. In a psychological study conducted by Alvarenga et al. (2014), this is further exemplified when they suggest that women presenting with disordered symptoms required individually tailored psychotherapy that focused on changing emotions, cognitions and behaviours. Indeed, this is one of the central features of recovery in the clinical literature and the focus of many discussions addressing women's uncomfortable relationships with food—the maintenance of a stable body weight (Kaye et al. 2000). While treatment efficacy varies and has not always been successful, the individualised treatment of women is a factor that generates some cause for concern in feminist discussions (Alvarenga et al. 2014; Malson 2009; Malson et al. 2009). Indeed, the strong focus on the individual, and on their genetic predisposition to eating disorders or their cognitive and behavioural patterns, rather than on the *meanings* ascribed to food and the female body, is one of the central criticisms of the traditional psychological approach to understanding women's problematic relationships with food, eating and their bodies (Malson 2009; Malson et al. 2009; Orbach 2006). In emphasising the individual, the psychological literature often overlooks or downplays the idea of larger social, cultural and environmental factors that may play a role in reinforcing these messages. It also places an inordinate amount of attention on the appearance of the female body to indicate successful 'treatment' without questioning their own tendency towards body-centrism.

In their article entitled *Beyond Psychopathology: Interrogating (Dis) Orders of Body Weight and Body Management*, Malson et al. (2009) argue that the psychological literature overlooks the importance of sociocultural factors by focusing too strongly on the individual and their presentation of symptoms. Specifically, they argue that a prevailing neoliberal rhetoric around health and well-being operates behind psychological discourses, where women who police their bodies and relate to food in a pathological way are seen as individuals with problems and unhealthy bodies, rather than individuals who "take on board wider cultural understandings of body, health and identity and make them their own" (p. 334). This distinction is crucial to this book and to subsequent chapters, as cultural discourses are problematised for their promotion of disordered, body-policing narratives. Malson et al. (2009) explain that

> [w]ithin neo-liberal rhetoric "body problems" such as obesity or anorexia are interiorised as individual concerns and methods of converting such problematic bodies into healthy ones are located in changing people's behaviours and attitudes to food and exercise (p. 332).

The individualistic project of psychological interventions overlooks the cultural antecedents of women's conflicted relationships with food and the scrutinising of their bodies. Rather than focusing on individual psychopathology and treatment, a number of feminist researchers have instead focused on the influence of popular cultural discourses in instantiating and normalising harmful body-policing messages to women.

THE DOMINANCE OF FASHION AND BEAUTY CRITIQUES IN FEMINISM

Feminist researchers who question why women police their bodies and subsequently their food intake focus their attention on the sociocultural discourses that reinforce these 'disordered' messages. Sociocultural theory, or a focus on the social and cultural factors operating behind women's anxious relationships with food and eating, is currently seen as the most robust theoretical framework for understanding women's 'disordered' relationships with food and their bodies (Harper and Tiggemann 2008). Sociocultural theory is used by most feminist researchers who question cultural discourses that reinforce, and sometimes promote, body-policing narratives to women. According to Harper and Tiggemann (2008), the sociocultural model provides an overview of the way the media operate to reinforce a (largely) unrealistic thin-ideal to women, an ideal that has its links to pathological eating behaviours. One type of sociocultural discourse that feminist researchers are fixated on is the fashion and beauty discourses, and the role they play in reinforcing harmful and sexist messages to women. Writers such as Bartky (1990), Bordo (2004) and Grogan (2008) argue that the fashion industry's promotion of the thin-ideal contributes to a host of physical and psychological conditions in women, such as eating disorders and body-image disturbance (Diest and Perez 2013; Harper and Tiggemann 2008; Monro and Huon 2006; Morry and Staska 2001). Through the promotion of a 'thinspirational' image of female beauty, one that relies on a size zero or lollypop-shaped body (i.e., where the head of the model appears larger than the emaciated frame of her body), those responsible for producing fashion and beauty discourses are often implicated by feminist researchers to be responsible for women's body-surveillance practices and their related anxiety about food (Ahern et al. 2011).

The feminist and psychological literature on the practice of body policing, thus, focuses strongly on how fashion and beauty discourses construct and perpetuate harmful gender roles through the emaciated and often digitally modified image of the female body. Despite the importance of this literature, I argue that this approach to understanding body-policing practices in women is an example of body-centrism, an approach that I will argue relies too heavily on those who, according to Malson (2009, p. 135), "stand as metonyms of culture," such as "Kate Moss, Victoria Beckham, Gianni Versace or Jean Paul Gaultier," and not enough on the way food can be gendered in popular discourses to reproduce the same harmful messages (Malson 2009; Probyn 2008).

Rather than scrutinising other discourses that may also be responsible for reinforcing women's anxieties about their bodies, feminist and psychological researchers come together in their condemnation of the fashion and beauty industries, and argue for the diversification of female bodies in the media as a solution. These researchers' focus on the sociocultural factors that harm women demonstrates that the images portrayed in fashion and beauty magazines promote a body shape, and thus a standard of femininity, that is unrealistic and unattainable for most women (Grogan 2008; Tebbel 2000; Wolf 1990). They attribute the development of body-policing practices and disordered eating behaviours among women to exposure to magazines, television programmes and music videos (and thus, images of emaciated, surgically enhanced and digitally modified versions of ideal femininity) (Barnard 2014; Bordo 2004; Tebbel 2000). As Bordo explains in her 2004 edition of *Unbearable Weight*, there is no way to ignore the power of these seemingly innocuous images, referring to them as an unavoidable part of women's lives that operate on an implicit, hegemonic level. "Like the water in the goldfish bowl [that is] barely noticed by its inhabitants," Bordo (2004) explains, digitally modified images of women's bodies "go down so easily, in and out, digested and forgotten" (p. xiii). Many feminist researchers, thus, argue that women are taught to police their bodies through their repeated exposure to ema-ciated images of the female body and their normalised exposure to the 'thin-ideal' (Grogan 2008).

The psychological literature, partially influenced by feminist research, strengthens this contention by arguing that the 'thin-ideal' found in fash-ion magazines reinforces anxiety about one's body, which in turn divorces women from their relationships with food and eating (Calogero et al. 2005; Harper and Tiggemann 2008; Swami et al. 2010). Studies conducted on the influence of the thin-ideal show that it is inextricably linked to pathological eating behaviours in women (Harper and Tiggemann 2008). Indeed, in a study conducted by Vandenbosch and Eggermont (2012), they explain that "exposure to sexually objectifying media ... trigger[s] a chain of psychological events among media users that may lead to various mental and physical health issues" (p. 869). Ahern and colleagues (2011) specify that these health issues concern women's relationships with food and eating. In their study, they argue that women who internalise the thin-ideal found in fashion and beauty discourses are significantly more likely to restrict their food intake in conjunction with expressing anxieties about, and surveillance over, their bodies. Indeed, these findings are echoed in a number of psychological studies (e.g., Calogero et al. 2005; Grabe et al. 2008; Harper and Tiggemann 2008; Kroon and Perez 2013). The thin-ideal, however, cannot be accounted for in all non-clinical women. Ahern and colleagues (2011) suggest that "the current trend for size zero and the rising profile and popularity of visibly underweight models and celeb-rities suggests that there may be individual differences in the level of thin-ness idealised in non-clinical samples" (p. 296). Rather than attributing women's obsessive surveillance of their bodies to discourses other than those relating to the image of the body, psychological researchers place much of their attention on the individual differences between women rather than on the influence of other social and cultural discourses, such as those relating to food.

Indeed, the obsession with scrutinising the way that women's bod-ies are presented in popular culture has manifested in a number of counterproductive ways. Over the last decade, size acceptance arguments have come to the fore as one popular way of addressing the body-policing thin-ideal currently proliferating mainstream fashion and beauty discourses. As Melinda Young (2005, p. 249) argues in her analysis of the thin-ideal in contemporary magazines, fashion and beauty discourses "hold a pedagogic function for women, proffering an obsessive, problematic representation of femininity," one that relies on women to conform to stringent body-policing practices. The solution she offers is to diversify images of women in the media, giving women a range of body shapes to identify with in an effort to promote a positive body image. These sentiments are echoed by feminist writer Sonya Brown in the same edition of *Feminist Media Studies*. Brown (2005) argues that the term 'size acceptance' has become "theoretically fashionable" (p. 246) in the feminist and mainstream media over the last two decades, but has not addressed what it set out to accomplish. Rather than abandoning the notion of size acceptance as a positive idea but an impractical solution, Brown (2005) argues that fashion and beauty magazines use the term plus-size on models who reflect the normal proportions of women in everyday life, and that the term plus-size should, in fact, reflect women who are considered overweight. There is, however, evidence to suggest that the fashion and beauty industries have co-opted the body-centric perspectives of current feminist literature, achieving praise for their use of 'real' women. As Malcolm Barnard (2014) explains in reference to the state of contemporary fashion, "larger bodies and larger models [are coming into fashion] and being used in catwalk shows and advertising. These larger bodies are sometimes called 'real' bodies, and they are sometimes said to belong to 'real' women" (p. 110). Rather than looking for alternative, yet equally powerful, ways that women are encouraged to police their bodies, feminist writers focus on the images presented in fashion and beauty discourses and, incidentally, argue that changing these images will lead to decreases in women's anxieties about their bodies.

These approaches have begun to enter the mainstream. Indeed, there is evidence to suggest that policy-makers, the general public, and the fashion and beauty industries themselves have embraced this body-centric solution to tackle the pernicious thin-ideal (Brown 2005; Murray 2013; Papies and Nicolaije 2012; Tiggemann et al. 2013). In 2003, international beauty company *Dove* released its successful The Real Truth About Beauty campaign, targeting women aged 18 to 64. The campaign, marketed extensively in both Western and non-Western countries, set out to expose the digital airbrushing techniques of contemporary beauty advertisements and to redefine what 'real' women look like. Through telephone interviews and public surveys, researchers at Dove found that "75 percent [of women] want representations of women to reflect diversity through age, shape and size" (Murray 2013, p. 84), which they concluded was the result of the pernicious 'thin-ideal' currently proliferating throughout Western advertising. To address these corporate body-policing attitudes, Dove later went on to launch its Campaign for Real Beauty, which used a diverse range of body shapes and sizes to emphasise what they referred to as 'real' women—women who were traditionally overweight, had freckles and had age lines. While commercially successful, there has been little evidence to suggest that the promotion of a so-called plus-size body, such as Dove's Campaign for Real Beauty, reduces women's surveillance over their own bodies and, subsequently, improves their relationships with food. In fact, in a recent and persuasive study conducted by Papies and Nicolaije (2012), the promotion of plus-size bodies in fashion and beauty discourses actually appears to reinforce body-policing attitudes among women. They explain that "comparing oneself to a plus-size model may have deflating effects if one feels rather similar to the model" (p. 76). Indeed, placing more attention to the weight and shape of the body appears to indirectly reinforce self-surveillance and restrictive eating behaviours in women, regardless of whether or not the image in question has been modified to meet realistic standards.

Similarly, body centric approaches to understanding women's hyper-surveillance of their bodies is by discussing potential warning labels on digitally airbrushed images. In 2009, the Voluntary Industry Code of Conduct launched its own initiative in Australia in an effort to reduce women's dissatisfaction with, and surveillance over, their bodies. The 'National Advisory Group on Body Image' was developed with the aim of targeting media images by "using a diverse range of models of healthy weight, ensuring that models are over 16 years of age, limiting the use of digital technology, and [...] making consumers aware of the extent to which media images have been digitally altered" (as cited in Tiggemann et al. 2013, p. 46). Some researchers, such as Tiggemann and colleagues (2013), argue that these methods, while seemingly beneficial, only offer a short-term solution to women. Testing the reliability of their claims, namely, that warning labels serve as a protective factor, Tiggemann and colleagues (2013) found that the opposite was true. They found that women who were exposed to warning labels on digitally modified images were at greater risk of engaging in self-policing practices than those without warning labels. By increasing the visibility of the body in fashion and beauty magazines, it seems that women are encouraged to self-objectify and compare themselves directly to the digitally airbrushed images. As Bordo (2004) explains, knowing that an image is not real does not serve as a strong enough protective mechanism from developing anxiety over one's body. The answer, thus, may not be in changing or diversifying images, but rather in focusing on other discourses that contribute to body-policing attitudes in women, and in understanding that the culture of self-surveillance constructed for women manifests in multiple discourses.

In this book, I aim to build on the feminist literature that acknowledges that the body-centric approach to analysing discourses is outdated and somewhat ineffective (Malson 2009, p. 135; Probyn 2008). Supporting this argument, in her article on the limits of size acceptance arguments in feminist discourse, Elspeth Probyn (2008) argues that it is puzzling that feminist theorists continue to focus on the visual contours of the body rather than on the sociocultural meanings embedded in food, an object that seems disembodied from women's lives in much of the feminist literature thus far. Specifically, she states that "the fixation on the image [of the body] tends to fix bodies in the sense that it renders understandings of bodies as static" (p. 401), and adds that feminist critiques of the fashion and beauty industries offer an "extraordinarily thin" (p. 402) analysis of women's often complicated and nuanced relationships with food and their bodies. As a suggestion, Probyn (2008) calls for a greater awareness of the way that food is gendered and, generally speaking, politicised in contemporary Western culture, and calls for an end to the "hyper-surveillance to what bodies look like" (p. 402) in the feminist and psychological literature thus far. Similarly, in *Critical Feminist Approaches to Eating Dis/Orders*, Malson (2009) emphasises the need to turn to other cultural sources for the answers, arguing that the exclusion of other popular discourses in the feminist literature on body-consciousness, body-dissatisfaction and disordered eating behaviour is "bizarre" (p. 135). Rather than focusing on the size, shape and general appearance of fashion and beauty models, Malson (2009) argues that feminist critiques of discourses should move the conversation into other discourses that impart body-policing narratives to women. Given that women's relationships with food and eating are adversely affected by their internalisation of cultural narratives that encourage them to be anxious about their bodies, it is useful to contemplate whether or not gendered discourses on food and eating also play a part in reinforcing harmful body-policing norms. This book contributes to the feminist literature by implicating discourses on food and eating themselves in perpetuating body-policing narratives, an area of research that, upon closer inspection, is long overdue.

MAKING FOOD THE MAIN COURSE

In stark contrast to the academic discussions pointing to the dangers of fashion and beauty discourses in propagating anxious and self-policing narratives through the thin-ideal, and the psychological literature that individualises women's disordered relationships with food and their bodies, there is relatively little attention being paid to the way food-related discourses influence women's surveillance of, and dissatisfaction with, their bodies. This is surprising, as food is said to play an unavoidably central role in women's lives, affecting them on individual, social, cultural, gendered, classed, racial and historical levels (Probyn 2000). Indeed, food is seen in sociological literature as a powerful cultural symbol, and it is used in a number of contexts to strengthen gendered stereotypes about women, casting them as nurturers, neurotic undereaters, or hysterical overeaters (Popa 2012). Feminist writers from a number of ideological perspectives argue that, across historical periods, women have been principally responsible for preparing food for others (Lawson 2011; Mitchell 2010; Neuhaus 1999; Scholes 2011), that they restrict their food intake more in comparison to men and that they experience eating disorders at a significantly higher rate than their male counterparts (Orbach 2006; Tebbel 2000; Wolf 1990). Given that women's relationships with food and eating are inextricably and quantitatively linked to their tendency to anxiously watch over their bodies, and that food itself occupies a significant place in the gendered norms of women's lives, it is surprising that so few feminist sources have critically analysed food discourses as possible arbiters of body-policing messages.

Focusing on the significance of food is of particular importance when it comes to understanding both how and why food discourses have been relatively absent in academic discussions on women's body surveillance. In their article on the gendered construction of foodie culture, Cairns et al. (2010) use the term food femininities to describe the gender-specific ways that women relate to food. They argue that through their everyday interactions with food, women express gendered ways of interacting with food that often cast them as nurturers or in quintessentially maternal roles. In this book, the term food femininities is used to refer to the roles that women assume in their various relationships with food, as nurturers, restrictive eaters and disordered eaters, and how these relationships are fundamentally harmful to women. While the feminist literature does address women's relationships with dieting, cooking and their experiences with eating disorders as being driven by gender norms and inequalities, it does not specifically implicate food discourses to the promotion and reinforcement of these self-policing narratives. In this book, I highlight food discourses as an important focus of study, as the way we culturally discuss food represents a hegemonic form of discourse that remains conveniently absent in critical discussions about women's rights, yet simultaneously appeals to women through a number of seemingly innocent and distinct guises.

Before outlining how the feminist literature discusses the significance of food in women's lives, it is important to delineate between the different types of feminism and how they approach this issue. The different types of feminist understandings play a role in comprehending how the discussion of popular food discourses have progressed throughout the years. In *Feminist Thought: A More Comprehensive Introduction* (2009), Rosemarie Tong explains that "feminism is not a monolithic ideology and ... all feminists do not think alike" (p. 1). Three dominant forms of feminist inquiry that are employed in analysing the gendered significance of food are liberal feminist, radical feminist and post-modern/post-structural feminist approaches. Contemporary liberal feminist approaches, according to Tong (2008), focus on individualism and the attainment of gendered justice. Rather than focusing on the collective goals of women, liberal feminist scholars place primary emphasis on maximising the individual women's choices.

Radical feminism, by contrast, acknowledges that "it is not just patriarchy's legal and political structures that must be overturned on the way to women's liberation. Its social and cultural institutions must also be unrooted" (Tong 2008, p. 2). When feminist scholars take a radical feminist perspective, they focus on the structures of male dominance and the extent to which women are subordinated under social institutions. Postmodern (and post-structuralist feminist) approaches to research, by contrast, challenge both liberal and radical approaches, focusing instead on the notion of multiple truths (and multiple versions of gender). Debates on the following areas of what I will term food femininities are often split along familiar feminist lines, with liberal approaches emphasising individual choice, radical approaches emphasising patriarchal oppression and material inequalities, and post-structural discourses emphasising the polysemic nature of texts. Given that the texts I analyse in this book (namely, diet books and cookbooks) are done through a multitude of feminist perspectives, it is important to emphasise how, to date, no feminist studies have adopted the specific approach I am taking, which is to view the relationship between discourses on food and eating and the perpetuation of harmful body-policing narratives through the concept of food femininities.

DIETETIC FOOD FEMININITIES: DIETING AS A GENDERED PHENOMENON

Dieting has long been considered a gendered phenomenon because it is marketed and appeals to a largely female audience (Drew 2009; Orbach 2010). While numbers vary from source to source, it is estimated that the diet industry itself is worth between $40 billion and $100 billion in the United States alone (Drew 2009; Orbach 2010), and that the average woman spends 17 years dieting in her lifetime (London 2012). The relationship between femininity and food restriction is, thus, one that is defined by self-discipline (Bartky 1990; Bordo 2004; Orbach 2006). Unlike the study of cooking and cookbooks, however, dieting (and the diet industry) has held a central role in feminist discussions of food and eating in women. A large body of feminist literature reveals that dieting (and, by association, the diet industry in general) is a harmful cultural phenomenon that reinforces self-objectifying attitudes in women. By contrast, in this book I will argue that there is a new, feminist-inflected discourse on dieting that tends to focus on dieting and, by extension, the diet industry as potentially empowering discourses for women. Diet books have also incorporated feminist terminology, which has not been subject to as much scholarly investigation. Thus, the feminist literature appears to be somewhat divided on what role dieting plays in women's lives.

The vast majority of feminist sources indicate that dieting behaviours are symptoms of women's subordinated cultural status (Bartky 1990; Bordo 2004; Grogan 2008; Orbach 2006; Wolf 1990). As Cairns et al. (2010) explain, the frequent interplay between the food women ingest and the bodies they wish to inhabit creates a fundamental disjunct that leads to food restriction behaviours:

In addition to historical associations between femininity and restraint, dominant representations of women's bodies have worked to further distance
women's food practices from the pursuit of food pleasures, idealising a femininity based upon diet and restriction, rather than indulgence (p. 593).

This narrative of restriction, rather than enjoyment, helps to define wom-
en's gendered relationships with food based on control rather than on
pleasure. Feminist writer Caroline Knapp (2003) discusses this gendered
phenomenon in her posthumously published book *Appetites*. She argues
that women learn from an early age that they live in the "World of No"
(p. 11) when it comes to food and eating, meaning that they learn to
police their appetites according to restrictive gender norms. Naomi Wolf
(1990) adds to this notion in her iconic book *The Beauty Myth* when she
politicises women's restrictive eating behaviours by referring to them as
the most "potent political sedative" (p. 187) of the twentieth century,
adding that women engage in dieting behaviours not out of choice, but
out of obligation to conform. Much of the available feminist literature
indicates that dieting is a form of self-policing patriarchal control over
women that oppresses them by complicating their relationships with food.
  Feminist writers drawing on post-structural and specifically Foucauldian
conceptions of discipline and power have made strong contributions
to understanding the gendered appeal dieting has for women. In particular, writers such as Bartky (1990) and Bordo (2004) use the ideas
presented in Foucault's technologies of power, as ways to conceptualise
women's restrictive behaviours around food and eating. They employ the
Foucauldian concept of the 'docile body' as a medium of social control.
Briefly, Foucault's (1979) writing on the technologies of power posits the
'docile body' as the body disciplined by culture and the self to become
a primary locus of social control. Bordo (2004) emphasises Foucault's
theories of 'power', 'discipline' and 'self-surveillance' in her iconic feminist book *Unbearable Weight*. She refers to his theory of 'docile bodies',
that is, bodies that have been "regulated by the norms of cultural life"
(p. 91), to demonstrate how femininity is inscribed onto women's bodies
through the rhetoric of 'self-control'. She refers to the restrictive dietary
practices that women engage in as evidence of the disciplinary regimes of
patriarchal oppression. She explains that

[t]hrough the pursuit of an ever-changing homogenising, elusive ideal of
femininity – a pursuit without a terminus ... female bodies become docile

bodies – bodies whose forces and energies are habituated to external regulation, subjection, transformation, "improvement" (p. 91).

Bordo (2004) ties restrictive eating behaviours to the quest for the thin-ideal. She uses a feminist post-structuralist understanding of docile bodies to argue that patriarchal societies construct women's bodies as docile by encouraging dieting practices. In *Femininity and Domination*, Bartky (1990) also applies a gender-specific focus to Foucault's theory of 'docile bodies'. Speaking in reference to women's restrictive dietary practices, Bartky (1990) argues that women are required to internalise the gaze of the "panoptic male connoisseur" (p. 72) in order to maintain the boundaries of heteronormative ideal femininity. This panoptic gaze, she argues, permeates into various facets of women's lives, affecting their relationships with not only their bodies but also food. Dieting is identified as one of the dominant ways that women's behaviours are monitored under a panoptic disciplinary gaze. Bartky (1990) explains:

> Dieting disciplines the body's hungers: Appetite must be monitored at all times and governed by an iron will. Since the innocent need of the organism for food will not be denied, the body becomes one's enemy, an alien being bent on thwarting the disciplinary project (p. 66).

Bordo (2004) and Bartky (1990) adopt a feminist post-structural analysis to dieting, drawing on psychoanalytic understandings. Their work presents dieting as a way of divorcing women from their appetites, reflecting a form of tacit disciplinary control over women's bodies that leads to an ongoing state of self-policing behaviours and even psychopathology.

However, the feminist orthodoxy on dieting has shifted somewhat in more recent academic discussions (e.g., Coleman 2010; Heyes 2006). In particular, some contemporary feminist writers position dieting behaviours in women as empowered lifestyle choices rather than indications of patriarchal oppression. In her article on dieting as a technology of the self, Heyes (2006) distances herself from Bartky's (1990) and Bordo's (2004) use of the term docile bodies and their focus on self-surveillance, instead preferring to focus on women's dietetic relationships with food as a form of askesis, or self-care. Drawing on Nikolas Rose's (1996) assertion that technologies of the self comprise three different parts, the epistemological (knowing oneself), the despotic (mastering oneself) and the attentive (caring for oneself), Heyes (2006) argues that feminist understandings of dieting place an overemphasis on the despotic elements of women's restrictive food practices, leading to a myopic understanding of the issue or presenting women who engage in dieting as passive victims. Heyes (2006) offers an alternative conceptualisation of dieting, suggesting that the examination of the epistemological and attentive technologies of the self plays an equally important role in understanding women's engagement with dietary practices. She explains further that in an attempt to characterise dieting as a counterproductive, patriarchal behaviour, "feminists may have elided the details of the capabilities it can develop" (p. 137). She suggests that feminists should instead focus on dieting as a form of self-affirming behaviour in order to be able to resist it. Referring to her own ten-month enrolment in the Weight Watchers weight-loss programme, Heyes (2006) posits herself as an active and willing participant. She explains that unlike the soldier in Foucault's conceptualisation of docile bodies, "the dieter can withdraw at any time without explanation or penalty" (p. 137). This notion of personal agency and self-determination is one that defines contemporary depictions of dieting behaviours in women, where the choice to engage in dieting is marked by narratives of self-empowerment, rather than of oppression.

Similarly, in her article on dieting temporalities and the experience of online weight watching, Coleman (2010) implies that feminist analyses focusing on the docile body ignore the notion that dieting can be a "bodily and embodied practice" (p. 268) for women. Coleman (2010) suggests that dieting empowers women's relationships with food by increasing their sense of agency. Framing her analysis of the *Weight Watchers* programme as a study of women's agency, Coleman (2010) argues that women who used the online version of *Weight Watchers* conceived of it as a lifestyle choice rather than as a weight-loss diet. Engagement with the online version of the weight-loss programme is therefore reconceptualised as a progressive and self-affirming decision that women made, catering to the growing demands of the twenty-first-century woman.

Indeed, the cultural shift in the way feminist theorists understand dieting has very much been informed by the changing role of 'femininity' in contemporary Western culture. According to Dubriwny (2012) in her book *The Vulnerable/Empowered Woman: Feminism, Postfeminism and Women's Health*, the twenty-first-century woman is defined by her vulnerability only in the context of her empowerment. The vulnerable–empowered subject is thus the woman who acknowledges she is physically vulnerable to illness, disease and disorder, but empowered by the individual health and aesthetic choices she decides to make. Dubriwny (2012) argues that narratives of women's health have changed to incorporate individualism, personal responsibility and the strengthening of some more traditional gender role stereotypes. Speaking in reference to the contradictions of the vulnerable–empowered subject, Dubriwny (2012) explains:

> As subjects who make choices, women are represented in discourses about their health as free to construct their own lives, to take responsibility for their bodies, and to craft better selves. However, their choices are not limitless; their choices are shaped by highly gendered expectations of womanhood ... [and] prevailing market forces (p. 24).

Thus, as dieters, women in contemporary culture are depicted as being empowered by the perceived dietary choices they make. Reflecting changes in feminist theory, there is evidence to suggest that the diet industry has followed suit and framed dietary texts as gendered scripts for vulnerable–empowered subjects. As Drew (2009) explains, the diet industry holds a malleable place in the cultural landscape and is capable of reflecting changes in the political climate through a re-visioning of women's eating behaviours. Winch (2011) adds to this notion by arguing that the framing of contemporary diet books as texts espousing empowerment reflects just how much feminist theory has permeated popular cultural discourses. Indeed, while feminist analyses have previously focused attention on the harms of the diet industry in perpetuating body-policing gender narratives among women, these theories have not examined the current empowered perspectives evident in contemporary diet books. To address these issues, I will provide a different kind of study of contemporary, feminist-inflected diet books and discourses on women and food. Indeed, I will radicalise discussions of diet culture by talking about its contemporary manifestations and use of feminist terminology to reinforce a newly palatable culture of body policing.

Culinary Food Femininities: Cooking as a Gendered Phenomenon

Like dieting, cooking is considered a largely gendered phenomenon that holds a contentious place in the feminist literature, and is an important food discourse worthy of further examination (Greer 1999; Supski 2006). When cooking is discussed in the feminist literature, it is typically presented as a mere facet of domesticity or as a secondary symptom of women's cultural subordination (Friedan 1963; Oakley 1976). Some prominent feminist writers attribute cooking to the gendered oppression of women, arguing that its other-oriented status stands in the way of women's cultural emancipation (e.g., Oakley 1976). Others, however, perceive cooking as a valuable source of gender identity, one that strengthens, rather than oppresses, women's experiences in the world (Supski 2006). Despite debates among feminists, the literature on women's relationships with cooking and, indeed, with food more generally is undoubtedly part of a highly gendered phenomenon. The cultural scripts that women use to maintain and reinforce these gendered ways of being can be found throughout cookbooks (Lawson 2011; Scholes 2011), and, as I will discuss further in Chap. 5, serve a function in maintaining harmful body surveillance among women.

The feminist literature dating back to the second-wave feminist movement represents cooking, and indeed women's responsibilities in the kitchen, as symptoms of women's domestic servitude and gendered oppression (Friedan 1963; Greer 1971; Oakley 1976; Summers 1975). Distancing themselves from essentialist arguments pointing to women's natural proclivity for selflessness through cooking, these and later feminist writers turned their attention to the socially constructed nature of woman as feeder and nurturer. Betty Friedan (1963), one of the founding figures of the second-wave feminist movement, famously documented the harmful effects of domesticity in her seminal book *The Feminine Mystique*. Through a series of in-depth interviews and cultural observations, Friedan (1963) exposed the myth of the happy housewife as a caricature of ideal femininity rather than a one based on women's lived experiences. Her path-breaking book, although peppered with references to women's culinary responsibilities, views women's relationships with food and cooking as merely an incidental part of their subordination, not as a role that carries central significance of its own.[1] This is a theme that resonates throughout other feminist texts critiquing domesticity of the time (e.g., Greer 1971; Summers 1975). In *Housewife*, for example, feminist writer Ann Oakley (1976) radicalises Friedan's (1963) argument by calling for an abolition of gender and, thus, of traditional gender roles that keep women subservient. Emphatically decrying the notion of the 'happy housewife' as "a form of antifeminism ... a rationalisation of inferior status" (p. 233), Oakley (1976) calls for a post-patriarchal society that abolishes women's domestic responsibilities, such as cooking, entirely. These highly influential texts, in conjunction with other feminist works of the time, make reference to cooking as a gendered act, but fail to adequately identify it as a central feature of women's gendered relationship with their bodies. Rather, cooking is perceived as an extension of domesticity, and domesticity is seen as a subordinated gender role ascribed to women.

Women's relationships with cooking, however, should be viewed as culturally significant in their own right and reflective of their relationships with their own bodies and appetites. As Cairns et al. (2010) explain in their engaging article on gender and foodie culture, the "social and cultural meanings attached to food serve to perpetuate unequal gender relations" (p. 592). Even when the meanings behind food do not translate to "unequal gender relations" (p. 592), they are still capable of influencing the reinforcement of other gender roles. Addressing how food has become an important component of women's gender socialisation has, thus, been an important task in contemporary feminist writing on food, cooking and gender norms. In *The Whole Woman* (1999), feminist scholar Germaine Greer dedicates a chapter of her book on the gendered components of food, cooking and eating, and, in doing so, repositions feminist arguments to argue that "food is a feminist issue" (p. 56). Greer (1999) refers to the way that food and cooking have been essentialised to women due to their reproductive capabilities and, without ignoring culture, positions women's culinary responsibilities as significant forms of gender expression in their own right. One of her stronger arguments is that women are becoming divorced from their culinary relationships with food because they associate it with gender oppression.

Sociologist Sian Supski (2006) also argues that women's relationships with food and cooking are not always confined to their cultural subordination but are also expressive of the power women experience in the home. Interviewing Australian women of multicultural backgrounds, Supski (2006) found that many of her participants saw cooking, for themselves and their families, as gendered expressions of love and care. From Supski's (2006) perspective, cooking is a positive expression of gender identity, and serves to empower women rather than oppress them. Whether cooking is seen as a symptom of oppression or as an expression of love and care varies according to the feminist lens one is looking through. However, one factor that remains constant in the feminist literature is that cookbooks are rich cultural scripts that socialise women into certain gender roles, some of which may be actively more harmful than others (Ferguson 2012; Lawson 2011; Mitchell 2010; Scholes 2011).

Cookbooks offer women different gendered scripts to conform to, resist, and identify with. Indeed, some feminist sources indicate that studying cookbooks as gendered scripts is a useful way to analyse cultural changes (Mitchell 2010; Scholes 2011). As Lawson (2011) explains in her engaging article on the performance of gender in culinary discourses, cookbooks can be seen as cultural narratives that perpetuate and reproduce gender norms. The culinary discourses available to women are, thus, part of their culinary food femininities, which change according to the era.

Feminist sources analysing cookbooks written prior to, or during, the second-wave feminist movement indicate that these texts strengthen, and sometimes resist, traditional food femininities associated with care and nurture (Ferguson 2012; Neuhaus 1999). These studies reveal that cookbooks written by women, for women, contain "political battle[s]" (Ferguson 2012, p. 696) within them, with Neuhaus (1999) suggesting that they represent a fantasy-type version of traditional femininity, rather than one based on reality. She states:

> Post WWII ... cultural representations of "traditional" women completely fulfilled by their roles as devoted and nurturing mothers spoke to the *expectations* or desires of society, not necessarily on reality (p. 537).

Indeed, from this perspective, it can be contended that culinary texts offer women a caricature of themselves, one that idealises certain aspects of gender while ignoring others that are considered unpleasant or mundane. Much of the contemporary feminist literature on cookbooks points to their increasingly fantasy-like appeal. Mitchell (2010) refers to the authors of contemporary cookbooks as food celebrities, and argues that their widespread appeal lies in their ability to express empowering gender norms. Indeed, more recently, the feminist literature has discussed popular cookbooks, and their celebrity authors, in terms of their irony and empowerment. Hollows (2003), for example, describes food celebrity Nigella Lawson as a dominant culinary figure in the popular imaginary, using her title of domestic goddess as a tongue-in-cheek way to describe women's fantasies of cooking like a 1950s housewife but remaining a liberated modern woman. Genz and Brabon (2009) play with Friedan's (1963) *The Feminine Mystique* to invent the term 'mystique chic' to describe this very notion. The contemporary feminist literature on cookbooks, thus, indicates that being in the kitchen has become a way to reinforce gender stereotypes and that cookbooks are the cultural script from which these messages become disseminated. Given the ever-changing role of cookbooks in contemporary Western culture, especially in regard to gender norms, they are considered a fertile area for study, as evident in the chapters to follow, especially with respect to their potential to reinforce messages of body anxiety to their largely female audiences.

FEMINIST FOOD FEMININITIES: FEMINIST CONSCIOUSNESS AS A GENDERED PHENOMENON

Feminist texts politicising women's relationships with food seem like an unlikely source of data as they are said to expose, rather than reinforce, body-policing cultural narratives; however, their influence on other, more pervasive food discourses brings into stark attention some of the assumptions embedded in their own gendered narratives of food and eating. The feminist literature indicates that both recent cookbooks and diet books are peppered with feminist references that, in many cases, prematurely celebrate women's emancipation from harmful food femininities. These texts rely on what appears to be a feminist perspective without politicising the reason why women engage in dysfunctional relationships with food in the first place. Indeed, influential feminist theories politicising women's disordered relationships with food and their bodies have been instrumental in challenging harmful stereotypes and, seemingly, not perpetuating them. Through the mantra 'the personal is political', voices from the second-wave, such as Susie Orbach, and those influenced by the second-wave and associated with the third-wave, such as Naomi Wolf, situate women's personal dissatisfactions with food into broader social, cultural and 'political' terms. This shift from pathologising the individual to acknowledging the power of sociocultural factors has been accepted as one of the primary methods of understanding women's problematic relationships with food (Bordo 2004). However, an important question remains: Do iconic feminist voices politicising women's relationships with food themselves impart food femininities that reinforce body-policing gender norms? As I will argue further in Chap. 6, iconic feminist texts are potentially another rich source for the interrogation of individualised body-surveillance messages and for their influence on new trends in culinary and dietary texts.

Specifically, I am interested in evaluating influential feminist texts politicising women's relationships with food, as they serve as an indirect method of consciousness-raising and are said to produce a protective feminist consciousness in women. The 'consciousness-raising' refers to the practice of "encouraging self-awareness" (Vanderford 2009, p. 97) in women through critical group discussion. According to Pilcher and Whelehan (2004), consciousness-raising was practised by women in the late 1960s and early 1970s as a way to share their experiences and situate their 'personal' struggles (e.g., with food and body-policing practices) within a broader, political context. As explained by Vanderford (2009), consciousness-raising during this time actively demonstrated the feminist adage "the personal is political" (p. 98), which helped women acknowledge that their conflicted relationships with food and their bodies were part of a culturally reinforced, rather than individual, phenomenon (Bordo 2004; Kadish 2012; e.g., Orbach 2006; Wolf 1990).

However, consciousness-raising practices have changed through the years (Sowards and Renegar 2004; Vanderford 2009). Vanderford (2009) explains how a cultural shift in the late 1970s changed the way consciousness-raising was practised by women, moving from the otherwise collective nature of group discussions into the solitary act of reading self-help texts. Sowards and Renegar (2004) describe "contemporary consciousness-raising" (p. 538) practices as "sharing personal stories in public venues like books and magazines, sharing experiences and reading feminist theory in classrooms, consuming popular culture, exploring issues of diversity and new audiences, and creating new options for self-exploration" (p. 541). Despite reinforcing the notion that women's eating behaviours should be politicised and discussed from a sociocultural perspective, some influential feminist texts on women's eating behaviour can also be seen as reinforcing individualist, self-help narratives among women.

Despite their solitary makeover, iconic texts are seen to represent a type of protective mechanism for women, increasing their awareness on how gendered scripts operate throughout popular culture to divorce them from their appetites. Some psychological researchers propose that the discourses on food and eating that iconic feminist texts convey serve to empower women by reinforcing a feminist consciousness. This has led to psychological researchers hypothesising the link between feminist identity and a reduction of disordered eating behaviours and body-policing practices among women (Green et al. 2008; Guille and Christler 1999; Hurt et al. 2007; Murnen and Smolak 2009; Peterson et al. 2008; Sabik and Tylka 2006; Tiggemann and Stevens 1998). While some researchers have identified a link between possessing a feminist consciousness and a reduction of 'disordered' eating behaviour, others have argued that the relationship between feminist consciousness and a healthy relationship with food and eating is weak, which is one of the reasons why interrogating feminist perspectives on food culture is important to the future of feminist discussions of food culture.

Murnen and Smolak (2009) attribute the weak relationship between feminist identity and disordered eating to the cultural pervasiveness of the 'thin-ideal', relying on a body-centric explanation behind women's 'disordered' relationships with food. They explain that "perhaps there is not a strong correlation between a developing feminist identity and a sense of self independent of cultural pressures about the body. After all, these pressures are very strong" (p. 193). Indeed, the impact of fashion and beauty discourses in perpetuating harmful ideals is important; however, the weak relationship between feminist consciousness and a reduction in disordered eating among women cannot simply be attributed to the thin-ideal. An interesting observation is made by Green et al. (2008) who attribute this weak relationship to feminist discourses themselves, asking whether feminist messages about food and eating are responsible, at least in part, for instilling body-policing messages among women and reinforcing their conflicting narratives about food.

In summary, popular food and eating-related discourses are fertile areas to study as they reference food in a way that reinforces potentially harmful gender roles in women. The chapters that follow contain analyses of cookbooks, diet books and iconic feminist texts to identify the food femininities that are conveyed within them, and whether or not these versions of femininity reinforce harmful body-policing narratives among women. Much of the current literature on body-policing narratives in popular discourses is premised on a body-centric understanding of self-objectification and women's disordered relationships with food, where the image of the female body in fashion and beauty magazines is said to be the strongest sociocultural predictor of body-policing narratives. This body-centric approach to analysing discourses does not include the influence of other, equally important cultural sources in perpetuating the same message. Rather, feminist studies implicating the dangers of fashion and beauty discourses often attribute harmful body-policing attitudes to the lack of plus-size models or warning labels on digitally altered images. Additionally, the psychological literature focusing on women's relationships with food and their bodies focuses on the topic from the optic of disorder and, thus, individualises the problem rather than looking at the broader cultural structure in which women reside. Given that cultural initiatives aimed at minimising body-policing gender narratives in the media have been deemed unsuccessful and even myopic according to some commentaries (e.g., Malson 2009; Probyn 2008), and that the psychological treatment for eating disorders has received mixed outcomes (Alvarenga et al. 2014), it is important to focus on and analyse other discourses in order to broaden the academic and cultural understanding of how certain cultural messages operate to reinforce women's anxious relationships with food and their bodies. Given that women experience body policing in conjunction with dysfunctional eating behaviours, it is important to establish whether popular food discourses available to women offer advice that perpetuates the rigid surveillance of their bodies. While the literature on cookbooks, diet books and iconic feminist texts has been studied separately, and has not looked at their potential to reproduce messages that encourage women to monitor their body weight and shape, this book takes up the task of studying all three genres for their harmful discursive contributions. In the following chapter, I provide a rationale for studying cultural narratives about food and eating through an emancipatory and revised radical feminist analysis on food discourses (Lazar 2004).

NOTE

1. In one interview, Friedan (1963) discusses domesticity and the workforce with one of her participants while they were busy kneading bread. In many examples, cooking is part of the backdrop of women's lived experiences of domesticity, but not mentioned with any explicit importance throughout the book.

REFERENCES

Ahern, A. L., Bennett, K. M., & Hetherington, M. M. (2011). A qualitative exploration of young women's attitudes towards the thin ideal. *Journal of Health Psychology, 16*(1), 70–79.

Alvarenga, M. S., Koritar, P., Pisciolaro, F., Mancini, M., Cordas, T. A., & Stagliusi, F. B. (2014). Eating attitudes of anorexia nervosa, bulimia nervosa, binge eating disorder and obesity without eating disorder female patients: Differences and similarities. *Physiology and Behaviour, 131*, 99–104.

American Psychiatric Association. (2013). *Diagnostic and statistical manual of mental disorders: DSM-5.* Arlington: American Psychiatric Association.

Barnard, M. (2014). *Fashion theory: An introduction.* Hoboken: Taylor and Francis.

Bartky, S. L. (1990). *Femininity and domination: Studies in the phenomenology of oppression.* New York: Routledge/Taylor & Francis Group.

Bordo, S. (2004). *Unbearable weight: Feminism, Western culture, and the body.* Berkeley: University of California Press.

British Psychological Society. (2004). *Eating disorders: Core interventions in the treatment and management of anorexia nervosa, bulimia nervosa, and related eating disorders.* Leicester: British Psychological Society.

Brown, S. (2005). An obscure middle ground: Size acceptance narratives and photographs of "real women". *Feminist Media Studies, 5*(2), 246–249.

Bruch, H. (1973). *Eating disorders; obesity, anorexia nervosa, and the person within.* New York: Basic Books.

Cairns, K., Johnston, J., & Baumann, S. (2010). Caring about food: Doing gender in the foodie kitchen. *Gender and Society, 24*(5), 591–615.

Calogero, R. M., Davis, W. N., & Thompson, J. K. (2005). The role of self-objectification in the experience of women with eating disorders. *Sex Roles, 52*(1–2), 43–50.

Coleman, R. (2010). Dieting temporalities: Interaction, agency and the measure of online weight watching. *Time Society, 19*(2), 265–285.

de Vries, D. A., & Peter, J. (2013). Women on display: The effect of portraying the self online on women's self-objectification. *Computers in Human Behaviour, 29*(4), 1483–1489.

Drew, P. (2009). Dieting. In J. O'Brien (Ed.), *Encyclopaedia of gender and society* (Vol. 1). London: Sage.

Dubriwny, T. N. (2012). *The vulnerable empowered woman: Feminism, postfeminism, and women's health.* Piscataway: Rutgers University Press.

Dworkin, A. (1974). *Woman hating: A radical look at sexuality.* New York: E. P. Dutton.

Ferguson, K. (2012). Intensifying taste, intensifying identity: Collectivity through community cookbooks. *Signs, 37*(3), 695–717.

Fitzsimmons-Craft, E. B., & Bardone-Cone, A. M. (2012). Examining prospective mediation models of body surveillance, trait anxiety, and body dissatisfaction in African American and Caucasian college women. *Sex Roles, 67*(3–4), 187–200.

Foucault, M. (1979). *Discipline and punish: The birth of the prison.* England: Penguin Books.

Fredrickson, B. L., & Roberts, T.-A. (1997). Objectification theory. *Psychology of Women Quarterly, 21*(2), 173–207.

Fredrickson, B. L., Roberts, T.-A., Noll, S. M., Quinn, D. M., & Twenge, J. M. (1998). That swimsuit becomes you: Sex differences in self-objectification, restrained eating, and math performance. *Journal of Personality and Social Psychology, 75*(1), 269–284.

Friedan, B. (1963). *The feminine mystique.* Harmondsworth: Penguin Books.

Genz, S., & Brabon, B. A. (2009). *Postfeminism: Cultural texts and theories.* Edinburgh: Edinburgh University Press.

Grabe, S., Ward, L. M., & Hyde, J. S. (2008). The role of the media in body image concerns among women: A meta-analysis of experimental and correlational studies. *Psychological Bulletin, 134*(3), 460–476.

Green, M. A., Riopel, C. M., Skaggs, A. K., & Scott, N. A. (2008). Feminist identity as a predictor of eating disorder diagnostic status. *Journal of Clinical Psychology, 64*(6), 777–788.

Greer, G. (1971). *The female eunuch.* London: Paladin.

Greer, G. (1999). *The whole woman.* London: Doubleday.

Grogan, S. (2008). *Body image: Understanding body dissatisfaction in men, women, and children.* New York: Routledge.

Guille, C., & Chrisler, J. C. (1999). Does feminism serve a protective function against eating disorders? *Journal of Lesbian Studies, 3*(4), 141–148.

Harper, B., & Tiggemann, M. (2008). The effect of thin ideal media images on women's self-objectification, mood, and body image. *Sex Roles, 58,* 649–657.

Heyes, C. J. (2006). Foucault goes to weight watchers. *Hypatia, 21*(2), 126–149.

Hollows, J. (2003). Feeling like a domestic goddess: Postfeminism and cooking. *European Journal of Cultural Studies, 6*(2), 179–202.

Hoyt, W. D., & Ross, S. D. (2003). Clinical and subclinical eating disorders in counselling center clients: A prevalence study. *Journal of College Student Psychotherapy, 17*(4), 39–54.

Hurt, M. M., Nelson, J. A., Turner, D. L., Haines, M. E., Ramsey, L. R., Erchull, M. J., & Liss, M. (2007). Feminism: What is it good for? Feminine norms and objectification as the link between feminist identity and clinically relevant outcomes. *Sex Roles, 57*(5–6), 355–363.

Jeffreys, S. (2005). *Beauty and misogyny: Harmful cultural practices in the west.* East Sussex: Routledge.

Kadish, Y. A. (2012). The role of culture in eating disorders. *British Journal of Psychotherapy, 28*(4), 435–453.

Kaye, W. H., Klump, K. L., Frank, G. K. W., & Strober, M. (2000). Anorexia and bulimia nervosa. *Annual Review of Medicine, 51,* 299–313.

Knapp, C. (2003). *Appetites: Why women want.* New York: Counterpoint.

Kroon, V. D. A. M., & Perez, M. (2013). Exploring the integration of thin-ideal internalisation and self-objectification in the prevention of eating disorders. *Body Image, 10*(1), 16–25.

Lawson, J. (2011). Food legacies: Playing the culinary feminine. *Women and Performance: A Journal of Feminist Theory, 21*(3), 337–366.

Lazar, M. (2004). *Feminist critical discourse analysis: Gender, power and ideology in discourse.* New York: Palgrave Macmillan.

London, B. (2012). *Over a decade of dieting: Women spend a staggering seventeen years of their lives trying to lose weight.* Retrieved from http://www.dailymail.

co.uk/femail/article-2204944/Women-spend-staggering-SEVENTEEN-years-lives-trying-lose-weight.html

MacKinnon, C. A. (1989). *Toward a feminist theory of the state*. Cambridge, MA: Harvard University Press.

Malson, H. (2009). Appearing to disappear: Postmodern femininities and self-starved subjectivities. In H. Malson & M. Burns (Eds.), *Critical feminist approaches to eating dis/orders*. London: Routledge/Taylor and Francis Group.

Malson, H., Riley, S., & Markula, P. (2009). Beyond psychopathology: Interrogating (dis)orders of body weight and body management. *Journal of Community and Applied Social Psychology, 19*, 331–335.

McKinley, N. M., & Hyde, J. S. (1996). The objectified body consciousness scale development and validation. *Psychology of Women Quarterly, 20*(2), 181–215.

Mitchell, C. M. (2010). The rhetoric of celebrity cookbooks. *The Journal of Popular Culture, 43*(3), 524–539.

Monro, F. J., & Huon, G. F. (2006). Media-portrayed idealised images, self-objectification, and eating behaviour. *Eating Behaviours, 7*, 375–383.

Morry, M. M., & Staska, S. L. (2001). Magazine exposure: Internalisation, self-objectification, eating attitudes, and body satisfaction in male and female university students. *Canadian Journal of Behavioural Science, 33*(4), 269–279.

Murnen, S. K., & Smolak, L. (2009). Are feminist women protected from body image problems? A meta-analytic review of relevant research. *Sex Roles, 60*(3–4), 186–197.

Murray, D. P. (2013). Branding real social change in Dove's campaign for real beauty. *Feminist Media Studies, 13*(1), 83–101.

Neuhaus, J. (1999). The way to a man's heart: Gender roles, domestic ideology, and cookbooks in the 1950s. *Journal of Social History, 32*(3), 529–555.

Oakley, A. (1976). *Housewife*. Harmondsworth: Penguin.

Orbach, S. (2006). *Fat is a feminist issue*. London: Arrow Books.

Orbach, S. (2010). *Bodies*. London: Profile Books.

Papies, E. K., & Nicolaije, K. A. H. (2012). Inspiration or deflation? Feeling similar or dissimilar to slim and plus-size models affects self-evaluation of restrained eaters. *Body Image, 9*(1), 76–85.

Peterson, R. D., Grippo, K. P., & Tantleff-Dunn, S. (2008). Empowerment and powerlessness: A closer look at the relationship between feminism, body image and eating disturbance. *Sex Roles, 58*(9–10), 639–648.

Pilcher, J., & Whelehan, I. (2004). *Fifty key concepts in gender studies*. London: Sage Publications.

Popa, T. (2012). Eating disorders in a hyper-consumerist and post-feminist context. *Scientific Journal of Humanistic Studies, 4*(7), 162–166.

Probyn, E. (2000). *Carnal appetites: FoodSexIdentities*. London: Routledge.

Probyn, E. (2008). IV. Silences behind the mantra: Critiquing feminist fat. *Feminism and Psychology, 18*(3), 401–404.

Rose, N. (1996). Identity, genealogy, history. In S. Hall & P. du Gay (Eds.), *Questions of cultural identity*. London: Sage.

Sabik, N. J., & Tylka, T. L. (2006). Do feminist identity styles moderate the relation between perceived sexist events and disordered eating? *Psychology of Women Quarterly, 30*(1), 77–84.

Scholes, L. (2011). A slave to the stove? The TV celebrity chef abandons the kitchen: Lifestyle TV, domesticity and gender. *Critical Quarterly, 53*(3), 44–59.

Sowards, S. K., & Renegar, V. R. (2004). The rhetorical functions of consciousness-raising in third wave feminism. *Communication Studies, 55*(4), 535–552.

Summers, A. (1975). *Damned whores and God's police: The colonisation of women in Australia*. Ringwood: Penguin Books.

Supski, S. (2006). 'It was another skin': The kitchen as home for Australian post-war immigrant women. *Gender, Place and Culture, 13*(2), 133–141.

Swami, V., Coles, R., Wyrozumska, K., Wilson, E., Salem, N., & Furnham, A. (2010). Oppressive beliefs at play: Associations among beauty ideals and practices and individual differences in sexism, objectification of others, and media exposure. *Psychology of Women Quarterly, 34*(3), 365–379. Dissatisfaction. *Body Image, 10*(1), 45–53.

Tebbel, C. (2000). *The body snatchers: How the media shapes women*. Lane Cove: Finch Publishing.

Tiggemann, M., Slater, A., Bury, B., Hawkins, K., & Firth, B. (2013). Disclaimer labels on fashion magazine advertisements: Effects of social comparison and body dissatisfaction. *Body Image, 10*(1), 45–53.

Tiggemann, M., & Stevens, C. (1998). Women's body figure preferences across the life span. *Journal of Genetic Psychology, 159*(1), 94–102.

Tong, R. (2008). *Feminist thought: A more comprehensive introduction*. Boulder: Westview Press.

Vandenbosch, L., & Eggermont, S. (2012). Understanding sexual objectification: A comprehensive approach toward media exposure and girls' internalisation of beauty ideals, self-objectification, and body surveillance. *Journal of Communication, 62*(5), 869–887.

Vanderford, A. (2009). Consciousness raising. In P. Greenhill, T. A. Vaughn, & L. Locke (Eds.), *Encyclopedia of women's folklore and folklife*. Westport: Greenwood Press.

Wilson, N. (2005). Vilifying former fatties: Media representations of weight loss surgery. *Feminist Media Studies, 5*(2), 252–255.

Winch, A. (2011). 'Your new smart-mouthed girlfriends': Postfeminist conduct books. *Journal of Gender Studies, 20*(4), 359–370.

Wolf, N. (1990). *The beauty myth: How images of beauty are used against women*. London: Vintage.

Young, M. (2005). One size fits all: Disrupting the commercialised, pathologised, fat female form. *Feminist Media Studies, 5*(2), 249–252.

CHAPTER 3

A Smörgåsbord of Food Femininities: How Gender Politics and Food Culture Combine

Words tell us, empirically, about: increases or decreases in equality; old inequalities in new guises; false power among members of an oppressed group; unconscious sexism, racism or other forms of inequality
(Kleinman et al. 2009, p. 49)

We should be weary of postulating a single gender-norm for women across cultures or even within a cultural group
(Haslanger 2002, p. 214)

Gendered discourses on food and eating are important sources of feminist inquiry, especially in relation to their capacity to promote, either implicitly or explicitly, harmful gender norms relating to self-surveillance. To date, much of the feminist literature explaining why women police their bodies has relied on a body-centric perspective, and emphasised the thin-ideal found in fashion and beauty discourses as the primary problem (e.g., Diest and Perez 2013; Harper and Tiggemann 2008; Monro and Huon 2006). In this book, I move away from the pernicious influences of the fashion and beauty industries and, instead, focus on the potentially harmful influence of popular food- and eating-related discourses. Given that women's relationships with food are routinely affected by their dissatisfaction with, and surveillance over, their bodies, it is reasonable to focus on the way food is discussed in mainstream culture and how it is marketed to women. Rather than being fixated on the image of the female body and viewing it as a source of data, I focus my analysis on the language that constructs

© The Author(s) 2017
N. Jovanovski, *Digesting Femininities*,
DOI 10.1007/978-3-319-58925-1_3

and perpetuates women's gendered relationships with food. As Kleinman and colleagues (2009) suggest, the way gender takes shape in popular discourses influences the way it is practically manifested. Rather than being manifested explicitly, many harmful gender norms are perpetuated in cultural discourses tacitly (Speer 2005). Indeed, as Haslanger (2002) explains, the way 'gender' itself is represented in cultural discourses can also be reinforced tacitly, where women are offered multiple types of femininity, referred to in this book as food femininities, which appear to simultaneously present empowering and oppressive messages in relation to food and their bodies.

Despite the veritable smorgasbord of food femininities on offer for women in contemporary Western culture, there appears to be no single overarching perspective used to prioritise, analyse or understand these discourses, and their tacit constructions of gender. As I explain later, this book uses radical feminist perspectives on gender to explore how body-policing messages currently operate throughout contemporary Western food culture. That is, emphasis will be placed on a more radical feminist perspective of patriarchy and gender, combined with the notion that gender has become fragmented and, deceptively, more diverse in a neoliberal, and increasingly individualistic, cultural climate. I argue in this book that the fragmenting of femininity in relation to food and eating serves to further complicate and mask the harmful body-policing messages promoted to women. By offering women a smorgasbord of gendered options to choose from, food- and eating-related discourses purport to empower women, but they may have the opposite effect. To outline how gendered discourses on food and eating rely on hegemonic messages governed by patriarchy and the oppressive notion of gender, this chapter will outline the theoretical framework for this book and provide a discussion of the importance of language, discourse, patriarchy and gender from a feminist perspective. This will be followed by a discussion of the method of Feminist Critical Discourse Analysis as proposed by Lazar (2004).

LANGUAGE AND DISCOURSE AS GENDERED

One of the dominant features of this book is the emphasis on language as a powerful tool used to construct and reinforce harmful gender norms. Specifically, it is argued that through language, women are advised to relate to food as a way to reflect anxieties about the appearance of their bodies, often in normalised or hegemonic ways. According to Rogers (2004), language is a powerful form of cultural practice, "reflect[ing] and construct[ing] the social world" through "constitutive dialectical, and dialogic" means (p. 5). Rather than considering language as a reflection of culture, it is useful to understand language as form of 'action' rather than a 'thing' (Speer 2005). As Weedon (1997) explains, "language is the place where actual and possible forms of social and political consequences are defined and contested" (p. 21). As such, it is useful to consider the way popular cultural sources use language by monitoring and analysing its political potency. The language that connects food and femininity, for example, holds political clues into why body-policing messages are marketed to women. Some feminists associate language with the construction and reinforcement of harmful gender norms, especially in the context of hegemonic cultural discourses (Baxter 2007; Lazar 2004; Speer 2005; Weedon 1997).

When language is shared by a number of significant cultural institutions, it is important to understand it in terms of discursive potential. In this book, it is argued that the study of popular cultural discourses reflects how language is gendered and used by male-dominated institutions to construct norms painting women's relationships with food and eating from a body-conscious, self-policing perspective. The definition of discourse, however, is not so straightforward and has generated a number of conflicting views within the arts, humanities and social sciences (Jorgensen and Phillips 2002). Broadly defined by Jorgensen and Phillips (2002, p. 1) as "a particular way of talking about and understanding the world (or an aspect of the world)," the term 'discourse' has also been described as, "all the phenomena of symbolic interaction and communication between people, usually through spoken or written language or visual representation" (Bloor and Bloor 2007, p. 6), a form of communication that occurs in specific institutional contexts (e.g., scientific discourse, legal discourse). A critical feminist analysis of discourse uses gender as an indication of how discourses operate to discipline and control women. According to Haslanger (2002), one of the primary methods of analysing and deconstructing discourses for their perpetuation of harmful gender norms is through a feminist approach. This involves an acknowledgement of how multiple discourses convey the same harmful gender norms in seemingly distinct ways, and how these discourses are both responsible for constructing and reproducing existing gender norms. It also acknowledges systems of male dominance as the primary force guiding these discourses.

Patriarchal Discourses and Harmful Gender Norms

Patriarchy, or the system of male dominance and female subordination, is an important concept in the feminist literature on harmful cultural discourses (Haslanger 2002). The concept of patriarchy is used repeatedly in this book to describe some of the sexist and regressive narratives present in food discourses. I argue that the gaze operating behind gendered discourses on food and eating reinforces body-policing narratives is a patriarchal one. As Weedon (1997) explains in reference to the cultural distinction between how men and women are socialised, the term 'patriarchal' refers to "power relations in which women's interests are subordinated to the interests of men" (pp. 1–2). From Weedon's (1997) perspective, patriarchal discourses are those that use language to actively subordinate women through their reinforcement of oppressive gender norms. Indeed, patriarchy defines how men and women perceive their place in society, playing a central role in the construction and perpetuation of gender in cultural interactions (Dickerson 2013). Unsurprisingly, the role of patriarchal discourses, especially those that instantiate and reproduce body-policing messages to female audiences, has been a topic of conversation in the feminist literature (Bartky 1990; Bordo 2004). In *Femininity and Domination*, Bartky (1990) argues that patriarchal domination relies on the dissemination of body-policing messages in multiple ways—messages that construct women's understandings of themselves as mere objects (Bordo 2004; Haslanger 2002; Speer 2005). Haslanger (2002), too, discusses radical feminist legal theorist Catherine MacKinnon's assertion that language and knowledge itself are governed by male objectivity, which is a form of objectivity that objectifies women by default. The challenge for feminist researchers has, therefore, been to expose patriarchal discourses and generate academic and public awareness of the pervasiveness of their messages. In my analyses of popular food discourses, I argue the notion that patriarchal discourses generate body-policing norms among women, and, specifically, that diet books, cookbooks and iconic feminist texts tacitly promote a body-policing narrative to women that operates from a hegemonic, male gaze.

The decision to focus on contemporary diet books, cookbooks and iconic feminist texts in this book rests, in part, on the notion that patriarchy operates to construct problematic messages about gender in subtle ways. The idea that patriarchy serves as a driving force behind discourses that promote self-objectification rests on what Speer (2005) refers to as the "subtle sexism" in cultural discourses (Speer 2005, p. 1), or on the notion that patriarchy "bubble[s] under the surface" (p. 2) of a particular discursive interaction. Speaking in reference to how oppressive patriarchal constructions of femininity remain hidden in discursive interactions, Speer (2005) explains how sexism in language is often tacit and less obvious to identify:

> Even while I may know instinctively that there is a "gender thing" going on, that what is being said is based in patriarchal understandings of women as "objects" who belong to men, or assumptions about normative feminine behaviour, it is, nonetheless, harder for me as a feminist seeking to "unpack" these claims, to point to what is said and find evidence that will help me say so with certainty (pp. 1–2).

One of the tasks of the feminist researcher is to expose how patriarchy operates *hegemonically* in popular cultural texts in subtle and complex ways to reinforce harmful attitudes about women. Uncovering the hegemonic power imbalances that manifest in gendered discourses on food is the primary aim of this book. Rather than being manifested explicitly, as they do in the emaciated bodies of fashion and beauty magazines, popular discourses on food and eating operate on a more tacit or implicit level. Lazar (2004) argues that uncovering patriarchal dominance in implicit texts is the primary task of the feminist researcher—to expose harmful gender norms in relatively unsuspecting places, and, ultimately, leading to the potential for an emancipatory counter-discourse.

One of the ways that I seek to accomplish this is through identifying the multiple ways that femininity is constructed and instantiated in food discourses. As explained by Haslanger (2002), one of the most successful ways that patriarchal discourses promote oppressive messages, such as sexual and self-objectification, is by reinforcing certain gender norms. These gender norms are often multiple, seemingly distinct, and sometimes presented as 'empowering' (Lazar 2004, 2009). Referring to these multiple gender norms as 'subject positions,' Weedon (1997) explains that:

> Gendered subject positions are constituted in various ways: by images of how one is expected to look and behave and by rules and behaviour to which one should conform which are reinforced by approval of punishment, through particular definitions of pleasure which are offered as natural and imply ways of being a girl or woman, and by the absence within particular discourses of any possibility of negotiating the nature of femininity and masculinity (p. 95).

Patriarchal discourses, thus, both construct and perpetuate harmful gender norms that place women in various subject positions, or gendered ways of being. These 'ways of being' in reference to food and eating, which are advertised in cookbooks, diet books and feminist texts marketed to women, provide women with a range of femininities to choose from, making them culturally palatable. However, rather than being empowering, Bartky (1990) argues that these socially constructed ways of being female appear to be freely chosen by women, and are inherently "global and suffocating" (p. 1) and difficult to ignore. Indeed, as she further explains, these idealised ways of being women encourage women to internalise a panoptic gaze over their bodies that is both normalised and deeply problematic at the same time. It is these gender stereotypes and norms that this book is particularly interested in identifying and investigating.

FOOD FEMININITIES: A RADICAL PERSPECTIVE

The identification of 'food femininities' is a central concept in this book. Cairns et al. (2010) first used the term 'food femininities' in their article on ethical consumption and food culture. They argued that there are multiple food femininities present in discourses on food and eating, but did not problematise the notion that food femininities exist. In this book, I argue that the idea that our relationships with food are gendered in multiple and seemingly distinct ways is problematic, in and of itself. Indeed, I adopt a radical feminist understanding of gender to do this. In the radical feminist literature, gender is understood as a hierarchy—a classificatory system that positions men as dominant, "strong, active, independent [and] rational," and women as submissive, "nurturing, emotional, cooperative, pretty, and so on" (Haslanger 2002, p. 214). Traditionally, gender is a viewed as a binary category, where 'masculinity' and 'femininity' are dialectically in opposition, and where men and women are stratified according to socially proscribed norms (Jeffreys 2005). Radical feminists view patriarchy as the system in which the gendered division of the sexes operates. In this book, I adopt radical feminist principles of gender, which position femininity as being harmful, and serve as a cultural reminder that women are part of the subordinated social class. Extending on these radical feminist understandings, I also adopt an understanding of gender where I argue that 'femininity' has become fragmented, taking on a number of seemingly disparate guises, a notion that emphasises the liberal-individualist and neo-liberal structures of contemporary Western culture. Departing from popular post-modern and post-structural ideas that would position multiple versions of femininity as transgressive, however, I argue that the multiplication of femininity is deceptive, as it provides women with what appears to be a veritable smorgasbord of culturally palatable 'food femininities' to choose from, but, as I will show, fundamentally reverts to sexist, body-policing narratives.

In this book, I rely on previous feminist analyses of body-surveillance norms and practices as a foundational benchmark. Bartky's (1990) research in *Femininity and Domination* and Bordo's (2004) work in *Unbearable Weight* provide an important basis for the major arguments presented in this book and how body-policing narratives are driven by multiple, socially constructed gender roles for women. One important element of this book is the understanding that patriarchy manifests in multiple versions of femininity to colonise the mind of the individual. As Dickinson (2013) explains, patriarchal narratives found in culture encourage their audience to "engage in self and other surveillance, moving along a narrowly prescribed path" (p. 103) that appears to be freely chosen, rather than constructed, for them. The dissemination of certain gendered ways of being, such as the 'mother,' the 'sex symbol,' and the 'hedonist,', for example, is perceived as a form of patriarchal control, giving the impression that gender roles are varied and freely chosen. At the same time, however, it is also important to acknowledge that women do not merely consume discourses, or contribute to cultural discourses, without some element of resistance. As Glapka (2014) explains in her critical discursive analysis of bridal magazines, "although this piece of research takes an openly critical approach to discourse and believes that media discourses reproduce gender-based inequalities, it does not claim that women are completely unaware of it" (p. 13). Rather, Glapka (2014) argues that women may play an active role in resisting the images and messages conveyed in popular cultural discourses, and that this resistance can be emancipatory. While this book does not seek to examine women's individual responses to the body-policing narratives found in diet books, cookbooks and iconic feminist texts, it does emphasise that the women *producing* these cultural narratives are not only complicit to patriarchal messages, but also able to resist these messages through various countercultural, or radical, messages. To analyse the data from a feminist perspective, one that acknowledges the nuances and areas of resistance in popular cultural discourses, I employ Lazar's (2004) Feminist Critical Discourse Analysis as a methodological framework, which acknowledges feminist research as a form of emancipatory praxis.

FEMINIST CRITICAL DISCOURSE ANALYSIS AS METHOD

Feminist critical discourse analysis (Feminist CDA) will be conducted on popular diet books, cookbooks and iconic feminist texts in the following chapters, with primary emphasis on the body-policing food femininities they espouse. The method of feminist CDA was first discussed by Michelle Lazar in her book *Feminist Critical Discourse Analysis: Gender, Power and Ideology in Discourse* (2004). An extension of a traditional critical discourse analysis, feminist CDA was developed as a form of qualitative inquiry that acknowledges gender as a site in which power relations reside (Lazar 2004). Using the same focus on ideological structures and power relations that are inherent in critical discourse analysis research, feminist CDA uses gender as the focal point of analysis, examining the various ways in which discourses enact and perpetuate harmful gender norms and promote inequalities between the sexes. The combination of feminism and critical theory allows for researchers to focus their attention more specifically on the cultural construction and pervasiveness of gender, and how it functions to control or limit women through discursive interaction.

Analysing data from a critical feminist perspective is not new. In fact, the ideas behind this kind of analysis have existed for some time in academia, but Lazar (2004) was the first to conceptualise feminist CDA. The critical component of feminist CDA was first introduced over three decades ago through traditional versions of CDA (Van Dijk 1993). The term critical is referred to by Rogers (2004) as the study of power relations in text and speech. Rejecting claims that espouse absolute truths and essentialist forms of knowledge (such as naturalism, rationality and individualism), the critical component of data analysis aims to "describe, interpret, and explain the relationship between the form and function of language" (p. 4). Form, in Rogers' (2004) account, refers to the "grammar, morphology, semantics, syntax, and pragmatics" of discourse (p. 4), while function refers to "how people use language in different situations to achieve an outcome" (p. 4). The combination of form and function drives critical discourse analyses. From a feminist perspective, Speer (2005) argues that the form and function of language operates to reinforce oppressive gender norms, which is why feminist researchers focus on gender as an important facet of discourses.

The feminist analysis of gender, and specifically on body-policing versions of gender, is the central part of the analysis presented in this book. Writers such as Lazar (2004) and Lehtonen (2007) explain why the inclusion of a feminist perspective is needed in critical discourse analyses pertaining to gender. Lazar (2004) refers to the importance of feminism in her conceptualisation of feminist CDA as an emerging discursive praxis. She explains that a specific focus on feminism provides researchers with the opportunity to highlight power imbalances associated with gender relations that would otherwise be obscured under the general framework of a critical discourse analysis. Lazar (2004) also explains that by placing a critical focus on unequal gender relations, the researcher exposes the hegemonic nature of gender inequalities and takes on the role of the consciousness-raiser by placing awareness on the issue. Lehtonen (2007), too, emphasises that feminism should be analysed as a political important field of study in its own right. Referring specifically to the application of feminist CDA to children's fantasy fiction, she explains that one of the benefits of applying a feminist analysis to the study of texts is the acknowledgement of gender as an ideological and/or hierarchical construct. Rather than merely describing gender under the general rubric of power relations, Lehtonen (2007) suggests that it may be useful to perceive it as a welcome alternative to critical discursive studies that focus on gender from a distance—studies that potentially and inadvertently ignore the hegemonic power structures behind text and speech. The critical potion of a feminist CDA focuses specifically on what Lehtonen (2007) refers to as the demystification or denaturalisation of sexist language. She explains that:

> One of feminist CDA's aims is to demystify taken-for-granted or common assumptions of gender by showing that these assumptions are ideological and obscure the power differential and inequality (Lehtonen 2007, p. 4).

Thus, in applying a feminist CDA, the primary focus is on the hegemonic, pervasive power of gender in oppressing women. Owing to the fluid nature of qualitative inquiry, there is no standard analytic procedure for conducting a feminist CDA. Rather, the use of feminist CDA in research is flexible and depends on how the analyst defines critical discourse within their own particular study (Rogers 2004).

There are, however, more established ways of following critical discourse analytic research, including Fairclough's (2001) five stages of CDA. Modelled upon Bhaskar's work on Explanatory Theory, Fairclough's (2001) five stages incorporate both negative and positive elements of the CDA process. The first three stages describe the negative portion of the analysis, where the identification, diagnosis and critical deconstruction of the central problem take precedence. The last two stages constitute the positive portion of the analysis, where opportunities for resistance and emphasising the emancipatory potential of the research project are discussed. The following is a brief description of Fairclough's five stages of CDA, where a feminist focus is adopted:

1. Identifying the central problem. In this book, the central "problem" is the lack of feminist and psychological literature implicating the role of cookbooks, diet books and iconic feminist texts in the dissemination of body-policing narratives.
2. Diagnosing the central problem through a feminist analysis of the data. A diagnosis of the data entails a feminist CDA on cookbooks, diet books and iconic feminist texts for their body-policing food femininities.
3. Examining why the dominant social order needs the problem in order to remain powerful. In this book, the dominant social order is patriarchal and entails an analysis of why the patriarchal social order needs body-policing attitudes to inform women's relationships with food.
4. Acknowledging the contradictions inherent in the texts, signalling potential areas where resistance may be possible. In this book, this requires a discussion of the places where the female authors position themselves from a politically assertive perspective, and how they occasionally resist, rather than reinforce, patriarchal conceptions of gender that require women to police their bodies.
5. Questioning how the analysis conducted will ultimately lead to social emancipation. In this book, this process requires a discussion on the importance of raising awareness of the multiple and pervasive nature of the food femininities available, and a deconstruction of the notion that body-policing attitudes are a normative component of women's relationships with food.

Having already established Stage 1 in Chaps. 1 and 2, Chaps. 4, 5 and 6 incorporate Stages 2 and 4 of Fairclough's (2001) proposed model. Specifically, Chaps. 4, 5 and 6 diagnose the central problem through an identification of the food femininities used by the authors, and an examination of the body-policing narratives they express. At the same time, however, these chapters also reflect possible sites of resistance where the authors of diet books, cookbooks and iconic feminist texts subvert oppressive gender stereotypes associated with food and eating. Chapter 7 incorporates Stages 3 and 4 of Fairclough's (2001) model. Thus, by looking at the similarities and differences between the diet books, cookbooks and iconic feminist texts, one is able to identify why the dominant social order needs body-policing attitudes to inform gendered discourses on food and eating, and the way in which all three genres resist certain harmful gender norms. Lastly, in the conclusion, Stage 5 of CDA of Fairclough's (2001) model focuses on how the findings of this book can contribute to a discourse of social emancipation or the promotion of a countercultural discourse on food and gender. The diagnosis of the central problem, where various food femininities are identified in contemporary food discourses, will begin with an examination of diet books, a popular genre that is perhaps the most explicit arbiter of contemporary Western notions of 'food femininity' and women's conflicting obsessions with both consumption and restraint.

REFERENCES

Bartky, S. L. (1990). *Femininity and domination: Studies in the phenomenology of oppression.* New York: Routledge/Taylor & Francis Group.

Baxter, J. (2007). *Positioning gender in discourse: A feminist methodology.* Basingstoke: Palgrave Macmillan.

Bloor, M., & Bloor, T. (2007). *The practice of critical discourse analysis: An introduction.* London: Hodder Arnold.

Bordo, S. (2004). *Unbearable weight: Feminism, Western culture, and the body.* Berkeley: University of California Press.

Cairns, K., Johnston, J., & Baumann, S. (2010). Caring about food: Doing gender in the foodie kitchen. *Gender and Society, 24*(5), 591–615.

Dickerson, V. (2013). Patriarchy, power, and privilege: A narrative/poststructural view of work with couples. *Family Process, 52*(1), 102–114.

Fairclough, N. (2001). The discourse of new labour: Critical discourse analysis. *Discourse as Data: A Guide for Analysis, 1*, 229–266.

Glapka, E. (2014). *Reading bridal magazines from a critical discursive perspective.* Basingstoke: Palgrave Macmillan.

Harper, B., & Tiggemann, M. (2008). The effect of thin ideal media images on women's self-objectification, mood, and body image. *Sex Roles, 58*, 649–657.

Haslanger, S. (2002). On being objective and being objectified. In L. M. Antony & C. E. Witt (Eds.), *A mind of one's own: Feminist essays on reason and objectivity*. Boulder: Westview Press.

Jeffreys, S. (2005). *Beauty and misogyny: Harmful cultural practices in the west*. East Sussex: Routledge.

Jorgensen, M., & Phillips, L. (2002). *Discourse analysis as theory and method*. London: Sage Publications.

Kleinmann, S., Ezzell, M. B., & Frost, A. C. (2009). Reclaiming critical analysis: The social harms of 'bitch'. *Sociological Analysis, 3*(1), 47–68.

Lazar, M. (2004). *Feminist critical discourse analysis: Gender, power and ideology in discourse*. New York: Palgrave Macmillan.

Lehtonen, S. (2007). Feminist critical discourse analysis and children's fantasy fiction – modelling a new approach. *Past, present, future – from women's studies to post-gender research*. Umea. Retrieved from http://semiotics.nured.uowm.gr/pdfs/feminist_critical_discourse_analysis_lehtonen.pdf

Monro, F. J., & Huon, G. F. (2006). Media-portrayed idealised images, self-objectification, and eating behaviour. *Eating Behaviours, 7*, 375–383.

Rogers, R. (2004). *An introduction to critical discourse analysis in education*. Hoboken: Lawrence Erlbaum Associates.

Speer, S. A. (2005). *Gender talk: Feminism, discourse and conversation analysis*. East Sussex: Routledge.

Van Dijk, T. A. (1993). Principles of critical discourse analysis. *Discourse Society, 4*(2), 249–283.

Weedon, C. (1997). *Feminist practice and poststructuralist theory* (2nd ed.). Oxford: Blackwell Publishers.

CHAPTER 4

Femininities-Lite: Diet Culture, Feminism and Body Policing

Feminist writer Naomi Wolf (1990) once famously declared that dieting in women is "the most potent political sedative" (p. 187) of the contemporary Western age—a sedative that has kept generations of young women out of the world of feminism and politics and into the grasp of the silence-inducing and pervasive diet and beauty industries. Despite the success of feminist writers drawing links between the defanging of feminist activism and the rise of diet culture for over four decades, research suggests that the diet industry continues to profit from women's insecurities about their bodies in the twenty-first century, and successfully rebrands itself according to changing cultural trends (Drew 2009; Orbach 2010). Estimates show that, collectively, the industry is worth between $40 billion and $100 billion in the United States alone (Drew 2009; Orbach 2010), with some reports stating that it has "come to be worth a sum which averages out to every adult citizen spending an estimated $600 a year on diet products" (Orbach 2010, p. 54). While feminist analyses of the diet industry have shown that it is explicitly associated with women's dissatisfaction with their bodies and the depoliticising of their lives, one issue that has not been addressed is how the diet industry manifests in the contemporary age, where harmful gender norms are made palatable to women through the promotion of feminist jargon. In this chapter, I examine the role that best-selling diet books play in reinforcing and normalising body-policing narratives in women. Specifically, I focus on identifying the food femininities promoted by Freedman and Barnouin (2005, 2007) in their books *Skinny Bitch* and *Skinny Bitch in the Kitch*, and Bridges' (2010, 2011) diet

© The Author(s) 2017
N. Jovanovski, *Digesting Femininities*,
DOI 10.1007/978-3-319-58925-1_4

books *Losing the Last 5 Kilos* and *Crunch Time Cookbook,* in an effort to understand how and why gender is used to reinforce narratives of body-anxiety in women.

A Feminist Diet?

A relatively new feature of diet books, and indeed an offshoot of make-over culture and its reliance on neoliberal and consumerist ideologies, is the application of feminist terminology typically associated with emancipa-tion and empowerment to the practice of weight-loss (Lazar 2009; Winch 2011). According to Lazar (2009), this trend has been more obvious in the fashion and beauty arena. Using *L'Oreal*'s famous campaign 'because you're worth it' as an example, Lazar (2009) argues that the frequent use of feminist-speak in discourses on beauty and self-improvement signifies a cultural shift in the way that beauty and dieting discourses are marketed to appeal to women. She explains that:

> Advertisers ... known for their opportunistic ability to read a society's pulse [and] respond adroitly by selectively appropriating social discourses, link the normative practice of beautification with an emancipated identity (p. 37).

The purpose of relying on narratives of empowerment in diet discourses (and other beauty discourses) addresses women's distrust in diet culture by framing the discussion as "women's [basic] right to be beautiful" (p. 38) rather than their need to fit to the culturally proscribed aesthetic standards. Some have referred to the phenomenon of using feminist terminology in discourses typically associated with women's disempowerment as a feature of post-feminist girlfriend culture. As Winch (2011) explains in her article on girlfriend culture and the cult of the makeover:

> Girlfriend culture does not develop female connections in order to defy patriarchal systems. On the contrary, it celebrates women networking the service of the postfeminist lifestyle industries which sell the allure of girli-ness, particularly through the mechanisms of makeover (p. 360).

One factor that reflects the newly feminist slant on diet culture is the notion that women are no longer victims of diet culture, and that the diet industry is not patriarchal but, instead, female-friendly. In stark contrast to influential feminist perspectives, such as those of Bartky (1990), Bordo (2004) and Orbach (2006), the contemporary and popular feminist understanding of diet culture is that it provides women with the opportunity to assert their agency through a range of beauty and health-related choices (Coleman 2010; Heyes 2006). Dubriwny (2012) refers to this contemporary feminist figure as the vulnerable–empowered subject, characterising her as someone whose body is vulnerable to ill health but who is individually empowered to make the appropriate health-related interventions. Defining the vulnerable–empowered subject of contemporary health discourses, Dubriwny (2012) states:

> As subjects who make choices, women are represented in discourses about their health as free to construct their own lives, to take responsibility for their bodies, and to craft better selves (p. 24).

The texts chosen for analysis in this chapter are all diet books and diet cookbooks published within a six-year period (2005–2011), and reflect Dubriwny's caricature of the vulnerable–empowered subject. Two American (*Skinny Bitch* and *Skinny Bitch in the Kitch*; Freedman and Barnouin 2005, 2007) and two Australian texts (*Losing the Last 5 Kilos* and *Crunch Time Cookbook*; Bridges 2010, 2011) were chosen on the basis of their popularity, and the popularity of their authors, both in Australia and overseas.

Freedman and Barnouin's *Skinny Bitch* (2005) and *Skinny Bitch in the Kitch* (2007) will be analysed in terms of the post-feminist position they adopt. Analyses will be conducted on the use of the words skinny and bitch as aspirational terms for women, as well as on the authors capitalising on women's body-consciousness through the promotion of a sexually objectified vegan food femininity. Bridges' diet book *Losing the Last 5 Kilos* and her diet cookbook *Crunch Time Cookbook* will be analysed for their liberal-individualistic perspectives. Analyses will be conducted on the self-surveillance and confession of both women's bodies and their eating behaviours throughout the discourse.

"DON'T BE A PUSSY": FREEDMAN AND BARNOUIN'S POST-FEMINIST FOOD FEMININITY

Rising in popularity after pop star Victoria Beckham was photographed clutching a copy while leaving a Los Angeles boutique, the *Skinny Bitch* diet book series has successfully capitalised on both the weight-loss and veganism trends circulating throughout contemporary Western culture in the twenty-first century. Published in 2005, with initially slow sales, *Skinny Bitch* sold over 1.1 million copies and spent 92 weeks on the New York Times Bestseller 'How-To' list (Moskin 2008; Rich 2007). Its authors, Rory Freedman, a former modelling agent, and Kim Barnouin, a former model, expressed that their motivation to create a vegan diet book was initially about animal rights, but gradually turned into a weight-loss manifesto. Owing to the unexpected popularity of their first book *Skinny Bitch*, the authors capitalised on the vegan diet book craze and published a series of diet cookbooks, calling for professional help of a 'cookbook consultant' to strengthen their credibility (Moskin 2008). Their corresponding diet cookbook, *Skinny Bitch in the Kitch: Kick-Ass Recipes for Hungry Girls Who Want to Stop Cooking Crap (and Start Looking Hot!;* hereafter referred to as *Skinny Bitch in the Kitch*), was published in 2007, and successfully sold over 270,000 copies in the year following publication (Rich 2007). One of the most obvious features of Freedman and Barnouin's (2005, 2007) diet books *Skinny Bitch* and *Skinny Bitch in the Kitch* is their construction of post-feminist notions of femininity to motivate women to adopt veganism.[1] Rather than taking a strictly animal rights approach, the authors rely on post-feminist tropes of femininity to sell their animal rights message.

While the term post-feminism is frequently used in both academic literature and popular media, there is no solid consensus about its meaning. According to Gill (2007), post-feminism has been broadly conceptualised as a historical shift after the feminist second-wave that simultaneously mourned and celebrated the political accomplishments. As explained by Barker (2004), post-feminists have selectively adopted certain feminist values (e.g., reproductive rights), but rejected others that critique patriarchal social structures that they believe are in their favour. For example, some post-feminists may argue that what was once said to oppress women, such as sexual objectification, can now be viewed as a form of female power, as it gives the impression that women in the twenty-first century have the right to "wield sexual power" (Barker 2004, p. 150) like never before.

While post-feminism may be prolific throughout Western advertising and the media, it has not come without its critics. One of the most widely employed critiques of post-feminism has come from various feminist sources who view it as a "new kind of sophisticated anti-feminism" (McRobbie 2011, p. 179). According to McRobbie (2011), post-feminism does not merely ignore the existence of feminism, but positions it as being dead. As Douglas and Michaels (2002) explain, the notion that feminism is redundant prematurely forecloses debates surrounding gender inequalities that prevail in the Western culture, and instead, tacitly ignores them by repackaging them as empowering. They state:

> What the hell is postfeminism, anyway? I would think it would refer to a time when complete gender equality has been achieved. That hasn't happened, of course, but we (especially young women) are supposed to think it has (p. 203).

One of the reasons why women are led to believe that gender equality has been achieved is through marketing and its pervasive emphasis on self-improvement. Winch (2011) uses the famous *L'Oreal* catchphrase 'because you're worth it' to emphasise how the cult of the makeover has been branded as a form of female empowerment. She states that, "rather than being an enforced victim of patriarchy, the makeover participant is coerced through a rhetoric of entitlement – she *is worth it*. The cultural function of the postfeminist makeover is to depict femininity as a commodity" (p. 361; original italics). Using the post-feminist argument of entitlement, in the following section it is suggested that Freedman and Barnouin's (2005, 2007) use of a post-feminist food femininity serves the function of capitalising on women's normative discontent (Rodin et al. 1984) with their bodies in order to spread a vegan/animal rights message. Perhaps one of the most striking features of their post-feminist persona is their use of the terms skinny and bitch as aspirational, and yet body-conscious, facets of attaining a vegan lifestyle.

Skinny

The word skinny is frequently used throughout both *Skinny Bitch* and its corresponding book *Skinny Bitch in the Kitch*. Its function within these texts is multifaceted, ambiguously serving as an idealistic title, a state of being and a type of body shape all in one. In the introductory paragraph of *Skinny Bitch*, Freedman and Barnouin (2005) idealise the state of being skinny by conflating certain types of body weight and shape to different states of being:

> Are you sick and tired of being fat? Good. If you can't take one more day of self-loathing, you're reading to get skinny ... This knowledge will empower you to become a skinny bitch (Freedman and Barnouin 2005, p. 10).

The authors position two extreme states of feminine bodily being: the 'fat' and "self-loathing" (p. 10) female body, and its "empower[ed]" (p. 10) skinny and unquestionably superior equivalent. The function of this dichotomy as a comparative tool for women is a common feature in post-feminist references to self-modification and the cult of the makeover. In their book on the commodification of post-feminist values, Douglas and Michaels (2002) demonstrate how powerful figures within the corporate media position women as active consumers, and thus, as empowered in the choices they make about their self-modification practices. Levy-Navarro (2012) describes this comparative process as the before and after shot that is typical of makeover programmes. She states that "the fat person is made into the 'before' to the glorious 'after' of the (precariously) thin person" (p. 340). This reinforcement of body-consciousness is said to encourage women to purchase cosmetic and weight-loss products (Douglas and Michaels 2002).

By designating women as either 'fat' or 'skinny,' Freedman and Barnouin (2005) limit the scope of options available for women to iden-tify with. The function of this dichotomy implicitly encourages women to engage in body policing, and as *Skinny Bitch* is, above all, a best-selling diet book, the assumption that their female audience is already 'fat' is made abundantly clear through their repetitive use of derogatory terms associated with 'fat':

> It's easier to socialise after you've had a few drinks. But being a fat pig will hin-der you sober or drunk. And habitual drinking equals fat-pig syndrome. Beer is for frat boys, not skinny bitches (Freedman and Barnouin 2005, p. 12).

> Your junk food has a shelf life of twenty-two years and will probably outlive your fat, sorry ass (Freedman and Barnouin 2005, p. 17).

In these excerpts, the authors depict 'fat' as both an abject part of the female body and a type of social identity. Winch (2011) argues that by labelling 'fatness' as a negative state of being, the authors of *Skinny Bitch* desig-nate being skinny as the ideal counter-aesthetic that represents "cleanliness, purity, health, energy, success and happiness" (p. 366). In other words, being skinny is positioned as the aspirational after shot that the reader has not yet achieved, but is encouraged to accomplish (Levy-Navarro 2012).

While the authors tout their scientific and research credentials, they make no such reference to what they biologically refer to as being 'fat' or 'skinny.'[2] Their female audience receives only a vague understanding of what being skinny literally constitutes, and while there appears to be no conclusive statement in either of their texts regarding the exact meaning of the term, the authors depict being skinny in the following way:

> It's time to strut your skinny ass down the street like you're in an episode of *Charlie's Angels* with some really cool song playing in the background. It's time to prance around in a thong like you rule the world. It's time to get skinny (Freedman and Barnouin 2005, p. 10).

By providing women with references to *Charlie's Angels* and the sexualised donning of a "thong," the authors depict being skinny as a post-feminist caricature of ideal femininity, one that is supposedly "empowered" (p. 10) by aesthetic choices, in this case, of choosing to be skinny. Despite their repetitive and overt preference for being skinny, Freedman and Barnouin (2005) emphasise on their website (www.skinnybitch.net) that being physically skinny should not be the driving force behind adopting their diet. They write:

> BTW: A Skinny Bitch is someone who enjoys food, eats well, and loves her body as a result. It has nothing to do with how much you weigh or what size you are! Skinny Bitches come in all beautiful shapes and sizes![3]

They also make a similar statement on the back page of *Skinny Bitch* (after the endnotes):

> P.S. Wait! We have a confession to make. We really couldn't care less about being skinny. Don't get scared or upset, you will definitely lose weight if you adopt the *Skinny Bitch* lifestyle. However, our real hope is for you to become healthy. We don't want anyone to get obsessed with getting skinny. When you eat right and exercise, you feel strong and healthy and confident ...

> Comparison is the thief of joy. No matter what we do, most of us will never look like supermodels or celebrities. And accepting that will make our lives a whole lot better. So what if there is only one standard of beauty perpetuated by Hollywood that you don't fit into? Don't buy into the bullshit. Take excellent care of the body you were blessed with, and love, love, love it! (Freedman and Barnouin 2005, p. 224).

While the authors use the word skinny liberally in both the title and content of their books, messages such as "we really couldn't care less about being skinny" (p. 224) and "it has nothing to do with how much you weigh or what size you are!" contradict their initial pre-occupations with being skinny and, in a sense, mask the original agenda presented in their books. Using Hollywood caricatures of femininity (e.g., *Charlie's Angels*) to convince the reader to adopt a 'skinny' lifestyle, the authors suddenly reverse these statements by suggesting that Hollywood standards of beauty are, in fact, "bullshit" (p. 224). Here, the female reader is expected to understand that the 'skinny' message conveyed is not literal, but ironic, and to prioritise their health rather than the perceived thinness of their bodies. According to Winch (2011), "this sudden ideological turnaround is typical of postfeminist popular culture where hyperbolic or ironic statements can be detracted with a laugh" (p. 368).

Despite the intended use of irony, however, Freedman and Barnouin's skinny message has been taken literally by some of their positive reviewers:

> Don't hate them – be them. The authors of *Skinny Bitch* offer women a no-holds-barred approach to being thin and fabulous – *Metro*.

> Any young woman who pays attention to this book will become healthier, thinner, and more powerful – *John Robbins, best-selling author of Diet For a New America and Healthy at 100*

> Read every last word. Healthy and skinny you will be – *Amy Joy Lanou, Ph.D., Senior Nutrition Scientist, Physicians Committee for Responsible Medicine*

While the authors retract their initial emphasis on the importance of being skinny, many reviewers fail to identify their intended message. Instead, their reinforced notion of skinny as a form of social identity is seemingly misunderstood when the reviewers use the word thin interchangeably with the skinny message. The function of encouraging women to be skinny in these excerpts becomes literal, and any tongue-in-cheek message about skinny as a state of being, rather than an indicator of body weight/shape, is lost. Winch (2011) explains that the post-feminist use of irony leaves women with a confusing set of questions about their self-worth, such as "should I or should I not be a skinny bitch? … Am I or am I not OK? Am I a fat maggot?" (p. 368). These questions, as well as their use of the word bitch, can be considered ironic, post-feminist messages.

Bitch

Besides adopting skinny as an aspirational term, Freedman and Barnouin (2005) also encourage their readers to identify with the term bitch. Bitch, coupled with the word skinny, becomes a type of honorary label describing women's positive relationships with food and their bodies. According to Kleinmann et al. (2009), the use of bitch in contemporary Western culture has shifted from being a negative label to a supposedly positive and empowering one. Drawing on references from popular culture, such as comedian Tina Fey's sense of pride in labelling herself a bitch on *Saturday Night Live*, Kleinmann and colleagues (2009) demonstrate that the term itself has been transformed to reflect empowerment for women (i.e., "the bitch persona").[4] In other words, the term bitch has said to have been reclaimed from its patriarchal origins.

Speaking in reference to the origins of the term bitch, Kleinman and colleagues (2009) emphasise that the word itself dates back to the 1400s where it was initially used to signify either a female dog or a sexually promiscuous women of low moral value. In contemporary Western culture, bitch remains a derogatory term describing women's social and sexual behaviours. Lyrics in popular music, such as Jay Z's 'Bitches and Sisters,' attest to the original derogatory meaning when he signifies that a 'bitch' is a woman to be disrespected (e.g., "Sisters get respect, bitches get what they deserve," Kleinmann et al. 2009, p. 56).

The term bitch is also used as a way for men to promote violence against other men. Kleinman and colleagues (2009) provide examples of how less dominant male inmates in prison systems are both physically and sexually abused, and how the use of the term bitch encourages other inmates to display violence towards these men through connotations of femininity (e.g., forcing them to wear make-up and adopting behaviours typically designated to women). The word bitch, then, can be understood as a type of language that signifies "men as systematically privileged, and women as disadvantaged" (Kleinmann et al. 2009, p. 49).

The post-feminist use of the word bitch, however, is purported to be a sign of female empowerment rather than a patriarchal slur against women. Ferriss and Young (2006) describe the popularity of third-wave feminist magazine *Bitch* as an example of this 'empowerment.' They state that *Bitch* gives women a "girl-friendly" (p. 91) guide to feminism that is less threatening than the messages conveyed by their second-wave feminist counterparts. By employing the word 'bitch' in daily use, women are said to be reclaiming it from its offensive patriarchal origins. Critics of the word bitch, however, argue that its increasingly acceptable use in society ignores the social harms that it inflicts upon women. Calling a woman a skinny bitch, for example, not only shows a veiled appreciation of her looks, but also signifies an envy of her, and therefore, an objectification of her body (Kleinman et al. 2009).

Freedman and Barnouin (2005) tacitly encourage both the objectification of others and oneself in their use of the phrase 'skinny bitch.' In an interview with the *New York Times*, Kim Barnouin, former model and co-author of the *Skinny Bitch* series, states:

> You know how you feel when a tall, thin, pretty woman walks by and something inside you wants to say, "That skinny bitch!"? ... The book [Skinny Bitch] takes that envy and anger and gives you a place to put it (as quoted in Moskin 2008, p. 3).

What Barnouin emphasises in this excerpt is a direct reinforcement of body policing, both of oneself and of other women. By identifying with and aspiring to *be* the skinny bitch, women's anger and envy towards her (and their objectification of her) become internalised. Here, Barnouin encourages women to objectify themselves (i.e., self-objectification) rather than others, and portrays this internalisation of negative feelings as a healthy alternative. As discussed in Chap. 2, a significant body of feminist and psychological research has been conducted on the dangers of self-objectification (Gurung and Chrouser 2007; Harper and Tiggemann 2008; Morry and Staska 2001; Tiggemann 2013). In particular, self-objectification has been shown to be strongly predictive of various forms of disordered eating behaviour (Diest and Perez 2013; Fitzsimmons-Craft and Bardone-Cone 2012; Monro and Huon 2006). Researchers such as Fredrickson and Roberts (1997) explain that women's body-policing behaviour stems from sexist, patriarchal messages surrounding femininity, where the sexual objectification of women serves as a societal norm rather than a problem. In *Skinny Bitch*, Freedman and Barnouin (2005, 2007) employ self-objectifying references as a way to promote a specific type of dietary identity, a post-feminist food femininity that "veers between bitchiness and identification ... [a] combination [that] is [both] highly emotive and punishing" (Winch 2011, pp. 361–362).

Post-Feminist Veganism

While Freedman and Barnouin (2005) emphasise the importance of a post-feminist and an implicit body-policing version of femininity in *Skinny Bitch*, Motoko Rich (2007, n.p.) of the *New York Times* emphasises that their book is less about weight loss than it is about animal activism, describing it as, "a vegan manifesto clothed as a weight-loss primer." Their vegan message has also been noted by other sources as being hidden under a veil of body-consciousness. As one reviewer from *People* (2007) magazine stated, their vegan agenda is barely stated throughout *Skinny Bitch*:

> Though what they're pitching is clearly a vegan diet, the sometimes funny, sometimes crude authors – an ex-model and an ex-modelling agent – don't mention the V-word right away, which feels sneaky (n.p.).

While the authors make their animal rights perspective clear throughout *Skinny Bitch*, devoting several chapters to critiques involving either the consumption of animals or animal products (e.g., 'the dead, rotting, decomposing flesh diet' and 'the dairy disaster'), they rarely use the word 'vegan' to describe themselves or, indeed, the diet they promote. One of the reasons why their vegan food femininity is masked by body-consciousness may be due to the shameful, unfashionable and feminist connotations associated with veganism.[5] According to Potts and Parry (2010), the word 'vegan' in Western culture has been associated with negative labels such as hippy and boring. Studies examining public opinions on veganism have shown a resistance to adopt it as a legitimate dietary practice (Cole and Morgan 2011). In their article on derogatory representations of vegans in UK newspapers, Cole and Morgan (2011) demonstrated that 74.3% of the articles analysed portrayed vegans as being oversensitive, hostile and likely to be engaged in a fad diet. Similarly, in an article on the heteronormative associations between meat-eating and sexuality, Potts and Parry (2010) demonstrate that hostile attitudes towards vegans were mostly directed towards women practicing the lifestyle, and were usually generated by "omnivorous heterosexual men" (p. 57). Given the knowledge that a significant number of omnivorous males find the veg*n lifestyle threatening (Potts and Parry 2010), and that veganism itself is touted as unfashionable and abnormal (Cole and Morgan 2011), some animal rights activists, including Freedman and Barnouin, have tried challenging negative stereotypes by turning veganism, and specifically vegan food femininities, into something sexy, and, thus, highly marketable.[6]

As explained by Deckha (2008), People for the Ethical Treatment of Animals (PETA), one of the most well-known animal rights organisations in the world, has been known to draw controversy for its racist and sexist advertising campaigns. She provides an example of sexist imagery in its anti-fur campaign entitled, 'I'd Rather Go Naked than Wear Fur.' Using former *Playboy* centrefold and *Baywatch* star Pamela Anderson as its poster girl, PETA relies on the imagery of soft-core pornography, and therefore on the sexual objectification of women to market its animal rights message. Deckha (2008) suggests that due to the sexually suggestive nature of its advertising, it can be argued that PETA is furthering its own political cause at the detriment of other equally important causes (i.e., feminism). While Freedman and Barnouin (2005, 2007) promote a less sexualised caricature of objectified femininity, they nevertheless adopt sexist and derogatory terminology to describe women and encourage body-consciousness through the lens of aestheticism. As one blogger for website *Veggie Girl Power* (2009) explains, her initial interest in the book was due to its emphasis on being skinny rather than on its vegan-friendly message:

> I picked up my copy of Skinny Bitch back in 2005 by pure accident. I liked the title, brief description and the fun cover. As I began reading the book, I quickly realised that OMG, this book is promoting a **vegan-lifestyle** – something I had only recently decided to embrace in full-force (Kathy, Veggie Girl Power 2009; original bold text).

As this blogger shows, the *Skinny Bitch* appeal is initially focused on the dietary and aesthetic ambitions of women rather than on their commitment to veganism. While the emphasis on being a 'skinny bitch' appears to initially outweigh the animal rights perspective, author Rory Freedman states that her primary motivation for writing the book was a "compassion for animals and the desire to help them" (Veggie Girl Power 2009, n.p.). This notion is exemplified in her interview with Jason Wachob (2010) of website *MindBodyGreen*, where she describes her animal activism as being the leading force behind the work:

> For many years I was a vegetarian and a vegan, but every time I would try to help someone who would complain to me about their diet it was really hard to get them to listen to me. I was at a conference where I saw more footage of factory farming and slaughterhouses, and I thought *I'm going to die if I don't do something to help these animals.* It occurred to me that humans very much love animals and don't want them to suffer, but they also don't want to sit there and read about their suffering, their pain, and how human involvement is contributing to that. So it occurred to me *if I would write a book, call it Skinny Bitch, and not give away that there was going to be anything about factory farming and slaughterhouses in the book, that women who are just living their lives who like shopping, who like watching Oprah, who like reading silly magazines, would pick up this book and it would change their lives,* and it would change how they treated animals (Wachob 2010, italics added).

In this excerpt, Freedman explicitly locates her intentions for writing *Skinny Bitch* as being contingent upon the rights of animals. Promoting a positive relationship between women and food, however, is presented as a secondary agenda, or more specifically, as one that can aid in promotion of animal rights. The demographic that Freedman targets is not the politically minded, critical-thinking feminist, but rather, the post-feminist consumerist woman. In fact, she even identifies her core demographic as women "who like shopping ... watching Oprah ... [and] reading silly magazines" (Wachob 2010). While she has not explicitly specified the name of this demographic, these women belong to the contemporary, post-feminist category of femininity.

Post-feminist depictions of ideal femininity often coincide with liberal ideologies that place choice above political analysis. In *The 'Fat' Female Body*, Murray (2008) depicts the dominant cultural perspective on obesity as being contingent upon notions of personal choice and responsibility. For example, people who find themselves labelled as obese have themselves to blame for their increase in body weight. The food choices they make are presented as being solely dependent upon their own level of personal responsibility. Murray (2008) argues that the liberal-humanist perspective encourages people within societies to become lipoliterate and to blame obese people for their dietary choices and the shape of their bodies, without acknowledging that their choices are specific to certain cultural contexts. According to Gilman (2009), self-help books stem from an industry that thrives off the liberal ethic of personal choice and responsibility. She states that the central premise of self-help culture is "that it is possible to manage one's life through reflection, discipline and routine" (p. 241). One of the ways that Freedman and Barnouin promote both liberal and post-feminist values in their diet books is by encouraging veganism through the strategically adopted phrase 'use your head.' Scattered explicitly throughout various chapter of *Skinny Bitch*, such as 'Give it Up' and 'The Dairy Disaster,' the phrase 'use your head' appeals to a specific kind of female audience:

> We sincerely hope that you will take the knowledge you've learned and put it to use from this moment on. YOU hold the power to change your life, and it's really so simple. Use your head, lose your ass (Freedman and Barnouin 2005, p. 191).

The self-help focused, body-conscious, post-feminist woman is the stereotype that Freedman and Barnouin (2005) rely on to further their vegan message (Winch 2011). The phrase 'use your head,' while touted as an empowering way to take back control of one's life, is also a tacit way to promote self-blame for decisions made that contradict the *Skinny Bitch* agenda. Murray (2008) suggests that liberal-humanist philosophies of personal choice are often used as a way to criticise people for their body weight and shape, especially if it does not fit socially acceptable models of beauty. If women are asked to 'use their heads' to understand the politics surrounding their consumption of food and the consequences of consuming these foods on their bodies, then they are also being asked to take responsibility for both their level of physical attractiveness and for the societal abuse of animals. Rather than staging a political protest to raise awareness on the violence against animals, women are being asked to take responsibility for their body weight through their own eating behaviour. By suggesting that "YOU have the power to change your life" (Freedman and Barnouin 2005, p. 191), it can be seen that Freedman and Barnouin depoliticise women's eating behaviour through the promotion of personal responsibility. The vegan lifestyle that they encourage plays on the physical insecurities of women rather than on their political potential.

Animalising Women

One of the methods the authors use to shame women for their contradictory diet practices is by applying non-human referents to them. Scattered throughout both *Skinny Bitch* and *Skinny Bitch in the Kitch*, Freedman and Barnouin (2005, 2007) use non-human referents as ways to describe women, and anthropomorphic referents as ways to describe animals. As explained in the previous sections of this chapter, the most common animal reference used in their books, that of the skinny bitch, has been depicted as an honorary label describing women's aspirational image of themselves. However, other non-human referents, such as pig, cow and pussy, have been used as explicit ways to insult women about their eating behaviour:

Try not to eat the entire batch of frosting before you put it on the cake, pig ("Vanilla Cake with Frosting"; Freedman and Barnouin 2007, p. 179).

You are a total moron if you think the Atkins diet will make you thin. Or, you are a gluttonous pig who wants to believe you can eat cheeseburgers all day long and lose weight (Freedman and Barnouin 2005, p. 39).

What if someone told you that you could easily change your life and have the body you want for the rest of your life? … All you have to do is follow a simple formula, and be willing to delay your gratification for a few months. A few months. That's it ... Don't be a pussy (Freedman and Barnouin 2005, p. 115–116).

By appropriating the words pig and pussy to describe women, Freedman and Barnouin (2005, 2007) show that non-human referents can be used as ways to insult women's eating practices. Pig, in these excerpts, carries with it the negative connotations of gluttony, laziness and 'fatness.' Pussy, on the other hand, depicts a person of weak motivational character, with an inability to delay gratification. While it may appear outwardly offensive to compare women to farm animals, the use of negative non-human referents to insult women and their eating behaviour is not, in itself, unusual. According to Van Oudenhoven and colleagues, animal references are the most common insults used against women, while derogatory terms describing men's genitals are the most common insults used against men (Van Oudenhoven et al. 2008). Freedman and Barnouin's use of non-human referents, though seemingly normative within Western culture, does, however, show some inconsistencies with their vegan/animal rights message. In fact, to insultingly describe a woman as a farm animal when one is devoting their diet book to the protection of animals does have implications on the way that both are treated within patriarchal culture (Adams 2010; Dunayer 1995, p. 12).

In the twentieth anniversary of her confronting book, *The Sexual Politics of Meat*, Carol J. Adams (2010) discusses the similarity between the mistreatment of animals and women through acts of physical and sexual objectification. Adams (2010) poignantly argues that the literal and metaphorical consumption of both relies on their repeated objectification or fragmentation in society. Once they are fragmented and emphasised for their parts rather than their whole self (i.e., animals depicted as meat and women depicted as their sexual organs), they are implicitly dehumanised. As Adams (2010) explains, dehumanisation often leads to various forms of violence (e.g., verbal, emotional, psychological, physical and sexual), as people become unable to empathise with those who are viewed as mere objects. She refers to this dehumanised persona as an absent referent throughout her work, and specifically in the context of the parallel violence that occurs in the case of both animals and women.[7]

In an interview with Tom Tyler (2006), Adams discusses the systematic abuse of animals and women by politicising the act of meat-eating:

All flesh eaters benefit from the labour of the bitches, chicks, (mad) cows, and sows whose own bodies represent their labour and whose names reveal a double enslavement – the literal reproduction forced upon them, and the metaphoric enslavement that conveys female degradation, so that we human females become animals through insults, we become the bitches, chicks, cows, and sows, terms in which our bodies or movements are placed within an interpretative climate in which female freedom is not to be envisioned (p. 122).

In this excerpt, Adams (as quoted in Tyler 2006) depicts the enslaved labour of female animals, such as cows, sows and chicks, as being directly related to the subordinate position of women within Western culture. By associating women with domesticated animals, it can be argued that one is implicitly labelling them as "soft, affectionate," and perhaps most prominently as "easily controlled" (Sutton 2012, p. 281). As Dunayer (1995) explains, comparing women to "denigrated nonhuman species" (p. 11) emphasises their place within patriarchal societies, namely, as objectified humans whose primary currency is their appearance, and, therefore, their ability to be consumed by the male gaze. From this perspective, Freedman and Barnouin's (2005, 2007) depiction of women as pigs, pussies and bitches serves the dual function of both promoting the objectified consumption of women and encouraging the post-feminist ideologies in shaping women's food femininities.

As explained by Winch (2011), Freedman and Barnouin's (2005, 2007) use of an ironic, post-feminist position, enacted in a "hyperbolic aggressive-intimate fashion" (p. 366), has allowed them to use non-human referents to describe women as negative in one instance, and positive in the other. In their diet cookbook *Skinny Bitch in the Kitch*, Freedman and Barnouin (2007) state:

We're total pigs and eating is, without a doubt, our favourite thing to do. We love eating so much it makes us mad. We have almost a violent passion for food. When we go out to eat, if something we order is really good, we talk about killing the chef. Or our pets. Or ourselves. Good food makes us want to die … you know, like the expression, "…to die for". But ironically, we also care about our health (Freedman and Barnouin 2007, p. 11).

Unfortunately, most people have no idea that they can enjoy food without getting fat, sick or sad. So it's our pleasure (oink, oink) to educate and feed the masses (Freedman and Barnouin 2007, p. 13).

When a vegan lifestyle is adopted, the negative use of the word pig somehow becomes transformed into something positive. What these excerpts illustrate is the interchanging nature of non-human referents throughout *Skinny Bitch*, which becomes curious upon closer inspection. While pig is viewed as a negative label when the diet adopted is a highly processed non-vegan one, it becomes positive when the readers adopt the *Skinny Bitch* message. The function of interchanging animal referents can be understood as an implicit attempt to reclaim negative non-human referents as something to be proud of.

The process of reclaiming previously sexist and derogatory references towards women has been discussed by some radical feminist writers. Mary Daly (1979), for example, appropriated the use of the terms witch and hag as ways to promote anti-establishment sentiments and a rupturing of patriarchal depictions of acceptable femininity (Sempruch 2004). As explained by Sempruch (2004), Daly transformed the word hag from a "victim of phallogocentric hegemonies" (p. 113) to "a female eccentric ... who deviates from established patterns and defines gynocentric cultural boundaries" (p. 118). She showed that words have the potential to be reclaimed when their origins are thoroughly explored. Freedman and Barnouin's (2005, 2007) use of non-human referents, however, can be seen as a contradiction to Daly's (1979) attempts to reclaim sexist vocabulary. Instead of attempting to take back the words pig and pussy for all women, regardless of their dietary preferences, the authors selectively reclaim the words for women who adopt the *Skinny Bitch* (and thus, vegan) diet. Women who do not adopt the diet, in this context, leave themselves open to being compared to abused domestic animals.

In an article for the British newspaper *The Guardian*, Gail Dines and Wendy J Murphy (2011) discuss the increasingly acceptable use of the term slut to describe women, specifically in the context of SlutWalk.[8] They argue that the efforts of protestors to reclaim the word slut from its derogatory origins were misguided, and that women should have been protesting about their safety and the misogynistic patriarchal systems in which they reside. In a similar sense, Freedman and Barnouin's (2005, 2007) depictions of women as pigs, pussies and bitches accentuate a protest against animal cruelty from a depoliticised, individualistic perspective. As Adams explains, animalising women and feminising animals are not considered acts of emancipation against patriarchy, but merely contribute to reiterating the sexual politics of meat (Adams 2010).

Anthropomorphising 'Food'

As well as assigning non-human referents to their female audience, Freedman and Barnouin (2005) also depict animals, nature and various types of food anthropomorphically. According to Karlsson (2012), anthropomorphism can be described as "the habit of attributing traits, *believed to be* uniquely or typically human, to non-human entities, such as ... animals" (p. 709). Bekoff (2008) explains that the anthropomorphism of animals serves as a useful way to remind people that "animals have rich and deep emotional lives" (p. 772). The anthropomorphism of animals has also been used as a tool for advertising companies to sell meat. As one blogger from website *Reverse Symmetry* (2011) explains, anthropomorphism in Western advertising assigns human characteristics to animals in an attempt to make their inevitable slaughter seem playful and cartoon-like. A chicken nugget, for example, may be shown fearing its imminent consumption by trying to run away from a person's mouth—an advertisement that depoliticises the act of killing chickens for human consumption and trivialising it to lighten the mood. In *Skinny Bitch*, however, Freedman and Barnouin (2005) use the anthropomorphism of animals as a way to increase and reiterate sympathy for their plight, devoting some chapters, such as 'You Are What You Eat,' to the anthropomorphic qualities of the animals people consume:

> Researchers at Bristol University in Britain discovered that cows actually nurture friendships and bear grudges (Freedman and Barnouin 2005, p. 74).

> Chickens are as smart as mammals, including some primates, claims animal behaviourist Dr. Chris Evans of Macquarie University in Australia. They are apt pupils and can learn by watching the mistakes of others (Freedman and Barnouin 2005, pp. 74–75).

> Pigs can play video games! They've been labelled more intelligent than dogs and three-year-old humans (Freedman and Barnouin 2005, p. 75).

The anthropomorphism used in these excerpts functions as a way to increase awareness about the sentience of animals rather than viewing them as depersonalised pieces of meat. It is clear that Freedman and Barnouin (2005) use anthropomorphism to further an animal rights message, but their descriptions of food (especially foods high in sugar) demonstrate their tendency to assign masculine and feminine properties to objects that are gender-neutral and without humanity.

In reference to the processing of foods such as flour, the authors make several anthropomorphic references:

Companies ... add these nutrients back into their refined, milled foods and use terms like "enriched" or "fortified". But there's no use trying to fool with Mother Nature. Our bodies cannot absorb these added-in materials with the same ease. Tragically, most cereals, pastas, rice, bagels, breads, cookies, muffins, cakes, and pastries have been bastardised in this manner (Freedman and Barnouin 2005, p. 24).

In this excerpt, two anthropomorphic references are made, both of which carry gendered connotations. The first reference to "Mother Nature" (p. 24) depicts the world as implicitly feminine and maternal. The second reference to "cereals, pastas, rice, bagels, breads, cookies, muffins, cakes, and pastries" (p. 24) presents baked goods as children, and their processing as a form of bastardisation. The term 'bastard' literally referring to "the fact of illegitimacy" (Hughes 2006, 18) depicts food as having been corrupted somehow by nature being perverted. The bastardisation of foods then, or the act of processing them, becomes coded as masculine—analogous to a father abandoning or neglecting his child. The foods that tamper with "Mother Nature" (p. 24) and bastardise the children of goodness (i.e., nutrients) are, therefore, often depicted as masculine. The following excerpts provide examples of the gendered anthropomorphism of white sugar:

Brace yourselves, girls: Soda is liquid Satan. It is the devil (Freedman and Barnouin 2005, p. 13).

The devil is lurking. Probably in places you wouldn't ever expect to find "him" (Freedman and Barnouin 2005, p. 27).

In these excerpts, Freedman and Barnouin (2005) demonstrate the gendered anthropomorphism of processed food, or, more specifically, the masculinisation of white sugar. Its (or his) presence in food depicts a panoptic gaze over women, where its devilish, and thus inherently bad, presence makes an innocuous appearance in all manner of unsuspecting foods. Maine and Kelly (2005) explain that, throughout most of Western culture, there is a general tendency to depict certain types of food as having moral attributes. They defined this phenomenon as the "morality of orality" (p. 30), where certain types of food are given moral and emotional labels that far exceed their practical value. The anthropomorphism of food is, thus, yet another way that Freedman and Barnouin (2005, 2007) construct a version of food femininity that transmits a moralistic gaze over women's eating behaviours.

The authors of the *Skinny Bitch* series use post-feminist versions of food femininity to reinforce and supposedly rectify women's body-conscious relationships with food. Specifically, they offer women the template for a vegan lifestyle that is contingent upon the aestheticism of their bodies, and the anthropomorphism and animalisation of their food and eating behaviours, respectively. Though they attempt to promote a type of food femininity that addresses and decreases women's body consciousness, their reiteration of terms like skinny and bitch as aspirational labels for women contradicts their otherwise healthy messages. Through the appropriation of the label skinny, as well as their use of derogatory non-human referents such as pig and pussy to describe women, Freedman and Barnouin portray a post-feminist food femininity. Their vegan diet plays on the objectification of women to prioritise the rights of non-human animals, thereby encouraging women to adopt a food femininity that is contingent upon body-consciousness and the promotion of a post-feminist aesthetic ideal. By adopting superficial feminist phrases about empowerment throughout their writing, Freedman and Barnouin abandon any feminist analysis of dieting, body-policing or consumption of meat.

"Just F---ing Do It": Bridges' Liberal-Individualist Food Femininity

Celebrity fitness trainer Michelle Bridges has become a household name in Australia since starring as the trainer of the red team on Australia's version of *The Biggest Loser* (Milsom 2012). Known for her controversial comments about weight and the details of her personal life and relationships, Bridges is generally perceived as a knowledgeable and respected figure in the personal training field. Since her time on *The Biggest Loser Australia*, she has penned a number of diet books and diet cookbooks, two of her best-selling books being analysed in this chapter. Her diet book *Losing the Last 5 Kilos: Your Kick-Arse Guide to Looking and Feeling Fantastic!* (hereafter referred to as *Losing the Last 5 Kilos*) became a number one best-selling book across all genres in Australia, and her *Crunch Time Cookbook: 100 Knock-Out Recipes for Rapid Weight Loss* (hereafter referred to as *Crunch Time Cookbook*) was also successful (www.michellebridges.com.au).

Her use of the phrase "Just fucking do it" (JFDI) as a motto, a modified version of *Nike's* tagline "Just do it," is examined in this chapter for its reinforcement of confession and panopticism as dominant forms of self-discipline. These techniques of (self-) discipline, I argue, are reinforced through the promotion of a liberal-individualist version of food femininity centring on feminist notions of choice and agency. As explained by Murray (2008), the liberal emphasis on individualism claims that "change lie[s] in the individual" (p. 5), thus placing primary responsibility on the person to change in themselves what is a deeply political issue. I argue that Bridges uses her modified phrase "just fucking do it," as well as other disciplinary mechanisms, to reinforce liberal-individualist food femininities in women, linking body-consciousness to women's identities about food and eating.

Just Do It: Deconstructing the Mantra

Based on Gary Gilmore's last words just seconds before being executed by firing squad (i.e., "let's do it"; Peters 2009), the phrase "just do it" has moved beyond its morbid origins and become emblematic of the "grit, determination, and passion" (p. 2) of sports-shoe giant *Nike, Inc.*[9] In 1988, more than a decade after Gilmore's famous last words, *Nike* was already profiting from the simultaneously simple, yet vague, message of "just do[ing] it." According to a mini case study conducted by the Centre for Applied Research (CAR 2010), *Nike's 'Just Do It'* advertising campaign was among the most successful in American history, going from "$877 million in worldwide sales to $9.2 billion in the ten years between 1988 and 1998" (p. 1). Part of the widespread appeal of the *Just Do It* slogan was *Nike's* use of irony in its portrayal of self-control and accomplishment—an irony that is conveyed in a post-modern package that appears to have a "detached, determined, unsentimental attitude" (p. 2). While some critics initially responded negatively to what they referred to as *Nike's* cold and somewhat sociopathic focus on achievement, the phrase *Just Do It* quickly became a part of everyday rhetoric (Dworkin and Messner 2002).

Just Do It Like a Woman

In the mid-1980s, women were among those most targeted by *Nike's* famous *Just Do It* advertising campaigns. Owing to the burgeoning fitness craze sweeping America at the time, women were purchasing *Nike* products as both fashion statements and ways to assert their female power through aestheticism (Centre for Advanced Research; Faludi 1993). According to Faludi (1993), the 1980s were an era where the slim, athletic physique served as an arbiter of women's cultural success and, therefore, of supposed emancipation from oppressive patriarchal roles, explaining the growing obsession with fitness as a beauty practice. As explained by Dworkin and Messner (2002), *Nike* used their simple message of *Just Do It* as a way to reinforce such notions of emancipation through the liberal-feminist construction of the superwoman. The 'superwoman,' according to Tischner (2012), was an aspirational image of ideal femininity—a character that was expected to fulfil all the duties of "domestic life, paid work and public life" (Tischner 2012, p. 139) with a sense of ease. The caricature of the superwoman was, thus, very much a product of liberal-individualist (and therefore liberal feminist) philosophies that espoused notions of choice and personal responsibility. Masked in an anti-establishment ethic, *Nike* was able to simultaneously convey both liberal-feminist notions of empowerment and mass-market reinforcements of body-consciousness through their *Just Do It* advertising campaigns:

> Couched in the logic of individualism … it seems that a woman needs only to enact her free will and "just do it" in order to "have it all"—But "doing it" the corporate individualist way involves a radical turning inward of agency towards the goal of transformation of one's body, in contrast to a turning outward to mobilise collective political purposes, with the goal of transforming social institutions (Dworkin and Messner 2002, p. 23).

Dworkin and Messner's (2002) quote clearly illustrates the depoliticised nature of "just do[ing] it." Rather than striving to "transform social institutions" (p. 23) keeping women subservient to the pressures enforced by the diet/beauty industries, the promotion of just doing *it* (that is, transforming one's body to fit socially acceptable standards) emphasises *it* as a liberal-feminist project of the self. Couched in a liberal-individualist framework, *Nike's* "intense, inwardly focused" (Centre for Applied Research 2010, n.p.) reinforcement of achievement, thus, emphasises *it* (i.e., achievement, control, choice, discipline and power) as an empowering state of being to strive towards.

Just Fucking Do What?

In an interview with Rosemarie Milsom (2012) of the *Weekender*, Bridges is depicted as the quintessential poster girl for a liberal-individualist ethic of choice and personal responsibility. Modifying *Nike's* famous mantra *Just Do It*, Bridges offers the alternative, 'Just Fucking Do It,' to reinforce her unquestionable and relentless commitment to health and fitness.

Her inclusion of the word "fucking" to *Nike's* famous mantra reflects what Milsom (2012) describes as a "tougher, cruder, Aussie take ... on *Nike's* famous slogan" (p. 8), a more urgent or, perhaps, casual take on the original. Monogrammed on both her hats and T-shirts, the initials 'J F D I' beg the question, 'what?' As Dworkin and Messner (2002) asked in their piece on *Nike's* liberal-feminist agenda: "just do *what?*" (p. 23), and perhaps more importantly, why do "it" at all?

Drawing on and reinforcing *Nike's* liberal-individualist (and sometimes liberal-feminist) promotion of just doing *it*, Bridges (2011) demonstrates what she refers to as consistency both in her herself and in her clients. In the introductory chapter of *Losing the Last 5 Kilos*, she states:

> Of all the questions that I am asked about exercise and healthy living ... there is one that endlessly haunts me: "So tell me, Michelle, how do you stay motivated?" When I hear it, I want to tear my hair out, because what I do is not about motivation, it's about consistency. **Motivation is about feeling—** determined, enthusiastic, frenzied, angry—and is therefore fickle and unreliable like a bad ex-boyfriend ... Consistency, however, **is about doing** ... It is that steady, yet relentless, journey to an end. It doesn't require profound thought. You quite literally **just do it.** In fact I have a T-shirt that makes the point a little more emphatically by boasting my favourite acronym on the front in bold letters: 'J F D I' (Bridges 2011, p. 35; original bold text).

Referring to her more emphatic version of *Nike's* original slogan, Bridges demonstrates that consistency, or "just fucking do[ing] it," is no more than an automatic process of self-discipline and routine. In fact, in an interview with Cornford (2012, n.p.) of *body+soul* magazine, Bridges suggests that women should refrain from thinking when it comes to health and weight loss in general and "just do!" This notion of automatic functioning, which is exemplified through the phrase "just fucking do it," is addressed in one interview when she is asked the question, "do you ever have days where you don't feel like training?" Bridges emphatically answers:

> Of course I do! But when those days turn up, I just slip into robot mode and get on with it. The moment you start bargaining with yourself ("oh, I'll train after work" or "maybe I'll have a day off and train longer tomorrow") you're in trouble (Bridges, as cited in Cornford 2012, n.p.).

Here, Bridges demonstrates that thought plays a very minor role in her own disciplinary success. In fact, the very notion that she "slip[s] into robot mode" to accomplish *it* is an important one in Bridges' reinforcement of a liberal-individualist position relating to food and her body. Much like *Nike's* portrayal of ideal femininity as a liberal-feminist construction of the superwoman, Bridges, too, demonstrates that successfully controlling one's body is contingent upon certain disciplinary practices that rely on the commitment of the individual. The ways in which this liberal-individualist position is enacted throughout her texts is through the promotion of a Foucauldian understanding of confession and panopticism. In the following sections of the chapter, confession and panopticism will be examined in relation to Bridges' liberal-individualist construction of food and body. First, however, confession and panopticism will be explained as residing in Foucauldian analyses of (self-) discipline.

Confession

Confession has been documented as a phenomenon that has risen in popularity in the last century through cultural mediums such as therapy and television talk shows (Landry 2009; Lynch 2009; Wilson 2003). Foucault (1978) was among the first theorists to acknowledge confession as a technique embedded in social hierarchies and power relations. He emphasised that rather than viewing confession as a private interaction between two equally esteemed parties, confession should be emphasised as an interaction between a powerful authority figure (one who decides what constitutes the truth) and the one who makes the confession (and thus reiterates their truth from a culturally acceptable narrative). Confession, from this perspective, is not merely the production of truth unmediated by external forces, but, rather, constitutes the reiteration of certain cultural norms. Wilson (2003) states that Foucault's theories of confession extend beyond theological accounts and into other social relationships (e.g., student–teacher, patient–doctor). She argues that confession even occurs in television talk shows (such as *Oprah*), where the encouragement of self-disclosure becomes a deeply feminine and emotional act of a self laid bare. A revelation of the shameful truth, thus, serves as both a perceived liberation from it and also a way to be controlled through the judgements of those listening. Murray (2008) argues that these, and similar, acts of confession found in medical practice are deeply engrained in liberal-individualist philosophies of choice and personal responsibility. From a liberal-individualist framework, people are depicted as producing their own, unmediated personal truths in a vacuum from societal norms and expectations, and are thus held accountable for their revelations. Many dietary discourses adopt multiple modes of confession, in conjunction with self-surveillance, as ways to encourage people's panoptic gaze over their bodies and eating behaviour (Carlisle Duncan 1994; Levy-Navarro 2012).

Panopticism (or Self-Surveillance)

Panopticism, the "power relations which manifest themselves as supervision, control and correction", was originally discussed by Foucault (1979) in his seminal work *Discipline and Punish: The Birth of the Prison*. Based on Jeremy Bentham's architectural model of a prison, Foucault (1979) described panopticon as:

> An annular building; at the centre, a tower; this tower is pierced with wide windows that open onto the inner side of the ring; the peripheric building is divided into cells, each of which extends the whole width of the building; they have two windows, one on the inside, corresponding to the windows of the tower; the other, on the outside, allowing the light to cross the cell from one end to the other. All that is needed, then, is to place a supervisor in a central tower and to shut up in each cell a madman, a patient, a condemned man, a worker or a schoolboy (p. 200).

According to Foucault (1979), the power of the panopticon lies in its capacity to induce self-surveillance. As each inmate is subjected to light, and thus visibility, the key purpose of the panopticon is to show the inmates that they are being monitored. The lack of visibility of the anonymous occupants in the watchtower functions to render the inmate helpless, and thus constantly in a state of self-policing their own behaviour. Initially touted as a more humane way to punish criminals, the panopticon was created as an alternative to the lightless dungeon that was successful at containing and punishing people, but failed to discipline them. Foucault (1979) argued that the state of self-surveillance reinforced by the panopticon extended beyond the prison system (and thus, the criminal) and into the greater social sphere (e.g., schools, hospitals), famously posing the question, "is it surprising that prisons resemble factories, schools, barracks, hospitals, which all resemble prisons?" (p. 228).

Some theorists have suggested that even without the architectural structures of the panopticon, panopticism is still possible (Bartky 1990). In her compilation of essays entitled *Femininity and Domination*, Sandra

Lee Bartky (1990) argued that the panopticon is, in fact, a construct that deserves a gendered focus. Instead of applying gender-neutral analyses to panopticism, she argued that studies should focus on feminism, and specifically on women's experiences of self-surveillance to achieve a more rich and nuanced understanding of the workings of panoptic discipline. Extending on what she regarded was Foucault's (1979) androcentric understanding of panoptic self-discipline, Bartky (1990) explains that those living in a body marked as female possess phenomenologically different expressions of self-policing behaviour than those living in a male one. Through prescriptive, gender-normative forms of aesthetic practices, such as the use of cosmetics and dietary products, women's bodies become normatively scrutinised and docile as a result. According to Rolfe and Gardner (2006), the notion of the docile body was initially emphasised by Foucault as being a direct result of the self-disciplinary function of the panopticon, and this was demonstrated through the behavioural restraint of the inmate, and not of their personal thoughts. The advent of the Enlightenment in the nineteenth century, which included the beginning of medical and psychiatric care, heralded an era where the docile body became replaced by the docile mind as a major disciplinary force in society. As explained by Rolfe and Gardner (2006), the docile mind was a useful way to achieve mass-surveillance simply through applying a panoptic gaze over people's thoughts in the form of self-reflection and, thus, in the act of confession.

Confessional Panopticism

According to Tell (2010), the connection between panopticism and confession is one of disciplinary power. He suggests that "confession is, as a technique of power, literally interchangeable with Bentham's panopticon" (p. 104) as both rely on some level of self-monitoring behaviour to exert control. Initially perceived as an attempt to reinforce self-policing behaviour through the use of panoptic structures such as churches, schools, medical and psychotherapeutic settings, the confession soon became a "a technology of examination" (p. 107), relying on the confessor's ability to police themselves through their supposedly 'private' and unmediated revelations about their thoughts and their bodies. Rolfe and Gardner (2006) state that the confession became a powerful medium of panoptic self-discipline by turning self-reflection into "a general strategy of self-restraint" (p. 597). Instead of being viewed as a liberating revelation of the truth, a truth that is unmediated by external forces, the act of confession implicitly served as a marker of panoptic control through its associations with liberal-individualist concepts such as choice and personal responsibility. As explained by Heyes (2006), the diet industry is one industry that profits from the liberal-individualist confessions and self-surveillance of its clients. She uses the popular weight-loss company *Weight Watchers* as an example by emphasising the clients' responsibility for their dietary choices through the introduction of 'Pro Points,' an example of how diet discourses have moved away from calorie-counting and notions of restriction. Reflecting on her own experiences of self-discipline with *Weight Watchers*, Heyes (2006) states that:

> Unlike prisoners or schoolchildren, we have elected to place ourselves under the care of this institution, and have only ourselves to blame if we fail to follow its good advice to the letter. The disciplinary practices of weight-loss groups are concealed in part by one of the most insidious dynamics in normalisation: the reification and subsequent internalisation of subject positions initially defined by mechanisms for the measurement of population (pp. 133–134).

The liberal-individualist position reinforced by *Weight Watchers* is similar to those depicted by Bridges in her diet books *Losing the Last 5 Kilos* and *Crunch Time Cookbook*. By acknowledging the liberal-individualist position that Bridges reinforces, it becomes evident that food, too, is used as a way to encourage women to police their bodies. Indeed, Bridges successfully utilises the notion of confession, and specifically the panoptic technique of confession, to reiterate a liberal-individualist food femininity that deliberately promotes body-consciousness in her female readers.

Self-Surveillance, Confession and the Female Body

In *Losing the Last 5 Kilos*, Bridges (2011) reinforces the need to stringently monitor and control both body weight and eating behaviour through various disciplinary mechanisms. She sets the scene for a body-conscious narrative when she states:

> Okay, we both know why you're reading this book—you want to lose the extra kilos that are between you and your ideal weight (p. 2).

In this excerpt, Bridges implies what Naomi Wolf (1990) referred to as the "one stone solution" (p. 186), an arbitrary unit of measurement that represents the discrepancy between a woman's actual and ideal self. The One Stone Solution, according to Wolf (1990), exists to perpetuate a normative discourse of body dissatisfaction in women, that the promise of shedding of a few kilograms will lead to a happier and more confident self. The central tenets of the One Stone Solution are that women are entitled to choose weight loss as a source of self-empowerment. Bridges (2011) applies this body-conscious narrative of the One Stone Solution to a relatively narrow demographic of women:

> Chances are you've picked up this book because you're sick to death of lugging around those extra kilos and you want to look and feel better. Maybe you've just had a baby, or the middle-age spread has snuck up on you, or you've lost a lot of weight but can't get the last five off. Or maybe you're desperate to get into your skinny jeans (or just any jeans!) (Bridges 2011, p. vi).

> It takes commitment, focus and discipline. Do you think that Jennifer Hawkins [Australian model] just turns up looking the way she does? Or all those Hollywood actors are just born lucky? Are you kidding? (Bridges 2011, p. vi).

Through the use of gender-specific references, such as baby weight, skinny jeans and Hollywood standards of beauty, Bridges identifies that her core demographic is young and female. Her reference to former *Miss Universe* Jennifer Hawkins in the second excerpt is another discursive device aimed at women, which serves as a comparative ideal for women to strive towards—not towards *looking* like Jennifer Hawkins per se, but towards applying her philosophy of "commitment, focus and discipline" (p. vi). Bridges (2011) also uses self-objectification as a way to reinforce what she refers to as "tenacity and self-discipline" (p. vi). She states:

> Take a photo of yourself in your underwear or swimmers. I know I'm really pushing the friendship here, but you'll be so glad you did this when you reach your goal (p. 43).

Under the rhetoric of friendship, Bridges implies that objectifying one's own body will potentially lead to an increase in (self-) discipline. Her female readers are explicitly encouraged to adopt a body-conscious narrative and to use the image of themselves in their underwear/swimmers as a catalyst towards achieving discipline and control. Here, Bridges adopts the disciplinary function of both self-surveillance and confession to reinforce women's sense of body-consciousness. As Freedman and Barnouin (2005, 2007) do in their *Skinny Bitch* diet books, Bridges uses the before picture of women's bodies in makeover programmes as a type of visual confession of their disciplinary failure. The roundness and fleshiness of the body becomes a metaphor for a general lack of control and responsibility (Levy Navarro 2012). Murray (2008) elaborates by stating that negative connotations surrounding the 'fat' female body are so strongly engrained in the cultural imaginary that the mere sight of body fat on a woman serves as a "virtual confessor" (p. 71) of her pathological relationship with food.

Bridges (2011) encourages her female audience to confess their newfound commitment to self-discipline in the 'How to Do It' section of *Losing the Last 5 Kilos*:

This is where you make your commitment out loud. This is about putting yourself at the top of the priority list and giving yourself as much time as you can give others ... Start by writing, "My commitment to lose 5 kilos in one month ... and I am prepared to do the work it takes to get there." Stick it up somewhere you can see it daily.

Now, call a family meeting and make sure you have everyone's full attention ... Be open and heartfelt about your goals for self-improvement, and how important it is that you achieve them. Although you don't need your family's approval and support to do this, it really *is* very helpful on a practical level if you have it. You need to explain that you will be eating differently and that as a family you will all be taking better care of your health and nutrition. Junk food will no longer be freely available. If and where the complaints start, remember that **you are the main role model** in your children's lives – showing them how to look after their nutrition is one of the greatest gifts you can give them.

Then share you goal with your friends. Call them, drop in and say hi or enter it on your Facebook page (Bridges 2011, p. 45; original italics).

In this excerpt, Bridges (2011) encourages her readers to perform a multifaceted confession, one that involves revealing one's newfound project of self-discipline to family, friends, co-workers and distant acquaintances. Much like the disciplinary function of visibility in Bentham's panopticon, Bridges' reinforcement of a multifaceted confession creates an environment of multiple gazes that the confessor inadvertently constructs through their weight-loss goals. The act of confession, in this instance, merely reiterates the disciplinary power of panopticism rather than creating it.

The explicit function of the confession is to increase self-discipline. However, studies have shown that the implicit consequences of persistent self-monitoring and confession can lead to an increase in body-consciousness and dysfunctional eating behaviour (Bringle 1989; Carlisle Duncan 1994). Levy-Navarro (2012) describes this type of confession as being reminiscent of the before shot in popular makeover programmes. The before shot of the 'fat' body carries negative connotations such as sloth, gluttony and unbridled hedonism. The 'fat' body required to confess, therefore, represents a confession of one's lack of willed self-restraint. Levy-Navarro (2012) explains that "there is something coercive about what they [the 'fat' person] are compelled to say about the 'before' self" (pp. 345–346) as it serves as a reminder of one's 'fatness' as a form of pathology. Nevertheless, the before shot can be compared to Bridges' (2011) reinforcement of the multifaceted confession, primarily through the assumption that revealing the truth about one's lack of self-discipline will set one free from it. Their aim, through both body and voice, is to become the esteemed after shot that is touted as the ideal.

Scattered liberally throughout both *Losing the Last 5 Kilos* (2011) and *Crunch Time Cookbook* (2010), Bridges is shown engaging in various fitness poses, displaying her athletically-sculpted physique as a comparative ideal for her readers to strive towards. In an article by Danielle Teutsch (2012) of the *Sydney Morning Herald*, Bridges is shown posing nude in a black and white photograph, covering her breasts with her hands with the words love, doubt, acceptance and vulnerable written across her body with black body paint. The article, entitled "The Naked Truth," depicts Bridges as a liberal-individualist caricature of ideal femininity, as one that has experienced body-consciousness but has not allowed it to dominate her 'true' self. Her confession of the 'truth' demonstrates her ability to self-present as somebody with a strong level of self-discipline and perseverance. She states:

> I was a bit of a chubby kid, but as so often happens, it dropped off when I started running around. I was into everything—debating, drama club, choir—and every sport you can imagine. I was captain of a lot of teams: netball, basketball, volleyball, water polo, hockey, soccer, touch football and softball. I played in both the boys' and the girls' teams. I even loved training. I started teaching fitness classes when I was 14, so I was aware of my body (Bridges, as quoted in Teutsch 2012, n.p.).

In this excerpt, Bridges inadvertently depicts herself as the aspirational after shot that has been cited in Levy-Navarro (2012). The image of her toned and taut body is enough to serve as a virtual confessor of self-discipline in its own right, and, therefore, makes her verbal confession "almost besides the point" (Levy-Navarro 2012, p. 345). As Grosz (1995) states, the body on its own can be said to possess the truth about a person simply through the culturally prescribed meanings attached to it. The verbal confession, however, adds nuance to the superficial image of the body. It depicts Bridges as a successful overachiever, providing her audience with a direct contrast to the shameful confession that they are asked to perform. In a sense, Bridges depicts her own confession as one that her audience should strive towards.

In presenting herself as the inspirational after shot of self-discipline, Bridges (as quoted in Teutsch 2012) also depicts herself as somebody who has experienced and conquered body-consciousness:

> I'm not going to pretend I didn't have insecurities as a teenager—I think every teenager does. I remember thinking that I would like to have a good set of boobs! (Bridges, as quoted in Teutsch 2012, n.p.).

> All my life I've hated my bum. It's big! It's like an African-American woman's booty.[10] But with maturity, I've learnt to love it (Bridges, as quoted in Teutsch 2012, n.p.).

By confessing that she, too, has had insecurities about her body, Bridges empathises with her female audience and the negative feelings they experience about their weight. Her body-conscious confession serves the dual function of both humanising herself in the eyes of her audience and emphasising what she refers to as "maturity." While it has not been explicitly outlined in these excerpts, the "maturity" that Bridges refers to relates to her self-discipline and her ability to "walk ... the walk" (Bridges, as cited in Teutsch 2012, n.p.) and, perhaps more prominently, "just f---ing do it" (Milsom 2012, p. 9). Bridges implicitly positions body-consciousness as a form of behaviour that teenagers and immature people engage in, and suggests that her way to rectify it is through a well-disciplined diet and controlled fitness regime. What she does not, however, mention is that body-consciousness is the driving force of the control and discipline she promotes. As explained by Murray (2008), the authority figure to whom one confesses one's 'fatness' to, often the doctor, is usually perceived as holding the authoritative power to assign certain truths to certain bodies.

While Bridges humanises herself through her own perceived body dis-satisfaction, her authoritative position makes her appear omnipresent in the eyes of her shame-confessing audience. In addition to employing self-surveillance and confession to the discursive depiction of the body, Bridges also uses the self-surveillance and confession of food and eating behaviour to construct her own brand of food femininity. She also uses food, in conjunction with the body, as a way to reinforce her idealised liberal-individualist food femininity.

Self-Surveillance, Confession and Women's Eating Behaviour

Besides reinforcing a narrative of bodily control and self-discipline, Bridges demonstrates a disciplinary gaze over women's food choices and eating behaviours. One of the more prominent ways she emphasises a liberal-individualist position is through the caloric properties of food. In *Losing the Last 5 Kilos*, she explains:

> I've always been blown away by how much exercise you have to do to work off calories: for example, a regular cappuccino (100 calories) and a berry muf-fin (500 calories) will take a 60-minute jog to burn-off; a glass of wine (120 calories) will take the equivalent of a 2 km power walk (Bridges 2011, p. 2).

In this excerpt, calories, like kilograms, are scrutinised for their negative impact on the body. Used as a form of bodily self-surveillance, the calorie takes on disciplinary characteristics that have little to do with its origi-nal meaning or purpose. As explained by Judd (2007), calories were first described strictly from a biological perspective, as a "scientific unit of mea-surement that describes the amount of energy contained in a substance" (p. 58). Owing to the increasing body-consciousness reinforced by the diet industry, the calorie began to take on dangerous connotations relat-ing to health and well-being. For women, in particular, counting calories has been associated with the notion of danger, and, specifically, with the process of withholding pleasurable dietary experiences to maintain a cer-tain type of weight and shape (Knapp 2003).

In her anorexia memoir entitled *Appetites: What Women Want*, Caroline Knapp (2003) refers to the process of calorie counting as the mathematics of desire, "a system of self-limitation and monitoring based on the fun-damental premise that appetites are at best risky, at worst impermissible, that indulgence must be bought and paid for" (p. 26). The notion that a woman must 'pay' for her indulgence in a 500-calorie muffin is made abundantly clear in Bridges' reinforcement of a liberal-individualist food femininity, where body-policing attitudes are conveyed through the symbol of the calorie and its potential impact on the body. The desire to look a certain way, thus, overwhelms the desire to feel good (or to take pleasure in food). In *Crunch Time Cookbook*, Bridges demonstrates this notion by emphasising that caloric surveillance is a way to maximise self-control:

> Adding up your daily calorie intake not only teaches you to identify calorie-dense foods, but also makes you feel that *you* are in control of your weight and your life (Bridges 2010, p. 5; original italics).

> To help you with calorie control, I have designed all the breakfast, lunch and dinner recipes so that you will only be taking in around 300 to 400 calories per serve (Bridges 2010, p. 5).

In this excerpt, Bridges positions herself as an authority figure, one who watches over her readers and their food choices through the design of a specific menu plan. While it does not seem as though Bridges is promoting a liberal-individualist position throughout these excerpts, she is tacitly conveying an authoritative stance. For example, by designing specific menu plans for her clients (and her readers), Bridges reinforces the notion of self-surveillance by effectively minimising people's chances of failure. Because each menu is designed by Bridges, a knowledgeable authority figure throughout *Crunch Time Cookbook*, the failure to follow the clearly set instructions becomes the responsibility of the dieter. In this respect, Bridges tacitly encourages the liberal-individualist politics of choice and personal responsibility through her authoritative structuring of a calorie-counting menu plan. One of the ways she reinforces the individuals' role in calorie counting is through the function of the food diary. In *Crunch Time Cookbook*, Bridges promotes the writing of food diary as the answer to weight management:

> I always create a menu plan for my clients—it's what they expect. But first I get them to keep a seven-day food diary. This is because the first step to controlling food choices is to identify them, and my clients need to know exactly what foods (and how much of them) have led to their weight and health issues (Bridges 2010, p. 24).

If Bridges uses calorie counting as a liberal-individualist strategy of bodily surveillance (and thus, self-control), then her promotion of food diaries serves as the confessional component towards (self-) discipline. According to Krause (2008), the objectivity of a food diary, literally an item-by-item description of food ingested throughout the day, is used as an effective means of encouraging discipline in its dieters. As Zepeda and Deal (2008) add, the popularity and efficacy of food diaries lies in their simplicity and their ability to lead to increases in self-awareness (and thus, self-monitoring behaviour). The constant recording of eating habits, thus, serves as a type of written confession. Bridges reinforces the notion that food diaries are analogous to confession when she states:

> I make it very clear to my clients that if they are overweight and they come to me with a food diary that reads like Mother Teresa's I will beat them over the head with it and tell them to stop wasting everyone's time! It's of no value and doesn't acknowledge the truth (Bridges 2010, p. 24).

Bridges makes reference to confession by emphasising food diaries as depicting the 'truth' about women's eating behaviour. As explained by Foucault (1978), the confession was used throughout history as a way to maintain (self-) discipline through the reiteration of cultural norms. In *The History of Sexuality – Volume 1*, Foucault (1978) describes the act of confession as:

> A ritual that unfolds within a power relationship, for one does not confess without the presence (or visual presence) of a partner who is not simply the interlocutor but the authority who requires the confession, prescribes it and appreciates it, and intervenes in order to judge, punish, forgive, console, and reconcile (pp. 61–62).

Applying Foucault's (1978) perspective of confession to the current analysis, Bridges is depicted as the all-knowing confessee, the authority figure that simultaneously listens to the truth and reconstructs it through a discursive repetition of a liberal-individualist food femininity that is dependent on body-policing narratives. The truth, in this context, is the supposedly objective confessions of a food diary, a depoliticised document that focuses solely on the individual's choices of food. What remains unspoken, however, is the way in which Bridges moralises food by promoting caloric surveillance and body anxiety. By suggesting that one's choice of food acknowledges the truth about one's body, Bridges reinforces the notion that food plays a pivotal role in women's experiences of body-consciousness. The food diary, then, cannot be viewed as an objective document (or confession), but rather, as one that is scrutinised for its cultural acceptability. In an excerpt of an edited version of a case study entitled "Diana –The Queen of Denial," Bridges' promotion of a liberal-individualist position, reliant on the panoptic and confessional mechanisms of self-discipline, is made apparent in her construction of Diana, an overweight woman, who refuses to confess the truth about her eating habits:

> I met Diana a couple of years back in a Sydney gym. I don't usually get tears from my clients until we're halfway through the first training session, but on this occasion I managed to excel myself and Diana was crying in the first two minutes of our initial conversation.
>
> Diana was quite overweight, and explained that she'd put the weight on with her first baby, and that it had stayed. In fact, it had compounded. Her words were: "I desperately want to lose the weight, I hate it."
>
> She was at the gym, which I thought was a good start, but obviously, she was struggling. She was telling me all the stuff that she thought I wanted to hear like: "I come to the gym three times a week, and I actually eat very healthy food."
>
> Experience told me that Diana wasn't trying to convince me, but was trying to convince herself. I knew that if she was telling herself she was trying hard to eat well and exercise, then her weight problem "wasn't her fault." It gave her permission to be a victim, and in doing so, allowed her to perpetuate her unhealthy lifestyle. So, I cut to the chase.
>
> "Okay. Tell me what you had for dinner last night."
>
> "Oh, um, spaghetti Bolognese – that's my kids' favourite."
>
> "Right. So what was your serving size and did you go back for seconds?" I asked.
>
> Bang. Her face told me everything. Her serving size was the same as her husband's – large. And, yes, she not only went back for seconds but finished off the kids' meals, because, hey, you can't waste food right? Then gradually it came out that she'd also had some garlic bread, half a bottle of wine and a little Easter egg or five after dinner.
>
> "But that's not a normal night's dinner!" she claimed.
>
> I wasn't sold. "You say you want to lose the weight desperately but you are knowingly sabotaging your efforts. You say you know what you need to do to get there, and yet you're not doing it. You *deserve to have whatever it is that you desire*. If you desire to get fit, feel healthy, feel sexy and lose some weight, then do it girlfriend! Stop talking about it and playing the victim and get on with it!" (Bridges 2010, p. 7).

The chosen case study exemplifies the disciplinary processes involved in encouraging women to adopt a liberal-individualist position in relation to food. As the title of the case study suggests ("Diana – the Queen of Denial"), Bridges characterises Diana as denying the truth about her eating habits. While Diana acknowledges that her weight has become a problem—complying with culturally normative scripts linking 'fatness' to pathology (Murray 2008)—her eating behaviour is not acknowledged in the same way. The need for Diana to confess her dysfunctional eating habits is analogous to the need to confess her 'fat' body as a problematic or pathological one. As explained by both Levy-Navarro (2009) and Murray (2008), the 'fat' body is itself a visual confession of both pathology and a lack of self-discipline. Without even uttering a single word, the 'fat' person has already confessed their dysfunctional lifestyle simply through their physical appearance. While Diana acknowledges her 'fat' body as one that needs changing, the need for her to acknowledge her eating behaviour, and its contribution to her body, is presented by Bridges as being a necessary component of her transformation.

The act of confession, as explained in the previous excerpt on food diaries, is once again presented as a tacit power dynamic between the confessor and the confessee. Bridges takes on the knowledgeable and authoritative role as personal trainer, a powerful position that has the capacity to "bring tears" to her clients. Diana, on the other hand, is depicted as the pathological victim of her own impulses, unable to identify where her diet is going wrong. Through her explicitly superior position, Bridges encourages Diana to confess the truth about her eating behaviour and, in doing so, promotes a liberal-individualist version of food femininity. As explained by Murray (2008), the act of confession cannot be distinct from individualist notions of choice and personal responsibility. She explains:

> What is most interesting … is the marking of the confessional … by a humanist logic. The patient/child/prisoner is invited into a space that is simultaneously marked by apparent autonomy, where the confessor is given the "opportunity" to reveal the truth of themselves, while at the same time, a disciplinary power functions to hear this confession, interpret it, and to produce a "truth" *for* the confessor (Murray 2008, p. 77).

In the case study presented, Diana is expected to confess her food choices and to produce a truth that complies with culturally constructed notions of healthy and unhealthy eating behaviours. The need for Diana to take on an identity that relies on choosing the proper way to eat is further bolstered by the advice that Bridges gives in relation to self-transformation. Using the liberal-feminist notion of entitlement, Bridges states, "You *deserve to have whatever it is that you desire"* (p. 7; original italics). While, on the surface, it may appear that Bridges is supporting Diana into taking ownership of her unhealthy food choices, what Bridges is actually conveying is a depoliticised understanding of Diana's life, and subsequently, a promotion of liberal-individualist values. Rather than acknowledging Diana's context as contributing to her overall food choices, Bridges orders Diana to, "stop talking about it and playing the victim and get on with it!" (p. 7). Bridges' tough-love approach with Diana, masked under the rhetoric of entitlement, is indicative of a liberal-feminist promotion of personal agency. Getting on with *it*, from this context, becomes analogous to Bridges' motto of "just fucking do[ing] it," a modified version of *Nike's* original that she has come to claim as her own. As established in an earlier section of this analysis, *it* is depicted as the technique of discipline that Foucault (1978, 1979) discusses, encompassing both panopticism and confession to maximise self-control. If Bridges encourages women to "just fucking do it," then she tacitly supports the notion that women's food choices are strongly contingent upon their own disciplinary choices. Much like *Nike's* liberal-individualist emphasis on entitlement and choice in their "just do it" advertising campaigns of the 1980s (Dworkin and Messner 2002), Bridges, too, employs notions of liberal-individualist to reiterate body policing in her female audience.

Throughout both *Losing the Last 5 Kilos* (2011) and *Crunch Time Cookbook* (2010), Bridges tacitly encourages women to adopt liberal-individualist notions of femininity in relation to food (and their bodies). Through her mantra of "just fucking do it," she emphasises individualist notions, such as choice and personal responsibility, and implicitly reinforces disciplinary practices, such as self-surveillance and confession, as ways to maintain choice and personal responsibility over food and their bodies. 'Just fucking do[ing] it' is presented as a reinforcement of disciplinary power and control over the self, which was enacted similarly in analyses of both food and the body. Self-surveillance and confession over the body were emphasised as confessions of the before shot self, of a body that needs modification, with the promotion of body-consciousness as a way to enforce transformation. Bridges, contrarily, is presented as the aspirational after shot, a caricature of an ideal woman who does not possess body-consciousness due to the perceived 'perfection' of her body. Food, too, was emphasised from a panoptic and confessional perspective.

Calorie counting is portrayed as a tacit form of bodily self-surveillance, and the caloric quantification of food in the form of food diaries was viewed as the confessional component of self-discipline.

In summary, Freedman and Barnouin's (2005, 2007) reinforcement of a post-feminist version of food femininity is somewhat analogous to Bridges' (2010, 2011) promotion of a liberal-individualist one. Both sources take a depoliticised perspective when they construct the relationship between women and food. Instead of analysing context, both sources place primary responsibility on the individual. Various body-policing mechanisms are employed in this depoliticised construction of food femininities. Freedman and Barnouin (2005, 2007) encourage women to adopt the phrase skinny bitch as an aspirational term to identify with, and use, non-human referents as a way to insult and tacitly victimise women who do not adopt a vegan lifestyle. Bridges, too, reinforces body anxiety through her gendered promotion of a liberal-individualist position. Using the phrase "just fucking do it" as an inspirational mantra, Bridges demonstrates that doing *it* is actually promoting a self-disciplinary gaze over food and the body through mechanisms such as panopticism (or self-surveillance) and confession. Regardless of the different food femininities emphasised, both of the diet sources present and normalise body anxiety in their female audiences, and do so through a thin veneer of 'feminist' empowerment. While body-policing narratives are somewhat expected in dietary discourses (Spitzack 1987), the messages promoted in this chapter are also found in other discourses relating to food and eating, such as cookbooks. While these texts tend to carry more celebratory overtones, they are also subject to body-policing narratives that are inherently couched in gender roles pertaining to women. The following chapter identifies cookbooks as popular cultural discourses that, in less obvious ways, reinforce a culture of body surveillance.

NOTES

1. I identify Freedman and Barnouin's (2005, 2007) version of food femininity as being contingent upon 'post-feminism.' It is important to note that Freedman and Barnouin (2005, 2007) do not explicitly state that their discourse is a post-feminist one, but other writers (such as Winch 2011) refer to their diet books as being part of the genre of 'post-feminist conduct books.' I refer to Freedman and Barnouin's (2005, 2007) relationship with food as being a 'post-feminist' one.

2. On the back cover of *Skinny Bitch*, Kim Barnouin has been cited as having a Master of Science degree in Holistic Nutrition. Winch (2011) notes that the degree is from an unaccredited university.

3. 'BTW' is the abbreviated version of the phrase 'by the way.'

4. American comedian Tina Fey presented a monologue on Saturday Night Live (SNL) commenting on the treatment of (then) presidential candidate Hillary Clinton. Fey stated, "What bothers me the most is that people say that Hillary is a bitch. Let me say something about that: Yeah, she is. So am I... bitches get stuff done" (Fey 2008; as cited in Kleinman et al. 2009, p. 63). Kleinman and colleagues (2011) argue that Fey's depiction of being a 'bitch' is, in fact, what is typically referred to as being a 'feminist.' Her preference to use the word 'bitch' attests to the social acceptance of the derogatory term in favour of the politically relevant term 'feminist.'

5. Carol J. Adams' (as cited in Tyler, 2010) connections between feminism and veganism will be discussed in the 'Animalising Women's Eating Behaviour' section of this book.

6. Here, I've used the term 'veg*n' to depict both vegetarian and vegan life-styles. The term was originally taken from Potts and Parry's (2010) article on 'Vegansexuality.'

7. In her interview with Steffen (2009), Adams explains that the term 'absent referent' refers to the ways in which people have difficulties realising the moral and ethical dimensions of eating 'meat' or watching consuming por-nographic images of women. In this sense, the animal- and the human-being become 'absent referents' from people's eating and sexual behaviours.

8. 'SlutWalk' is a protest that originated in Canada after a Toronto police officer publicly stated, in reference to sexual assault, that "women should avoid dressing like sluts in order not to be victimised" (Dines and Murphy 2011). The premise is that by adopting the use of the word 'slut' in daily rhetoric, women will be able to 'reclaim' the word from its sexist and oppressive origins and, thus, remove its power.

9. Gary Gilmore was a notorious serial killer in America who was executed by firing squad in 1977 for his crimes (Peters 2009).

10. While beyond the scope of this project, the racial implications behind Bridges' comparison of her buttocks to "an African American woman's booty" are significant (as quoted in Teutsch 2012, n.p). For further read-ing on the racial implications behind the denigrated bodies of women of colour, refer to book *Black Sexual Politics: African Americans, Gender, and the New Racism.*

REFERENCES

Adams, C. J. (2010). *The sexual politics of meat: A feminist-vegetarian critical theory* (20th anniversary edn). New York: The Continuum International Publishing Group Inc.

Barker, C. (2004). *The sage dictionary of cultural studies*. Thousand Oaks: Sage Publications.

Bartky, S. L. (1990). *Femininity and domination: Studies in the phenomenology of oppression*. New York: Routledge/Taylor & Francis Group.

Bekoff, M. (2008). Why "good welfare" isn't "good enough": Minding animals and increasing our compassionate footprint. *Annual Review of Biomedical Sciences, 10*, T1–T14.

Bordo, S. (2004). *Unbearable weight: Feminism, Western culture, and the body*. Berkeley: University of California Press.

Bridges, M. (2010). *Crunch time cookbook: 100 knockout recipes for rapid weight loss*. Melbourne: Penguin Books.

Bridges, M. (2011). *Losing the last 5 kilos: Your kick-arse guide to looking and feeling fantastic*. Australia: Penguin Books.

Bringle, M. L. (1989). *Confessions of a glutton*. Retrieved from http://www.religion-online.org/showarticle.asp?title=894

Carlisle-Duncan, M. (1994). The politics of women's body images and practices: Foucault, the panopticon, and shape magazine. *Journal of Sport and Social Issues, 18*(1), 48–65.

Centre for Applied Research. (2010). *Mini case-study: Nike's "Just do it" advertising campaign*. Retrieved from http://udoc.eu/docs/b0c524/mini-case-study-nike-s-%2522just-do-it%2522-advertising-campaign-center-for-applied-research

Cole, M., & Morgan, K. (2011). Vegaphobia: Derogatory discourses of veganism and the reproduction of speciesism in UK national newspapers. *The British Journal of Sociology, 62*(1), 134–153.

Coleman, R. (2010). Dieting temporalities: Interaction, agency and the measure of online weight watching. *Time Society, 19*(2), 265–285.

Cornford, M. (2012). *Spotlight on Michelle Bridges*. Retrieved from http://www.bodyandsoul.com.au/health/celebrity+profiles/spotlight+on+michelle+bridges,11815

Daly, M. (1979). *Gyn/Ecology: The metaethics of radical feminism*. London: Women's Press.

Deckha, M. (2008). Disturbing images: PETA and the feminist ethics of animal advocacy. *Ethics and the Environment, 13*(2), 35–76.

Dines, G., & Murphy, W. J. (2011). SlutWalk is not sexual liberation. *The Guardian, 8*(11). Retrieved from http://www.theguardian.com/commentisfree/2011/may/08/slutwalk-not-sexual-liberation

Douglas, S., & Michaels, M. (2002). *The mommy myth: The idealisation of motherhood and how it has undermined all women*. New York: Free Press.

Drew, P. (2009). Dieting. In J. O'Brien (Ed.), *Encyclopaedia of gender and society* (Vol. 1). London: Sage.

Dubriwny, T. N. (2012). *The vulnerable empowered woman: Feminism, postfeminism, and women's health.* Piscataway: Rutgers University Press.

Dunayer, J. (1995). *Animals and women: Feminist theoretical explanations.* Durham: Duke University Press.

Dworkin, S. L., & Messner, M. A. (2002). Just do ... what? Sport, bodies, gender. In S. Scraton & A. Flintoff (Eds.), *Gender and sport: A reader.* New York: Routledge.

Faludi, S. (1993). *Backlash: The undeclared war against women.* London: Vintage.

Ferriss, S., & Young, M. (2006). Chicks, girls and choice: Redefining feminism. *Junctures, 6,* 87–97.

Fitzsimmons-Craft, E. B., & Bardone-Cone, A. M. (2012). Examining prospective mediation models of body surveillance, trait anxiety, and body dissatisfaction in African American and Caucasian college women. *Sex Roles, 67*(3–4), 187–200.

Foucault, M. (1978). *The history of sexuality – Volume 1.* New York: Pantheon Books.

Foucault, M. (1979). *Discipline and punish: The birth of the prison.* London: Penguin Books.

Fredrickson, B. L., & Roberts, T.-A. (1997). Objectification theory. *Psychology of Women Quarterly, 21*(2), 173–207.

Freedman, R., & Barnouin, K. (2005). *Skinny bitch: A no-nonsense, tough-love guide for savvy girls who want to stop eating crap and start looking fabulous!* Philadelphia: Running Press.

Freedman, R., & Barnouin, K. (2007). *Skinny bitch in the kitch: Kick-ass recipes for hungry girls who want to stop cooking crap (and start looking hot!).* Philadelphia: Running Press.

Gill, R. (2007). Postfeminist media culture: Elements of a sensibility. *European Journal of Cultural Studies, 10*(2), 147–166.

Gilman, S. L. (2009). *Diets and dieting: A cultural encyclopaedia.* New York: Routledge.

Grosz, E. (1995). *Space, time and perversion: The politics of bodies.* New York: Routledge.

Gurung, R. A. R., & Chrouser, C. J. (2007). Predicting objectification: Do provocative clothing and observer characteristics matter? *Sex Roles, 57,* 91–99.

Harper, B., & Tiggemann, M. (2008). The effect of thin ideal media images on women's self-objectification, mood, and body image. *Sex Roles, 58,* 649–657.

Heyes, C. J. (2006). Foucault goes to weight watchers. *Hypatia, 21*(2), 126–149.

Hughes, G. (2006). *An encyclopaedia of swearing: The social history of oaths, profanity, foul language, and ethnic slurs in the English-speaking world.* Armonk: M. E. Sharpe.

Karlsson, F. (2012). Critical anthropomorphism and animal ethics. *Journal of Agricultural and Animal Ethics, 25*(5), 707–720.

Kleinman, S., Ezzell, M., & Frost, M. (2009). Reclaiming critical analysis: The social harms of 'bitch'. *Sociological Analyses, 3*(1), 46–58.

Knapp, C. (2003). *Appetites: Why women want.* New York: Counterpoint.

Krause, K. (2008). *Keeping food diary doubles weight loss.* Retrieved from http://abcnews.go.com/Health/Fitness/story?id=5327486&page=1

Landry, J.-M. (2009). Confession, obedience, and subjectivity: Michel Foucault's unpublished lectures on the government of the living. *Telos, 146,* 111–123.

Lazar, M. M. (2009). Entitled to consume: Postfeminist femininity and a culture of post-critique. *Discourse and Communication, 3*(4), 371–400.

Levy-Navarro, E. (2012). I'm the new me: Compelled confession in diet discourse. *The Journal of Popular Culture, 45*(2), 340–356.

Lynch, T. (2009). Confessions of the self: Foucault and Augustine. *Telos, 146,* 124–139.

Maine, M., & Kelly, J. (2005). *The body myth: Adult women and the pressure to be perfect.* Hoboken: John Wiley.

McRobbie, A. (2011). Beyond post-feminism. *Public Policy Review, 18*(3), 179–184.

Milsom, R. (2012). *The making of Michelle Bridges.* Retrieved from http://www.theherald.com.au/story/269538/the-making-of-michelle-bridges/

Monro, F. J., & Huon, G. F. (2006). Media-portrayed idealised images, self-objectification, and eating behaviour. *Eating Behaviours, 7,* 375–383.

Morry, M. M., & Staska, S. L. (2001). Magazine exposure: Internalisation, self-objectification, eating attitudes, and body satisfaction in male and female university students. *Canadian Journal of Behavioural Science, 33*(4), 269–279.

Moskin, J. (2008). *Still skinny, but now they can cook.* Retrieved from http://www.nytimes.com/2008/01/02/dining/02skin.html?pagewanted=all

Murray, S. (2008). *The 'fat' female body.* London: Palgrave Macmillan.

Orbach, S. (2006). *Fat is a feminist issue.* London: Arrow Books.

Orbach, S. (2010). *Bodies.* London: Profile Books.

People. (2007). *Books.* Retrieved from http://www.people.com/people/archive/article/0,,20060029,00.html

Peters, J. W. (2009). *The birth of 'just do it' and other magic words.* Retrieved from http://www.nytimes.com/2009/08/20/business/media/20adco.html?_r=0

Potts, A., & Parry, J. (2010). Vegan sexuality: Challenging heteronormative masculinity through meat-free sex. *Feminism & Psychology, 20*(1), 53–72.

Reverse Symmetry. (2011). *Anthropomorphic food sabotages itself.* Retrieved from http://revsym.blogspot.com.au/2011/05/anthopomorphic-food-sabotages-itself.html

Rich, M. (2007). *A diet book serves up a side order of attitude.* Retrieved from http://www.nytimes.com/2007/08/01/books/01skin.html?pagewanted=all

Rodin, J., Silberstein, L., & Striegel-Moore, R. (1984). Women and weight: A normative discontent. *Nebraska Symposium on Motivation, 32,* 267–307.

Rolfe, G., & Gardner, L. (2006). 'Do not ask who I am ...': Confession, emancipation and (self)-management through reflection. *Journal of Nursing Management, 14*(8), 593–600.

Sempruch, J. (2004). Feminist constructions of the 'witch' as a fantasmic other. *Body Society, 10*(4), 113–133.

Spitzack, C. (1987). Confession and signification: The systematic inscription of body consciousness. *Journal of Medicine and Philosophy, 12*(4), 357–369.

Sutton, L. A. (2012). Bitches and skanky hobags: The place of women in contemporary slang. In K. Hall & M. Bucholtz (Eds.), *Gender articulated: Language and the socially constructed self.* Hoboken: Taylor and Francis.

Tell, D. (2010). Rhetoric and power: An inquiry into Foucault's critique of confession. *Philosophy and Rhetoric, 43*(2), 95–117.

Teutsch, D. (2012). *The naked truth.* Retrieved from http://www.smh.com.au/lifestyle/the-naked-truth-20120807-23rz5.html

Tiggemann, M. (2013). Objectification theory: Of relevance for eating disorder researchers and clinicians. *Clinical Psychologist, 17*(2), 35–45.

Tischner, I. (2012). *Fat lives: A feminist psychological exploration.* Hoboken: Taylor and Francis.

Tyler, T. (2006). An animal manifesto: Gender, identity, and vegan-feminism in the twenty-first century. *An interview with Carol J Adams. Parallax, 12*(1), 120–128.

Van Oudenhoven, J. P., de Raad, B., Askevis-Leherpeux, F., Boski, P., Brunborg, G. S., Carmona, C., Barelds, D., Hill, C. T., Mlacic, B., Motti, F., Rammstedt, B., & Woods, S. (2008). Terms of abuse as expression and reinforcement of cultures. *International Journal of Intercultural Relations, 32*, 174–185.

Veggie Girl Power. (2009). Rory Freedman's veggie girl power interview. Retrieved from http://kblog.lunchboxbunch.com/2009/10/rory-freedmans-veggie-girl-power.html

Wachob, J. (2010). *Q&A with skinny bitch author Rory Freedman: Her spiritual journey that led to best-selling book.* Retrieved from http://www.mindbodygreen.com/0-1195/Q-A-with-Skinny-Bitch-Author-Rory-Freedman-Her-Spiritual-Journey-that-Led-to-BestSelling-Book.html

Wilson, S. (2003). *Oprah, celebrity and formations of self.* Basingstoke: Palgrave Macmillan.

Winch, A. (2011). 'Your new smart-mouthed girlfriends': Postfeminist conduct books. *Journal of Gender Studies, 20*(4), 359–370.

Wolf, N. (1990). *The beauty myth: How images of beauty are used against women.* London: Vintage.

Zapeda, L., & Deal, D. (2008). Think before you eat: Photographic food diaries as intervention tools to change dietary decision making and attitudes. *International Journal of Consumer Studies, 32*(6), 692–698.

CHAPTER 5

Cooking Up Femininities: Motherhood, Hedonism and Body Policing in Popular Cookbooks

Cooking has played a contentious role in feminist academic literature over the last four decades, with conflicting accounts about its significance in women's lives (Supski 2006). Some second-wave and radical feminist writers attribute cooking to women's social and cultural subordination, arguing that being responsible for food, and the domestic labour that accompanies it, renders women voiceless within male-dominated or patriarchal societies (Friedan 1963; Greer 1971; Oakley 1976). Other more contemporary feminist writers, however, influenced by liberal ideologies, perceive cooking as an act that signifies women's agency. From this perspective, being responsible for food and residing within a space to express their love and care, is seen as a powerful aspect of womanhood and not necessarily understood as an indicator of women's subordination or oppression (Supski 2006). Indeed, as magazine and television programmes show, the cultural fascination with the art of cooking—both domestic and professional—has intensified in the last couple of years (Seale 2012). Some have argued that this increase in culinary entertainment has heralded a return to the study of cookbooks as arbiters of important cultural messages about race, class and gender (Scholes 2011). As Neuhaus (2003) explains in her book *Manly Meals and Mom's Home Cooking: Cookbooks and Gender in Modern America*, the study of cookbooks reveals both implicit and explicit gender norms that function to construct and reinforce certain attitudes and behaviours in women. She explains that:

© The Author(s) 2017
N. Jovanovski, *Digesting Femininities*,
DOI 10.1007/978-3-319-58925-1_5

> Cookbooks echo a national debate about women's social roles in general and represent particular kinds of food and cooking as gendered. They help to reinforce the notion that women ha[ve] inherently domestic natures (p. 2).

Indeed, in this chapter, cookbooks are analysed for their gendered significance and studied on the basis of the food femininities promoted by their authors. The study of contemporary cookbooks combines the importance of domestic, selfless ideologies with more individualist, hedonistic narratives of pleasure (Culver 2012). In order to understand the cultural significance of cookbooks in the twenty-first century, especially in relation to the strengthening of often harmful gender norms, it is essential to understand how certain gender norms are used in culinary texts to appeal to female audiences (Neuhaus, 1999). It is also important to acknowledge that cookbooks can be a place for women to simultaneously escape from the restrictive and anxious food culture and be part of the same body-policing culture that permeates other food discourses such as diet books. I argue that the conflicting messages produced by contemporary cookbooks written by female food celebrities contribute to a confusing set of gender rules about food and eating (Bordo 2004; Popa 2012).

Using Food as a Mouthpiece

Some writers have argued that the food femininities depicted in culinary texts function to provide women with a voyeuristic, and fantasy-like, expression of femininity, one where women are given permission to cook elaborate or exotic meals and to enjoy the food that they prepare (Magee 2007). In his post-structuralist piece on the subject positions embedded in cookbooks, West (2007) explains,

> More than simply instrumental communication, like food itself, cookbooks and recipes invite readers into specific subject positions, some of which are more attainable than others ... Cookbooks provide cooks opportunities for communicating who they are and who they might want to be (p. 358).

From West's (2007) perspective, when women read cookbooks, they ingest not only the recipes, but also the gender norms that lie, often hidden, between the glossy food images.

In keeping with the idea that gender plays a significant role in constructing cookbooks and is reflected in the recipes promoted by cookbook authors, it is important to note that the cultural status of cookbooks has changed significantly to meet the demands of contemporary Western culture. The changes expressed in contemporary cookbooks have led to a potentially new set of tensions for women in their relationships with food (Mitchell 2010; Scholes 2011). As Mitchell (2010) explains in her article on the cult of the celebrity chef, popular figures in the media associated with food and cooking, otherwise known as food celebrities, transcend the instructional-style domestic cookery that was once a staple of cookbooks and television shows. Rather, contemporary food celebrities, such as Nigella Lawson, Jamie Oliver and Gordon Ramsay to name a few, communicate through food in a way that favours entertainment rather than sustenance, a phenomenon that Mitchell aptly describes as "glitter overwhelm[ing] substance" (p. 537).

The "glitter" that Mitchell (2010) speaks of relates to the personalities behind the cookbooks, and the influence of these personalities in reinforcing certain food femininities. Scholes (2011) refers to these personalities as "towering persona[s]" (p. 45), capable of reinforcing gendered lifestyles in addition to a series of recipes. The significance of female food celebrities is, thus, of central importance in this chapter. As Scholes (2011) explains, due to the celebrity status of celebrity cookbook authors, they are often referred to "companionably by their first names" (Scholes 2011, p. 45). In keeping with Scholes' (2011) suggestion, this chapter will refer to the food celebrities analysed by their first names.

In this chapter, I examine how the uncomfortable intersection of gender and food is reinforced by female celebrity cooks in mainstream, bestselling cookbooks. I also explore how the advice given to female audiences rests upon a narrative of both traditional and contemporary food femininities. It is the tension between the maternal (i.e., the traditional feeder) and the hedonistic (i.e., the contemporary eater) where body-policing narratives are expressed, an indication that the male gaze operates to colonise both women's ability to feed others and to feed themselves. Unlike popular diet books, cookbooks written by female food celebrities are publicised for their wholesome qualities, encouraging women to adopt nurturing qualities through food. The body-policing attitudes uncovered in cookbooks are, thus, less explicit and more complex than those expressed in the diet books analysed in Chap. 4. The tacit nature of cookbooks as arbiters of body-policing narratives is, therefore, an important analysis to consider.

The texts chosen for analysis are all cookbooks published within a ten-year period. Two Australian (Julie Goodwin and Poh Ling Yeow) and two British (Nigella Lawson and Tana Ramsay) authors are chosen on the basis of their popularity in both Australia and abroad. Nigella Lawson's cookbook *Feast* (2006) is chosen on the basis of the celebrity appeal of its author. As Hewer and Brownlie (2009) explain, Nigella's cookbooks carry a cultural significance that transcends her recipes. Her fame is often compounded by her regular guest appearances on television programmes such as *MasterChef* and other entertainment-based chat shows. Tana Ramsay, on the other hand, has achieved celebrity status through her comparison to her colourful celebrity chef husband, Gordon Ramsay. Her cookbooks *Real Family Food* (2009) and *Tana's Kitchen Secrets* (2010) are published as domestic, rather than professional, culinary texts and suggested by some to be a contrast to Gordon's celebrity persona (Lawson 2011). Julie Goodwin's *The Heart of the Home* (2011) is selected on the basis of her popularity on season one of *MasterChef Australia*. Receiving the winning title of *MasterChef Australia* in 2009, Julie's victorious episode attracted between 2.5 and 3 million viewers in 2009 (Townsville Bulletin 2009). Since then, Julie has become a household name in Australia, and regularly appeared on television programmes and advertisements (Seale 2012). Poh Ling Yeow, runner-up of *MasterChef Australia* 2009, and her cookbook *Poh's Kitchen: My Cooking Adventures* (2010), also gained fame through her association with the famous cooking competition. Poh's cookbook, based on her eponymous cooking show for the Australian Broadcasting Corporation, was published due to Poh's popularity among the Australian public (Gunders 2011).

"CRACKING THE COMBINATION LOCK": TANA'S MATERNAL AND HEDONISTIC FOOD FEMININITIES

Tana Ramsay is a British celebrity cook and wife of controversial celebrity chef and reality TV star, Gordon Ramsay. Her cookbooks, which mirror her television appearances, focus largely on her role as the mother of Gordon's four children, and reflect the tensions experienced by women who attempt to juggle their maternal responsibilities with their own desire for food and pleasure. Throughout *Real Family Food* (2009) and *Tana's Kitchen Secrets* (2010), Tana's maternal and hedonistic portrayals of food femininity reflect the importance of being responsible, which is both reflected in the patriarchal confines of her kitchen and in her own relationship with enjoying food. Tana's 'responsible' relationship with food and her body is bolstered by her public persona as a "busy mother of four"

(Beazley 2010, n.p.), one that is intrinsically monitored by the professional male gaze of her husband, Gordon. Juxtaposed against his colourful and often controversial public persona, Tana is represented as the "soft-spoken Ramsay" (Honey 2008, n.p.), the humble, domestic and unmistakably feminine version of Gordon's hegemonic masculine persona. According to Lawson (2011), Tana "has founded her niche market out of her status as Gordon Ramsay's wife and mother of their children" (p. 361) and, as such, relates to food in a way that emphasises an anxious type of responsibility, whether in relation to her children or to herself. It is through the theme of responsibility where Tana's anxious relationship with food and her body takes shape, and where the male gaze of her husband and the culinary culture in which she operates shape the appropriate ways she is expected to relate to food.

A key defining feature of Tana's cookbooks and, indeed, her maternal depiction of food femininity is her care-oriented and selfless relationship with food and cooking. In her recipe for 'Lamb Kidneys in Cream and Mushroom Sauce,' for example, Tana demonstrates how the narrative of responsibility (i.e., being responsible for nourishing *others*) is one that has been passed on by her mother through food:

> When I was a child, my mother used to serve this to us on toast. It's a great way to encourage children to eat kidneys. My mother was way ahead of her time, as these days offal of all sorts is the height of culinary fashion in the best restaurants (Ramsay 2010, p. 50).

Tana's recipe emphasises two dominant themes about her responsible maternal food femininity; firstly, that a mother's responsibility in the family is to nourish and protect her children through food, and secondly, that the role of domestic cooking is significant in its own right, and capable of influencing and competing with professional culinary figures and institutions. Both of these themes will be discussed.

Tana's maternal sense of responsibility in tending to her children's health and well-being through food is not unusual. Rather, it is best understood as a gender-normative approach for women in relating to food. In their article entitled, *Feeding the 'organic child': Mothering through ethical consumption*, Cairns et al. (2013) argue that mothers are culturally expected to provide their children with healthy and organic meals, and that women experience "pressure to consume ethically through their food work and mothering practices" (p. 98). Responsible feeding, from this perspective, plays an unavoidably central part in women's relationships with food and cooking. Indeed, as Cairns et al. (2013) identify, it was their female participants who expressed this normalised responsibility most, and that their role as mothers were implicitly, and sometimes anxiously, associated with neoliberalism. They explain that, "in a neoliberal context, where mothers are positioned as individuals responsible for ensuring their child's optimal development, the idealised figure of the organic child is a product of mothering practices ... [and] a discourse of ethical consumption" (p. 113). Indeed, in Tana's maternal version of food femininity, the motivation behind her responsible persona is driven by pre-existing cultural norms relating to women's essentialised nurturing properties, a gender role that is fuelled by patriarchal constructions and expectations of women, and the ever-present male gaze in women's lives. In *Tana's Kitchen Secrets* (2009), for example, the male gaze operating behind Tana's responsible version of food femininity is the gaze of the professional chef and sometimes even her husband, Gordon. I argue here the gaze operating behind Tana's anxieties over feeding her children is the same gaze that stifles her own enjoyment of food, and, subsequently, of her body. It is this gaze that constructs her anxious relationship as both a mother and as a woman who feels entitled to enjoy food.

Tana's comparison of maternal home cooking with the fashionable cuisines prepared "in the best restaurants" (p. 50) is one of the ways the male gaze permeates into her cookbooks. Indeed, one of the disempowering ways that Tana accentuates her maternal food femininity, and where the male gaze begins to solidly take shape, is through her involvement in the kitchen, which, from the outset, is presented as a space that does not belong to her. In the 'acknowledgements' section of *Real Family Food* (2009), Tana jokingly writes:

> Gordon, thank you for your patience and for letting me use your kitchen – thank God I cracked the combination lock! (Ramsay 2009, p. 257).

Breaking the second-wave feminist criticism that women are confined to their kitchens, Tana jokingly reveals that her own place in the kitchen is one that is dominated by her celebrity chef husband, Gordon. Indeed, as Tana herself explains in a piece written for *The Daily Mail*, she has two kitchens in her house, one belonging to her, and the other belonging to him. The main kitchen overlooking the garden contains a "custom-made two-and-a-half tonne industrial stove which cost €75000" (n.p.), one that

Gordon uses when entertaining guests or filming for his various television appearances. Tana's kitchen, which is located in the less picturesque basement of their home, is designated to the less glamorous task of cooking for their four children. In these examples, and strewn throughout her cookbooks, Tana's lack of creative space in the kitchen is reflected in her anxious relationship with food, both in preparing it and in eating it.

In her article on the gendered significance of the kitchen in Australia, Sian Supski (2006) emphasises the importance of the kitchen in framing women's place and significance in the home. She argues that in a time when women had little cultural and political power, the kitchen was seen as a place of solace where one could use food and domestic labour as a facet of strength and empowerment. Despite the contemporary cultural setting of her cookbooks, it seems that Tana's relationship with her own kitchen is one that is colonised by the professional male gaze of her husband, depicting her relationship with food as a site of surveillance and control. This is expressed when Tana is shown resisting Gordon's professional gaze when it comes to feeding their children:

> I am a true believer in steamed vegetables. Gordon thinks it takes too long, but he's wrong! (Ramsay 2010, p. 154).

Rather than expressing a confident, maternal relationship with food and cooking, Tana defends herself, a defence that emphasises Gordon's professional male gaze and highlights uncertainties in her expressions of responsible, culinary motherhood. As much as Tana asserts that Gordon is "wrong!" (p. 154) about the preparation of vegetables, his presence in her cooking is virtually unavoidable. It is this presence that also dominates Tana's own enjoyment of food.

Perhaps, unsurprisingly, Tana's own relationship with and enjoyment of food is also colonised by the male gaze. Without being explicitly referenced as such, the male gaze permeates her recipes when she begins to express her own desire for certain types of food. Despite being seemingly absent when she describes her enjoyment of food, the overarching presence of Gordon and his professional and masculine, objectifying gaze remain constant. Depicted in the British and international media as a "friendly rivalry" (Honey 2008, n.p.), Tana's relationship with her husband Gordon reflects tensions in the way that the professional male gaze occupies the life of the domestic cook, so much so that it impacts the domestic cook's own enjoyment of food and its preparation. Tacitly (and sometimes explicitly) positioned as Tana's culinary superior, Gordon's 'macho' presence in the kitchen is felt through-out *Real Family Food* (2009), juxtaposing against Tana's more anxious and unmistakably maternal relationship with food. As Scholes (2011) explains in her article 'A Slave to the Stove?', Gordon "is famous for his uber-macho attitude to cooking" (p. 50) and takes "every opportunity to contest his virility, as if penis size equates to cooking skills" (p. 51). His reputation in the kitchen, on the surface, is conveyed as a hard-hitting, belligerent and quintessentially masculine public persona. Tacitly, however, it is reflective of his own anxieties about the emasculating gendered connotations of cook-ing (Higgins et al. 2011; Scholes 2011). Gordon's anxieties and the devel-opment of his brand of food masculinity only seem to further exacerbate Tana's helpless and body-policing relationship with food, which reflects a tense, hierarchical and quintessentially gendered contrast.

Tana's own enjoyment of food is hampered by this power disparity. In *Tana's Kitchen Secrets* (2009), for example, she is shown repeatedly describing the food she enjoys as "a bit naughty" (p. 122), "a ... guilty pleasure" (p. 246) and "not for those watching their figure" (p. 122). The infantilising tone of Tana's enjoyment of food is coupled with the notion of guilt to produce a body-policing food narrative. The same responsible theme that resonates throughout her references to being maternal also plays a part in defining her hedonistic appreciation of food. In her recipe for 'Fish Pie,' for example, Tana demonstrates that she has earned her right to have three helpings:

> It's good to know how to make a comforting fish pie. You can use cheap sustainable fish such as Pollack [...] After a recent half-marathon I had three helpings (Ramsay 2009, p. 70).

Without explicitly referencing the male gaze, Tana alludes to its presence by stating that she has earned the right to "three helpings" following a "recent half-marathon" (p. 70). In defending her responsibility-driven right to comfort food, Tana reflects a dominant feature of contemporary, patriarchal Western culture and its fascination with disciplining women's hunger (Bartky 1990; Bordo 2004; Knapp 2003; Wolf 1990). As Knapp (2003) argues, monitoring one's hunger based on the amount one deserves to eat is a common component of women's disordered relationships with food and eating and, more importantly, a gendered one. Tana's adherence to the male gaze, taking shape in her conscious disciplining of her body, falls in line with Gordon's hegemonic masculinity and criticism of all things feminine. In her article entitled 'Balls Enough: Manliness and Legitimated

Violence in Hell's Kitchen,' Gabriella Nilsson (2013) argues that Gordon uses gender "as a sorting mechanism" (p. 656) in the professional world of cooking and relies on his hierarchical position in the kitchen to make judgements about both his male and female contestants, often using femininity as an insult. She further explains that in his reality TV shows, Gordon is frequently shown referring to his male contestants as 'pussies' and insulting his female contestants by making degrading comments about their appearance (e.g., "Sharon, go and put some more makeup on!") or calling them names such as "bimbo, bitch, Barbie [and] showgirl" (Nilsson 2013, p. 656). Bringing Gordon's hegemonic masculinity and criticism of all things feminine to light, it appears as though Tana's need to complete a "half-marathon" (p. 70) in order to receive comfort from food reflects the gendered positioning of herself in comparison to Gordon, as the juxta-posed masculine and feminine versions of the culinary world. As a way to justify this self-consciousness, Tana also produces a body-policing narrative in her cookbooks through a veil of humour. Speaking in reference to her 'Chocolate, Fruit and Nut Cookies' recipe, Tana explains that the dessert is:

> Based on my favourite chocolate bar, fruit and nut, these cookies are a fan-tastic energy boost. Well, that's my excuse! (Ramsay 2009, p. 262).

Once again, Tana's appreciation of food is moderated by her responsible consumption of it (e.g., the "fantastic energy boost" (p. 262)), which, implicitly, can be read as a body-policing narrative. The "fantastic energy boost" (p. 262) she receives from her favourite dessert is used to justify the pleasure she experiences from eating it. Indeed, Tana's attempts to conceal her anxieties about food and her body are masked by a veneer of tongue-in-cheek humour. In essence, humour serves as a way to normalise the harm and political potency of her message. In keeping with the notion that Gordon's patriarchal gaze hovers over Tana's maternal version of food femininity, it can be argued that the male gaze is also unsurprisingly present in Tana's enjoyment of food. This is a theme that bleeds into other culinary texts, despite obvious differences between authors.

CONSUMING THE 'YUMMY MUMMY': NIGELLA'S MATERNAL AND HEDONISTIC FOOD FEMININITIES

Unlike Tana, Nigella is shown outwardly challenging the roles that are commonly ascribed to women through food when she constructs a world where "it is possible to choose to care for yourself ... through taking time to feed yourself and choosing food you like rather than deferring to the choices of significant others" (Hewer and Brownlie 2009, p. 483). A journalist by trade, Nigella carved a name for herself as a self-proclaimed 'domestic goddess,' penning a series of successful cookbooks and hosting a number of cooking shows in the UK. Her sensual and seemingly hedonistic relationship with food has positioned her in the cultural imaginary as somewhat of a feminist icon; as a woman who values carbohydrates over counting calories. Despite her public persona, however, Nigella also shows signs of succumbing to the harmful, yet normative, preoccupation of body anxiety, and reflects this anxiety in tacit ways throughout her cookbooks.

In her cookbook *Feast* (2006), for example, Nigella veers from encouraging her audience to rejoice in their consumption of food, to being consumed by the gaze of the Other. Like Tana, Nigella's careful balancing of motherhood and hedonism reflects some element of the male gaze and, inadvertently, highlights tensions in the way she relates to food and her body. Unlike the responsible, care-oriented maternal food femininity that Tana depicts in her cookbooks, however, Nigella's brand of culinary motherhood occupies the relatively uncharted space between the "traditional stay-at-home-mummy ... [the] professional-entrepreneurial mummy ... [and the] yummy mummy" (Hewer and Brownlie 2009, p. 485). Instead of using food as a way to assert her motherhood, Nigella uses cooking as a way of playing with or reinventing maternal food femininities, or as Hewer and Browlie (2009) state, "drawing[ing] into a particular version of feminine identity, a branded subject position" (p. 483) that combines motherhood and hedonism. I argue here that Nigella's resistance to traditional food femininities associated with motherhood and selflessness is replaced by her hedonistic and sexualised appreciation of food, which obscures her sense of body consciousness and self-surveillance and, implicitly, obscures the male gaze, which continues to operate in her enjoyment of food. The male gaze that she resists in her maternal connection with food is the same gaze that colonises her hedonistic enjoyment of food with body-policing narratives.

Motherhood is one way that Nigella transgresses cultural boundaries. She resists the idealised notions of culinary motherhood through the food she prepares for her children and, specifically, for their birthday parties. This is one of the many indicators throughout *Feast* where Nigella paints herself as somebody who is not entirely comfortable with traditional, care-oriented feminine relationships around food, roles that have previously been touted as oppressive (e.g., Oakley 1976). She states:

I've covered this ground before, and with each year and indeed, each book. I'm inclined to make less of a fuss. Anything you make to be healthy or to feed them properly goes ignored and you end up throwing paper-platefuls of food wastefully into bin-bags at the end. Children like cake – or rather, the icing – and they like crisps, but I can't honestly say they want otherwise to eat at parties ... So, all I'd suggest you do is food that doesn't tax you at all; some little sausages (cooked in the oven, so no spitting from a pan) or bought mini-pizzas; now is not the time to put puritist pressure on yourself (Lawson 2006, p. 262).

Differentiating herself from the traditional caricature of the responsible and health-oriented mother, Nigella adopts a more casual approach to organising the food at her children's parties. Without conveying any shame or guilt about her lack of culinary puritanism, Nigella encourages women to relinquish their anxious relationships with food, cooking and, implicitly, with selfless nurturing. Nigella's transgression of traditional maternal food femininities makes her message more palatable to her largely female (and likely guilt-ridden) audience. In other words, by drawing on references to "crisps" and "bought mini-pizzas" (p. 262) in a cookbook intended to *teach* women how to cook, Nigella depicts herself as a welcome antithesis to the stereotype of the woman who has it all, a woman who is otherwise referred to as the superwoman, and divorces herself from what Hewer and Brownlie (2009) refer to as the "all too hectoring," "all too schoolmarmish" (p. 485) stereotypes of female food celebrities of the past (i.e., Delia Smith). Throughout *Feast*, Nigella explicitly resists the stereotype of the 'superwoman' by emphasising the drudgery involved in cooking food that will be "thrown ... wastefully into bin-bags at the end" (p. 262). She shows elements of second-wave feminist thinking by shattering the myth of the happy housewife and, instead, replaces it with a version that sees cooking in the context of fantasy, as a way to please oneself rather than emulating an essential, selfless and other-oriented stereotype of the ideal woman.

Despite her intentions, however, not all writers and social commentators agree that Nigella successfully subverts this cultural ideal. Some even argue that she contributes to perpetuating it (Shapiro-Sanders 2009). According to Brunsdon (2005), because Nigella explicitly disidentifies with the notion of the superwoman, she plays a part in reinforcing it, attaining superwoman status precisely through her imperfections. Indeed, as Shapiro-Sanders (2008) adds, Nigella's distinctive and often messy relationship with food obscures her successful, middle-class lifestyle, offering "permission to her audience to not be the domestic ideal," while simultaneously airing her 'flaws' and giving her target audience "permission to be themselves" (p. 152). Nevertheless, despite these criticisms, Nigella's resistance to the traditional and selfless domestic ideal inadvertently positions her relationship with food and cooking as a resistance to the traditionalist, male gaze. In fact, her relationship with food and cooking is one that seems to, on the surface, reflect her rebellion towards patriarchal expectations of women.

One of the key features of her subversive maternal position in relation to food is the resentment she experiences in enacting the role. Nigella makes no exceptions when she emphasises how difficult it is to maintain being maternal in relation to food. In doing so, she begins to depict her own needs and desires through her association of cooking with domestic drudgery. She states:

> I don't cook frenziedly for my children, and like many mothers, would be stricken most teatimes if there was no such thing as pasta, but at weekends I cook for them for the simple reason that meals need to be cooked and children must be looked after and I can combine the two (Lawson 2006, p. 238).

> I know these are quite a lot of trouble, but they are a real treat, and even such instinctive ingrates as children will truly appreciate it ("Chicken Pot Pies"; Lawson 2006, p. 240).

While elements of traditional motherhood are present (e.g., "meals need to be cooked and children must be looked after," p. 238), the main message behind Nigella's experiences of cooking point to the drudgery associated with feeding children or, as Nigella calls them, her "instinctive ingrates" (p. 240). Breaking from traditional conceptions of culinary motherhood, where the 'love' of the mother is outwardly and centrally expressed in the act of feeding, Nigella appears to transgress the normative expectations of motherhood (e.g., care, selflessness) by complaining that the expression of love and care through food is, inherently, a form of labour. The pragmatics of cooking for her children, and others, is seen to be part of Nigella's cultural appeal. It is these criticisms of traditional, selfless and other-oriented versions of culinary motherhood, however, where Nigella begins to reflect her own tensions with food itself.

In an interview with Josh Tyrangiel (2003) for *Time* magazine, Nigella discusses her iconic domestic goddess persona as having turned her into a type of caricature, or a domestic monster. She explains that "I was a journalist before … and sometimes I go to these chat shows and I'd just so much rather talk about al-Qaeda than how to cook a proper lamb" (n.p.). What this reveals is that cooking serves the dual role of fuelling her fame and yet stunting her intellectual credibility at the same time. Jenny Lawson (2011) reflects this cultural bind when she argues that food provides women with a catalyst to achieve social and cultural status, and has been used as a vehicle towards being "in the public view, watched and consumed" (p. 341). Nigella's relationship with food and cooking, as transgressive as it may seem, is her primary means of being acknowledged and culturally heard. The way she subverts these essentialised stereotypes of femininity is by enjoying the food herself and emphasising why she deserves to gain pleasure through food and eating.

Indeed, one of the major components of Nigella's celebrity image is her outward appreciation for tasting and enjoying her own cooking. Her role as an eater, and not just a feeder, has been argued to reflect her popularity among her many audiences, but especially among women, who have been socialised to monitor their food intake and body shape in a "world of no" (Knapp 2003, p. 11). Rather than providing women with a traditional snapshot of a selfless culinary femininity, one that involves the nurturing of family and friends above oneself, Nigella is shown actively inserting her own hungers and desires throughout *Feast* and, seemingly, transgressing patriarchal norms that dictate women's normative discontent with their bodies. In the following excerpt, Nigella uses an academic tone to legitimise her desire to feast. She states:

> In a 1999 research paper, a number of learned writers sought to describe and compare various attitudes to food. Subjects from France, Belgium, Japan and America were given several foodstuffs and required to give their immediate associations. To "chocolate cake" the Americans responded with "guilt"; the French countered with "celebration". (Just as to the word "cream", the Americans came out with "unhealthy" and the joyful French, "whipped".) In this context, I must declare myself firmly allied with the French. If chocolate cake is an indulgence, please don't consider it a sinful one: it is a confection to exult in, not to regret (Lawson 2006, p. 263).

Aligning herself with the "joyful French" (p. 263), Nigella situates her food narrative as one that is in direct opposition to the guilt-ridden Americans and, as such, constructs her hedonistic version of food femininity as one that conflicts with gender norms proscribing to women's 'normative discontent.' By emphasising the joy of feasting, Nigella poses a resistance to dominant body-policing gender narratives, presenting a seemingly carefree and entitled attitude to consumption. This message is also evident in her personal life, when she has, at times, emphasised her apparent dislike of anything related to weight loss. In an interview with Josh Tyrangiel (2003) for *Time* magazine, Nigella is depicted as a Rubenesque beauty, unashamedly proud of her hedonistic gustatory life-style. During the interview, she strengthens her hedonistic persona and confidently states that "people should stop demonising fat ... seeing food as something like medicine is a horrible idea, life's too short ... working out and eating lite are simply an impossibility" (n.p.). In keeping with the notion that 'fat' is acceptable for women to ingest, the following quotes highlight Nigella's apparent disregard for the 'dangers' of carbohydrate narratives and show elements of resistance to feminine norms involving calorie counting and body-monitoring behaviours:

> Any meal is better if there's a serious carb content ("Stir-Fried Rice"; Lawson 2006, p. 246).

> The food I like best at parties is the carb-rich stuff everyone falls for, having spent the evening virtuously turning down every mimsy little canapé (Lawson 2006, p. 399).

> This cake is not named for the bypass you might feel you'd need after eating it, but in honour of the four choc-factors that comprise its glory; cocoa to make the cake; chocolate chips or morsels to fold into it; a chocolate syrup to drench it once out of the oven; flakily sliced dark chocolate to top it before slicing. I love this for tea, even for weekend breakfast, or late at night when its melting squidginess tends to fall darkly to my white sheets – and I don't care. It's always wonderful as a pudding; put it on the table, ready to slice, alongside a bowl of strawberries and another of crème fraiche ("Quadruple Chocolate Loaf Cake"; Lawson 2006, p. 272).

Nigella's appreciation for food with "serious carb content" (p. 246) and her words of praise for a cake that can be compared to a quadruple "bypass" emphasise a message that conflicts with dominant and idealised narratives of healthy food femininities. Her apparent lack of anxiety over consuming foods that have otherwise been associated with a host of physiological conditions and aesthetic *faux pas* can be perceived as a welcome alternative. Indeed, it is her almost reckless sense of hedonism that contributes to the rising popularity of *Brand Nigella* (Hewer and Brownlie 2009).

Nigella's hedonism has been argued to offer her female audiences permission to enjoy their cooking and, implicitly, the permission to desire and care for oneself. The dominant way she conveys this message is through the sexualisation of eating (and of herself). In his article about the rising popularity of gastroporn, Magee (2007) argues that Nigella's cultural persona as a female food celebrity is one that is reliant on her sexuality, which is ultimately used as a way to legitimise her appreciation of foods high in fat, sugar and carbohydrates. Magee (2007) describes the contents of Nigella's website as a testament to her sexualised hedonistic persona. In one particular photograph, he describes Nigella wearing a tight black T-shirt, with the words 'English Muffin' emblazoned across her chest. The function of this image, he explains, plays on the otherwise repressive sexual nature of the British and the sexual connotations behind the word muffin, serving as a reminder that *Brand Nigella* is just as edible as the high-carbohydrate food she prepares. In a similar example, Scholes (2011) demonstrates that Nigella's "ultra-feminine" (p. 49) and sexualised persona serves to legitimise her enjoyment of foods otherwise considered unhealthy. In one example, Scholes (2011) describes Nigella's 'Trashy Food' section of *Nigella Bites* as an overtly sexualised, tongue-in-cheek example of how the guilt-free appreciation of food intersects with the notion of sexuality. Wearing a *Playboy* bunny T-shirt in one image and a pair of silk pyjamas in another, Nigella is shown flirtatiously tucking into a large bowl of what she refers to as "Slut's Spaghetti" (p. 49). The function of these images is clear; watching Nigella feast on food not only endorses her own hedonistic relationship with it, but also encourages the visual, and rather voyeuristic, consumption of her sexualised body.

Indeed, in her description of 'Quadruple Chocolate Loaf Cake,' Nigella relies on expressions of sexuality to legitimise her enjoyment of the cake, which she herself mentions is comparable to a heart attack. By drawing on references to its "melting squidginess ... fall[ing] darkly [on her] white sheets" (p. 272), Nigella successfully merges her physical appetites with the visual appetites of her audience. In doing so, she conflates and legitimises both the pleasures of eating (for her female audiences) and, simultaneously, caters to the heterosexual male gaze by encouraging viewers to voyeuristically consume her sexuality. It is this outward display of sensuality and hedonism that has led to some writers to refer to Nigella as a yummy mummy (Hewer and Brownlie 2009).

Nigella's conflation of sexuality with the desire to eat signifies her adherence to, and perpetuation of, the objectified and, arguably, oppressive

Western caricature of the yummy mummy (McRobbie 2006). In her article entitled "The Rise of the 'Yummy Mummy': Popular Conservatism and the Neoliberal Maternal in Contemporary British Culture," Littler (2013) describes the increasingly mainstream caricature of the yummy mummy as a figure that "symbolise[s] a type of mother who is sexually attractive and well groomed," a woman who "knows the importance of spending time on herself" and somebody who is "profoundly classed" (p. 231). The yummy mummy, from a contemporary cultural perspective, is seen as a progressive destabilisation of the traditional, and largely asexual, representations of motherhood and, as such, is often touted as a welcome alternative to the Virgin Mary archetype dominating Western culture for over two millennia. According to Hewer and Brownlie (2009), Nigella's yummy mummy persona is an amalgamation of the mother, the sister and the sex symbol, a seemingly refreshing image of culinary motherhood that avoids the asexual pitfalls of traditional, matronly and unsexualised motherhood (Douglas 2010). Rather than waiting for the culinary praise of her children or her partner, who remains largely absent throughout *Feast*, Nigella praises her own cooking through the experience of taste and pleasure in a sensual way. In a sense, Nigella capitalises on her own objectification in order to promote her hedonistic version of food femininity (Hewer and Brownlie 2009; Magee 2007; Scholes 2011).

Some writers argue that Nigella relies on a narrative of sex appeal to encourage a fantasy-driven, self-objectifying version of food femininity (Magee 2007; Mitchell 2010; Scholes 2011). In his article on the cultural appeal of celebrity cookbooks, Magee (2007) discusses the rising popularity of food pornography in popular culinary texts in the wake of, and during, the twenty-first century. Using the cult of the celebrity cook as an example, Magee (2007, n.p.) argues that food identities, such as Nigella Lawson, construct cookbooks as forms of pseudo-pornography for housewives, encouraging women to engage in a "voyeuristic exercise" that delves into the life of the author and, specifically, into her seemingly dangerous, yet enticing, appetites. Indeed, Nigella uses this technique all throughout her cookbooks, television programmes and public appearances. The image of her sneaking into the kitchen and rummaging through the refrigerator for leftovers, "licki[ng] her fingers" seductively and "flicking her hair" (Hesser 2002, n.p.) throughout the process, has not only been a topic of discussion among academics but has also been parodied by the media and various comedians (Whiting 2012). Indeed, as Hewer and Brownlie (2009) explain, Nigella's emphasis on hedonistic consumption is her primary method of selling her cookbooks and kitchen products. Through the very notion of being a food celebrity, Nigella simultaneously commodifies her recipes and, perhaps less obviously, herself (Hewer and Brownlie 2009). Indeed, I argue that her commoditisation, and objectification, of herself is one way that she reinforces her female audience to self-police their bodies.

Cashmore and Parker (2003) explain commodification as a phenomenon when they describe the cult of the celebrity. They argue that "the commodification of the human form ... the process by which people are turned into 'things', things to be adored, respected, worshipped, idolised, but perhaps more importantly ... consumed" (p. 251) is one of the consequences of being in the public eye, especially for women. Although often unwanted, the commodification of celebrities (and their bodies) serves as a way of bringing them into the public eye. Indeed, evidence of Nigella's relationships with food and eating appear to be moderated by the male gaze, and the commodification of her body, all throughout *Feast*. One of the ways this is depicted is through her reference to the physical consequences of overeating. Nigella displays a conflicted relationship between desire and body consciousness, for example, when she discusses her recipe for "Sprauncy Christmas Eve Supper for Eight." She states:

> The thing to remember is that while feeling a welcoming abundance is wonderful, a seasonal sense of overstuffed bloat is not (Lawson 2006, p. 43).

As Shapiro-Sanders (2008) explains, Nigella's sexualised, hedonistic appreciation of food is challenged by her gender-normative, yet destructive, surveillance over her body. While Nigella persistently shows herself enjoying food and appreciating the act of feasting, the fact that she reminds her readers about the all-too-common "sense of overstuffed bloat" (p. 43) that comes after feasting diverts attention away from her enjoyment of food and onto the narrative of body surveillance. In fact, Nigella shows a mixed reaction to food as both a source of pleasure and empowerment, and, at the same time, a potentially destructive, body-altering object. Exemplified in Shapiro-Sanders' (2008) chapter entitled *Consuming Nigella*, Nigella candidly admits that:

> For all my long-held beliefs that fat was a feminist issue, that the modern tyranny of the scales was both ideologically and physically damaging, and that intolerance of the unthin was dangerous, I have to admit that I felt awful when I put on weight after the birth of my first child and better when I lost it (Lawson 1998; as cited in Shapiro-Sanders 2008, p. 155).

Indeed, Nigella's relationship with her body is one that mirrors the feelings that many contemporary Western women experience over their own bodies, and even her own mother's decade-long abuse of her own body through experiencing both anorexia and bulimia (Khokhar 2011). In what appears to be a sign of body consciousness, Nigella breaks from her hedonistic version of food femininity to the process of her weight loss. Her more recent and dramatic weight loss, from a size 16 to a size 12 (PR Newswire 2012), can be perceived as an example of the tensions embedded in carrying a hedonistic version of food femininity in contemporary Western culture. In an article for tabloid British newspaper *The Sun*, Nigella confesses that:

> I have indeed lost weight ... Almost a year ago, I had a very glamorous operation, a double bunionisation. I couldn't walk to the fridge afterwards. Actually it's quite a good diet, not because I stopped eating, because you can say to someone "Can you get me a slice of cake?", but because it's kind of embarrassing to say "Could you get me a second slice of cake?" (Lawson, as quoted in Whiting 2012, p. 2).

Nigella's hedonistic food femininity, well publicised as that which separates her from the weight-obsessed narratives of contemporary Western femininity, comes under threat when revelations about her weight loss begin to surface. Indeed, the difficulty she faces in merging the space between maternal and hedonistic appears to be due to living in a culture that embraces only certain aspects of women enjoying food. As Cheryl Day (2009) explains, Nigella's voluptuous body is—almost—excused for carrying excess weight because she represents the confusing space between the mother and the seductress. The upper part of her body displays fat in culturally acceptable places (e.g., breasts), and the bottom half of her body remains conveniently hidden behind the kitchen bench, which is why her message is both palatable to some and offensive to others at the same time. This feature is evident all throughout *Feast* where Nigella's upper body gains prominence over her lower half, a theme that is mirrored in tabloid media articles glamourising Nigella's voluptuous curves. In her piece for the *Daily Mail*, Liz Jones (2011) romanticises Nigella's body and outlines, in detail, the appropriateness of where her 'fat' resides. She states:

> Nigella ... has taken a long hard look in the mirror [and] seen what can be exposed and what needs to be covered up ... She always avoids trousers ("a--e too big"), and above all steers clear of anything "tent-like" or

remotely baggy. She knows her waist is small, so she never wears smocks or shifts … On top, she always wears something fitted at the bodice: she knows a sloppy sweater over big breasts only serves to make them look matronly (Jones 2011).

Jones' (2011) evaluation of Nigella is not surprising; indeed, it has been well established that the link between the maternal and the sexual is one fraught with difficulty, with some arguing that the two terms, taken together, signify two different people rather than the same woman (e.g., Montemurro and Siefken 2012). In Jones' quote, by matronly covering her breasts in a sweater, Nigella loses her yummy mummy persona and, both simultaneously and implicitly, her right to enjoy food. In fact, throughout *Feast* (and her other cookbooks and television programmes), Nigella is only allowed to engage in hedonistic eating when it is contained by her sexuality, when her breasts are "fitted at the bodice" and when her "small waist" is accentuated.

According to Littler (2013), part of the appeal of the yummy mummy is her ability to merge the maternal with the sexual. This has been perceived by some, such as Douglas (2010), as a positive step for women. However, as Littler (2013) accurately points out, the 'yummy mummy' is only allowed to consume when she is considered visually and aesthetically palatable herself. Littler (2013) explains that:

[The yummy mummy] reverses the idea of the mother as devouring monster; the hungry, castrating monstrous feminine that populates psychoanalysis, flipping the trope around so it is instead the mother herself who is not only edible but also a diminutive tasty morsel (p. 234).

Nigella's hedonistic relationship with food is, thus, strongly related to her sexuality and the voyeuristic consumption of her body. Nigella walks on a tightrope of acceptable and unacceptable food femininities, fearing that she will become the Oedipal, "devouring monster" (p. 234) by engaging in dieting herself. While she somewhat successfully subverts the traditional maternal expectations ascribed to women and food by acknowledging her own desires, a task which has been touted by some as a feminist act, her anxieties around food and eating remain, albeit in the background, as a theme throughout *Feast*. When she compares the food she prepares and consumes to a "quadruple bypass" and makes cursory references to avoiding "the bloat," she is implicitly reinforcing a narrative of normative discontent that is already pervasive in mainstream Western culture.

Rather than resisting this message, she subtly normalises it by casually referencing it in her language. While she resists the patriarchal confines of domesticity and turns them into a fantasy-type performance, she nevertheless only experiences hedonism when it is coupled with restraint.

'IT MUST BE IN MY BLOOD': JULIE'S MATERNAL AND HEDONISTIC FOOD FEMININITIES

In stark contrast to Nigella's subversion of the traditional domestic ideal, Julie Goodwin presents herself as the antithesis to the contemporary and fashionable domestic goddess. Julie is an Australian television personality, best known for taking out the title of the first season of *MasterChef Australia* and appearing in various advertisements for cooking and cleaning products. Julie's place in the home, and specifically the kitchen, is where her traditional and maternal versions of food femininity are reinforced. Indeed, Julie is shown repeatedly asserting herself as somebody who expresses care through cooking and feeding others. Unlike Nigella, who uses her sexual palatability and voyeuristic depiction of food, Julie's cookbook demonstrates a comparatively humble, asexual depiction of culinary motherhood, one that relies on the stereotypes that second-wave feminist writers, such as Betty Friedan (1963) and Ann Oakley (1976), aimed to eradicate in their famous texts. Her own enjoyment of food, unlike Tana and Nigella, seems to be relatively unaffected by the male gaze but, rather, seems to serve as a protective mechanism that the other writers in this chapter have not demonstrated.

Julie's cookbook, affectionately titled *The Heart of the Home* (2011), questions her female readers about what makes their house a home. Julie is quick to describe her grandmother, who she lovingly refers to as her "Nan," as the heart of her home, and describes her mother as one of her most significant culinary influences. In doing so, she frames her version of food femininity as one based, first and foremost, on the notion of maternal care:

> Mum was always throwing dinner parties. Some were finger food, some were sit-down dinners, but for the bigger crowds she would cook a buffet-style feast ... There was always a lot of laughter and music ... So, I come from a party-throwing background and it must be in my blood (Goodwin 2011, p. 122).

Julie invites her audience to share her warm memories and, in doing so, frames her own relationship with food from a traditional, care-oriented perspective. Indeed, Julie's description of her mother demonstrates that caring for and entertaining others through food is an idealised part of a woman's culinary persona. Julie's distinctive construction of a maternal food femininity, as influenced by her mother, is accentuated as something that is innate or, as she states, "in my blood" (p. 122), an essentialised component of her womanhood. As Scholes (2011) explains in her article on the gendering of culinary culture, female food celebrities tend to construct themselves in the media to reflect the nurturing qualities of their cooking, steering clear of the professional connotations associated with the craft. Indeed, in Julie's case, her essentialised and maternal version of food femininity serves as her primary culinary identity, even when she is placed in the context of and succeeds within a professional—and predominantly masculine—cooking arena such as *MasterChef Australia*. As cited in Sydney Morning Herald (2009), Julie's involvement in the professional world of food and cooking, as evidenced in her participation and success in the first season of reality television cooking show *MasterChef*, is very much defined by her maternal, care-oriented persona. She states:

> I just want it to be a warm and welcoming place that people love to be in and I want to cook food, when people leave my restaurant I want them to feel like they've been loved (Goodwin, as cited in Cranston 2009, n.p.).

Julie's emphasis on making her diners "feel like they've been loved" demonstrates how difficult it is for women to divorce the maternal from the professional world of cooking. Indeed, as Greer (1999) explains in *The Whole Woman*, the underlying expectation on women (and especially mothers) to be other-oriented and to provide love through food is considered both antiquated and normative in Western advertising and everyday rhetoric, a caricature of idealised femininity that has undergone revisions but has ultimately proven difficult to budge. Julie reinforces this perspective through her essentialised and almost innate relationships with food and cooking. And while it appears as though she chooses to adopt the selfless nurturing of the traditional maternal role, the gaze operating behind her maternal construction of food femininity is an unmistakably patriarchal one.

Throughout *The Heart of the Home*, Julie's essentialised and maternal version of food femininity is reinforced and moderated by the male gaze of her husband and teenaged sons. Scattered throughout and between her recipes, Julie's husband Mick is shown reinforcing her traditionally maternal relationship with food:

> Eating great food has always been one of the ways we have enjoyed time together. I remember our first Valentine's Day. Jules' parents went out for the night so that she could cook me a romantic dinner. She made a huge cheesy lasagne and bought Coronas. She knew the way to my heart. It was a memorable evening (Goodwin 2011, p. 155).

> One Mother's Day we invited mum, Jules' mum and sister, and all the family to our place for a celebration lunch. We had to bring the outdoor setting indoors to fit everyone at the table, which Jules set beautifully. She made the most enormous baked dinner – it was great (Goodwin 2011, p. 17).

Julie's husband Mick enters her culinary narrative as the male gaze, scrutinising her cooking and, implicitly, reinforcing her essentialised, maternal relationship with food. Mick's observation that "Julie knows the way to [his] heart" (p. 155) through food clearly reinforces the norm that women express love through feeding, and while showing appreciation of her culinary expressions of love and care, he does not appear to play any role in assisting Julie throughout the process. Rather, Mick is depicted as an appreciative bystander, rather than an attentive, active and equal cooking partner.

The stereotype of the distant, yet appreciative, male gaze is not new. In her chapter on the intersection of food and gender, McLean (2013) argues that the role men play in reinforcing food femininities onto women is "a major component of female identity" (p. 255). She explains that men's preferences for certain meals and experiences tend to dominate women's cooking choices so much so that family meals become "masculine meals" (p. 255; as cited in Sobal 2005, p. 142). McLean (2013) explains that, "such dynamics produce and reinforce a patriarchal structure" (p. 255) that positions women in roles that cater to men's needs. In the aforementioned excerpts, Mick's preference for certain meals dominates Julie's culinary repertoire, positioning her relationship with food as one predicated upon the care and nurture of others. This notion is further reinforced by Julie's conflation of relaxation and domestic labour:

> Nature abhors a vacuum (so do I, Nature, so do I). In the same way, the calendar abhors a Sunday with nothing scheduled ... So, if I see an opening in the calendar I will often nab it and schedule a relaxing day – what my

teenage sons call a "chillaxin' day". This can take a number of norms but my favourite is going to Mass, then heading home to prepare a feast, and finally enjoying a lazy afternoon on the back deck (Goodwin 2011, p. 1).

In this excerpt, Julie positions herself within a traditional maternal food femininity, one that views domestic work, such as cooking, as a way of relaxing rather than a form of domestic labour. Her use of the term "chillaxin'" (p. 1), a term borrowed from her teenage sons, reflects Julie's submission to the male gaze. Rather than using the term "chillaxin'" (p. 1) in the way her sons would, where "enjoying a lazy afternoon on the back deck" (p. 1) would take precedence over a Sunday morning filled with cooking, Julie frames her domestic labour as an extension of her relaxation. Julie's construction of relaxation as an opportunity for cooking, and her inaccurate use of the term "chillaxin'" which she borrows from her sons, indicate that her maternal relationship with food relies on traditional markers of ideal femininity.

Feminist writers and activists around the time of the second-wave movement, such as Betty Friedan (1963) and Ann Oakley (1976), both criticised and denounced the role of the happy housewife as a mythical creature. In her iconic book *The Feminine Mystique* (1963), Friedan explicitly describes the role of the happy housewife as an idealised caricature of femininity, an oppressive gender norm that exists to make women feel deficient by advertising companies in order to sell household products. Similarly, in *Housewife*, radical feminist writer Ann Oakley (1976) denounces the role of the happy housewife too by associating it with female subordination. From these perspectives, Julie's traditional maternal food femininity, one that is both moderated by the male gaze and refers to domestic labour as a form of relaxation, is a clear indication and narrative of women's continued subordination in mainstream culinary texts.

Rather than seeing herself as a mythical creature, however, Julie sees herself as the down-to-earth counterpart of the contemporary domestic goddess, and instead of relying on the sexualised connotations associated with contemporary culinary hedonism, Julie's appreciation of the food she prepares seems to be mostly about her own enjoyment. In her recipe for 'Vanilla Slice,' for example, Julie is shown revelling in its sweetness:

This involves a few different processes but is completely worth it. Thick, cold vanilla custard, crispy pastry, passionfruit icing ... heaven (Goodwin 2011, p. 187).

Julie's appreciation for the "heaven[ly]" (p. 187) qualities of her 'Vanilla Slice,' and her descriptive focus on its rich ingredients, points to the hedonistic and guilt-free pleasure she receives from eating. In contrast to Tana and Nigella's culinary narratives of hedonism, Julie describes her enjoyment of food throughout *The Heart of the Home* (2011) with no indication of shame or guilt whatsoever. Indeed, initially, it can be argued that Julie's hedonistic food femininity, unlike her maternal relationship with food, is not influenced by the male gaze at all. However, upon closer inspection, it becomes evident that Julie's lack of guilt over enjoying food and feeling comfortable about her body is precisely that which warrants the most intense public criticism.

In 2012, for the cover of Australian women's magazine *New Idea*, Julie posed in a bathing suit along with three other female television personalities in an effort to raise awareness about bodily diversity in the media. What followed from Julie's participation in the shoot was a host of scathing criticisms, the most prominent from *Sunday Times* columnist Ros Reines (McLean 2012). According to McLean (2012), Reines criticised Julie's participation in the shoot for promoting what she referred to as an "irresponsible" (n.p.) (i.e., abject, unhealthy and overweight) body weight and shape, arguing that she, "owes it to her children to downsize" (n.p.). Julie's responded to Reines' comments by stating:

> It fascinates me that my health can be commented on by someone who has absolutely no medical data on me ... I am grateful to my body, for the three children it has given me, for its strength and ability to work long hard hours, and for its robust good health (Goodwin, as cited in McLean 2012).

Julie's comments directed at Reines, and her other critics, inadvertently call attention to the Western phenomenon of lipoliteracy. As Murray (2008) explains in her book *The 'Fat' Female Body*, 'lipoliteracy' refers to the, "cultural meanings that we have come to attach, for the most part, preconsciously, to 'fat' bodies" (p. 13) as unquestionable and therefore, unspoken truths. This particular form of weight discrimination is suggested to be so pervasive that it has been normatively distributed throughout both lay opinions and in medical publications on weight (e.g., Yalom 2005; as cited in Murray 2008). Indeed, Reines' criticisms of Julie's weight as an indicator of her health are part of a broader lipoliterate culture that positions the 'fat' female body as an indicator of dysfunction.

When Julie thanks her body for "the three children it has given [her]" (McLean 2012), she is demonstrating an awareness that her maternal experiences have legitimised her body size/shape. Unlike Nigella, who relies on the sexual palatability of her domestic goddess persona, Julie seems to successfully merge her hedonistic desires with the maternal accomplishments of her body without any sense of body consciousness or self-policing behaviour. When applying Julie's hedonistic relationship with food to Littler's (2013) discussion of the yummy mummy, the contemporary, sexualised caricature of ideal motherhood, it becomes evident that Julie's weight, unrestricted enjoyment of food and general asexual public image become interpreted as a type of cultural subversion, and even a taboo. As Littler (2013) explains, part of what makes the yummy mummy an acceptable caricature of femininity is the fact that she nurtures both male and female appetites, that is, she encourages women to be pleasure-seeking creatures and encourages men to objectify them. The role of the yummy mummy is, thus, not necessary a subversive one, but, rather, one that conforms to the *status quo*. Julie's hedonistic relationship with food, then, can be regarded as being threatening for its monstrous qualities, that is, for her unrestricted appetite for food and for her lack of body consciousness. While Julie's maternal food femininity is very much embedded within traditional and oppressive caricatures of food femininity, her hedonistic relationship with food, which seems to elide gender altogether, protects her from the influence of the male gaze. Despite criticisms made by prominent figures in the Australian media, such as Ros Reines, Julie's reluctance to perpetuate a narrative of body policing can be regarded, on the surface, as a form of cultural subversion. However, what remains dominant throughout *The Heart of the Home* is that her essentialised culinary motherhood serves as a protective mechanism against the highly sexualised and objectified body of the yummy mummy, and calls to question whether total resistance to feminine gender norms in relation to food and eating is even possible.

Becoming a "Certified Feeder": Poh's Maternal and Hedonistic Food Femininities

Poh Ling Yeow is an Australian celebrity cook and painter of Chinese–Malaysian ancestry, best known for being runner-up and losing to Julie Goodwin in the first season of *MasterChef Australia* (Gunders 2011).

Unlike Tana, Nigella and Julie, who are all Caucasian mothers and operate primarily from the confines of their domestic kitchens, Poh's migrant background, her travels outside of the home and her status as a woman with no children serve as critical points of difference. I argue here that Poh's Othered persona plays a role in accentuating a type of food femininity that, on the surface, transgresses gender norms associated with cooking (Scholes 2011). However, rather than assuming Poh's diverse ethnic background and single status serve as protective mechanisms against the patriarchal confines of food femininity—the same framework that casts women as selfless nurturers and body-policing victims—this analysis reveals how Poh, too, inadvertently mirrors the narratives of motherhood and body consciousness that the other female authors in this chapter convey. Despite Poh's unique exterior, her success in the television studio kitchen of popular entertainment rests somewhat on her repetition of the well-known maternal and restrained hedonistic versions of food femininity found in other female culinary narratives. Indeed, Poh's kitchen still appears to be colonised by the male gaze of the professional chef, and her enjoyment of food is stifled by being viewed through this gaze.

Throughout *Poh's Kitchen My Cooking Adventures* (2010), and her eponymously titled cooking show for the Australian Broadcasting Corporation (ABC), Poh is frequently shown weaving between maternal and hedonistic versions of food femininity in a way that emphasises the tensions associated with her authentic Asian culinary role and her role in the patriarchal genre of the professional celebrity chef. The term authenticity, in this book, does not refer to Poh's essentialised relationship with Asian cuisine, but, rather, it relates to what Gunders (2011) describes as "a politically valued construction that operates ideologically and discursively to create meaning" (p. 90). In *Poh's Kitchen* (2010), her assimilation of Eastern and Western culinary influences, and her attempts to merge the traditionally feminine art of domestic cooking with the professional, male gaze of the chef, is seen as evidence of the gendered conflicts she experiences both in preparing and consuming food authentically.

Like Julie, Poh's celebrity status as an amateur cook, bolstered by her runner-up status on the first season of *MasterChef Australia*, emphasises themes of domesticity and authenticity, which are tensely intermingled with the heightened cultural status of the professionally trained, and often male celebrity chefs that she works with (Gunders 2011; Seale 2012). Indeed, Poh's amateur relationship with food is depicted as being predicated upon her Asian heritage, which reminds the reader that when they watch Poh cook Asian cuisine, they are also consuming her cultural heritage and the professed authenticity that comes with it. Unsurprisingly, tensions emerge when Poh's Asian heritage combines with her associations with the professional culinary world. One of the dominant ways that this relationship with food is depicted in *Poh's Kitchen* (2010), where her Eastern and Western influences seemingly collide, is in her description of her formative cooking influences. She states:

> Growing up with a mum and Koo Poh or great aunt (who's made a career of shoving mountainous plates of food in front of me with the instruction – "eat it all!") are what has turned me into a certified feeder (Ling Yeow 2010, p. 8).

This excerpt illustrates two important themes that resonate throughout *Poh's Kitchen* (2010). Firstly, it emphasises that her maternal influences play a seminal role in constructing her own relationship with food, and secondly, it shows how the professional male gaze colonises her thinking when she proclaims that she is "certified" to enact this role. Poh's inclusion of her mother and great aunt as her dominant food influences plays an important function in her narrative of culinary motherhood. Namely, her mother and Koo Poh represent the maternal, traditional and authentically Asian qualities of her cooking, the same qualities that are touted in Western depictions of culinary motherhood, such as care, selflessness and other-orientedness. Like the other female food celebrities analysed in this chapter, and regardless of whether she is a mother in the literal sense, Poh's relationship with food is strongly informed by all things maternal. It is only when Poh declares that she is a "certified feeder" (p. 8) that tensions in her food narrative begin to emerge, signifying an uncomfortable overlap between her formative maternal influences and the professional, 'certified' qualities of her male counterparts and participation in the competition-focused *MasterChef Australia*. By proclaiming her 'certified' status as a "feeder," Poh strips the care-driven, maternal qualities of her cooking abilities and turns them into a type of honorary qualification. In doing so, she breaks from her authentic food femininity to include the competitive, achievement-driven perspective of the patriarchal chefs that surround her. Indeed, by referencing her maternal qualities in terms of certification, Poh ignores the other reasons behind her love of food.

In an interview for *Lifestyle Food* (2011), Poh is shown reflecting on her cultural heritage and its influence over her culinary journey:

> Desperately wanting to assimilate as a child migrant, I shed everything that made me feel different in my new country. In my 30s, I suddenly realised that food is the vehicle that can help me keep in touch with my past, the history of my ancestors. It is a way I can still bond with the generations before me, even with the loss of traditional values and language (Yeow, as quoted in Lifestyle Food 2011, n.p.).

Poh's reinvigorated love for food and her authentic preparation of it are informed by community and ancestry rather than by achievement and certification. Indeed, the complex interplay between the authentic, domestic and unmistakably maternal food femininity that Poh reinforces, juxtaposed against the professional and usually male celebrity chef who is often shown standing beside her, is one of the ways that the male gaze penetrates *Poh's Kitchen*. All throughout her cookbook, which is loosely based on her television show, Poh is often shown interacting with male celebrity chefs and combining her own authentic knowledge with their professional culinary expertise. In the following excerpts, Poh positions her maternal relationship with food in conflicting ways by describing the cooking styles of two prominent Australian culinary figures Neil Perry and David Thompson, respectively. She states:

> Neil Perry has taught me so much, dare I say it, about cooking Chinese food (Yeow 2010, p. 66).

> [David Thompson] learnt to cook the traditional Thai way from women, not chefs, by watching, touching and tasting (Yeow 2010, p. 124).

While Poh acknowledges that professional chefs, such as David Thompson, learn their trade through the authentic influences of the maternal, she also asserts that her knowledge of Chinese cuisine is based strongly on the teachings of Western, male chefs. In these excerpts, Poh positions herself as an amateur, as somebody who has the potential to prepare 'authentic' Asian food, but is only just beginning to learn this craft from the predominantly male masters of Australian food culture. Poh's depiction of herself as an amateur reflects her humble beginnings on *MasterChef Australia* and the fame that has accompanied it.

According to Seale (2012), the *MasterChef* title is just one of the many ways that Australian reality television has perfected the art of the makeover. She explains that the *MasterChef* franchise, and all its amateur home cook contestants, "activates the 'makeover' genre" by promising to "transform amateur cooks into professionals" (p. 28). The main task of

the makeover reality television format is to present the amateur as someone who is "rehearsing the professional" (p. 29) and to give exposure to
people who would otherwise fall within the cracks of Australian celebrity culture. Poh's celebrity appeal during the screening of *MasterChef*
was noticed by the ABC, earning her a television show with some of
Australia's most well-respected and renowned chefs. As Gunders (2011)
argues, Poh's place within celebrity food culture produces tensions in the
way that she reinforces her 'authentic,' maternal version of food femininity, especially when she is challenged by the male celebrity chefs who she
has on her show as guests. In one example, Gunders (2011) describes
Poh's interaction with chef David Thompson regarding the authenticity
of canned coconut cream in a traditional Thai dish:

> In the second episode of *Poh's Kitchen* ... the presenter tried to get renowned
> Australian chef David Thompson to admit that using tinned coconut cream
> in Thai cuisine was acceptable. Having spent the first part of the show labo-
> riously making the essential ingredients from fresh coconut, the celebrity
> chef refused to answer, even when Poh begged him to say "yes" (p. 88).

While Gunders (2011) argues that Poh is allowed to stray from the traditional qualities of the dish and still remain an authentic pan-Asian voice,
what is of more interest in this book is the gendered distinction between
Poh and guest chef David. Despite David being a guest in Poh's television
kitchen, her need to turn to him for advice about Asian cuisine and, as
Gunders (2011) suggests, to "beg" (p. 88) him to agree with her culinary
knowledge is telling. Playing out a good-cop–bad-cop scenario, David is
presented as the strict disciplinarian, following recipes in a staunch, conventional and, arguably, inauthentic way. Poh, by contrast, is relegated to
the maternal role of the good cop, easing her audiences into Thai cuisine
and allowing them to use coconut cream rather than expecting them to
expertly create it on their own. In stereotypical fashion, her other-oriented
status as a carer prompts her to doubt her own culinary abilities. Indeed,
Poh represents herself as somebody who carefully and selflessly eases her
Australian audiences to Asian cuisine, while David is depicted as the male
culinary gaze. The male gaze, manifested through Poh's uncomfortable
merging of her Eastern and Western culinary influences, is also present
when she begins to assert her own desires and appetites for food.

   In stark contrast to the traditional depiction of feeding she describes
early in her book involving her mother and great aunt presenting her

with "mountainous plates of food" (p. 8) to enjoy, Poh's hedonistic relationship with food in *Poh's Kitchen: My Cooking Adventures* is relatively subdued. In fact, her desire to eat conforms less to the indulgent, care-oriented influences of her home country and more with the Western stereotype of femininity and restraint. Speaking in reference to her recipe for 'Sinful Scrambled Eggs with Sourdough Toast' and 'Soft-Boiled Eggs with Parmesan Soldiers,' respectively, Poh states:

> Every time I make this, and it's probably a lot more than I should, I do feel like I'm going straight to hell (Yeow 2010, p. 15).

> I used to love soft-boiled eggs with soldiers as a kid. In Malaysia, we'd always have them only par boiled, with slightly runny whites, soy sauce, white pepper and heavily buttered white toast. It's a really lovely kiddy food memory I wanted to play on, so I thought why not parmesan soldiers. It's as naughty as eating French fries for brekky (Yeow 2010, p. 20).

Despite her otherwise subversive racial Otherness and the authenticity of her cooking, Poh's relationship with food is very much dependent on the normative Western tradition of body surveillance and self-policing. By drawing references to going "straight to hell" (p. 15) and being a bit "naughty" (p. 20) for enjoying food, Poh's hedonistic food femininity is defined by restraint, a theme that is not unusual in contemporary Western culture (Popa 2012). Even when she recollects memories of eating soft-boiled eggs prepared by her father in Malaysia, Poh still retains the oppressive Western stereotype of body consciousness that women face, focusing on the guilt and surveillance women experience about eating rather than merely enjoying the meal.

Like Nigella, however, Poh does illustrate that body-policing attitudes (and, indeed, food-policing attitudes) are counterproductive. She states:

> I am slavishly addicted to baking frequently ... It's just so nice to have something a bit cheeky to have with coffee in the morning or tea in the afternoon if a friend drops by. Personally, I've come to realise that in the long run, it's much healthier to be a bit naughty and happy, rather than to be "good" and miserable, not to mention those horrible lapses where you find yourself tucking into a dirty burger with all the trimmings and then a chaser of chips, lollies and chocolate, all in the one sitting. Aaaargh, the self-loathing that follows ... you should've just eaten the small slice of banana caramel pie the night before! (Yeow 2010, p. 10).

Like Nigella, Poh demonstrates a form of gendered knowledge when she explains how women in contemporary Western culture are oppressed by their conflicted relationships with food and eating. While she encourages women to take pleasure in food, a clear demonstration of her hedonistic version of food femininity, Poh also refers to the enjoyment she takes out of eating as naughtiness. By allowing herself to have small doses of sinful foods, she avoids "the self-loathing that follows" (p. 10), otherwise known as a binge-eating episode. While her advice to the audience is based on hedonism and an encouragement to eat, it is also peppered with elements of sinfulness and guilt. Poh's hedonistic and quintessentially gendered relationship with food is similar to Tana's in that they both emphasise guilt as a central theme in their relating to food, despite their racial and maternal differences. Indeed, removing the adventurous, single, Asian qualities of Poh's authentic public persona, the analysis is this chapter shows that she is no different in being influenced by the male gaze than the other women studied. Her maternal and hedonistic versions of food femininity remain colonised by the often professional male gaze.

The food femininities analysed in this chapter, drawn from a variety of female food celebrities and across cultural demographics, reflect similarities in the way that food is both normatively and problematically prepared and consumed by women in popular cookbooks. It was evident in all the texts that the male gaze, which is implicated in women's domestic servitude and their anxious pre-occupations with their bodies, colonises both the maternal and the hedonistic aspects of women's culinary experiences. In contrast to some of the previous feminist literature on either the oppressive (e.g., Friedan 1963; Oakley 1976) or agentic (e.g., Supski 2006) qualities of cooking and domesticity, I have shown in this chapter that female food celebrities in popular cookbooks are not only constrained to their kitchens, but are also dominated by the male gaze in their relationships with food and eating. As mothers and hedonists, the women analysed in this chapter presented versions of food femininity that ultimately relied on some element of body consciousness. With the exception of Julie, the right to assert one's enjoyment of food is peppered with the same male gaze that operates behind women's selfless, care-oriented relationships with food. As Teodora Popa (2012) argues in her article on consumption and hedonism, the contemporary Western woman is defined by her restrained hedonism, that is, her ability to assert her right to consume and, simultaneously, her need to control her own consumption.

Indeed, the food femininities unearthed in this analysis point to an implicit narrative of body policing that contributes to a culture of restrained hedonism, a culture that has the potential to harm women. In the next chapter, the implicit continuation of these narratives is analysed in an unlikely source: through an examination of iconic feminist texts and their analysis of women's beauty and eating practices.

REFERENCES

Bartky, S. L. (1990). *Femininity and domination: Studies in the phenomenology of oppression*. New York: Routledge/Taylor & Francis Group.

Beazley, M. (2010). *Tana's kitchen secrets*. Retrieved from: http://www.publishersweekly.com/978-1-84533-550-2

Bordo, S. (2004). *Unbearable weight: Feminism, Western culture, and the body*. Berkeley: University of California Press.

Brunsdon, C. (2005). Feminism, postfeminism, Martha, Martha, and Nigella. *Cinema Journal, 44*(2), 110–116.

Cairns, K., Johnston, J., & MacKendrick, N. (2013). Feeding the 'organic' child: Mothering through ethical consumption. *Journal of Consumer Culture, 13*(2), 97–118.

Cashmore, E., & Parker, A. (2003). One David Beckham? Celebrity, masculinity, and the soccerati. *Sociology of Sport Journal, 20*(3), 214–231.

Culver, C. (2012). A pinch of salt and a dash of plot: The power of narrative in contemporary cookbooks. *Journal of the Australasian Universities Language and Literature Association, 118*, 33–50.

Day, C. (2009). Does my bum look big in this? Reconsidering anorexia nervosa within the culture context of 20th century Australia. *Surveillance and Society, 6*(2), n.p.

Douglas, P. (2010). Yummy mummy and the medicalised milkmother. *Hecate: An Interdisciplinary Journal of Women's Liberation, 36*(1/2), 119–135.

Friedan, B. (1963). *The feminine mystique*. Harmondsworth: Penguin Books.

Goodwin, J. (2011). *The heart of the home*. North Sydney: Random House.

Greer, G. (1971). *The female eunuch*. London: Paladin.

Greer, G. (1999). *The whole woman*. London: Doubleday.

Gunders, J. (2011). Authenticating the kitchen: 'Poh's kitchen' and 'Jamie's great Italian escape'. *Metro Magazine: Media and Education Magazine, 167*, 88–94.

Hesser, A. (2002). *Culinary critique: Sex and the kitchen*. Retrieved from: http://www.nytimes.com/2002/01/09/dining/culinary-critique-sex-and-the-kitchen.html

Hewer, P., & Brownlie, P. (2009). Culinary culture, gastrobands and identity myths: 'Nigella', an iconic brand in the baking. *Advances in Consumer Research, 36*, 482–487.

Higgins, M., Montgomery, M., Smith, A., & Tolson, A. (2011). Belligerent broadcasting and makeover television: Professional incivility in Ramsay's kitchen nightmares. *International Journal of Cultural Studies, 15,* 501–518.

Honey, K. (2008). *Tana Ramsay the soft-spoken chef.* Retrieved from: http://www. thestar.com/life/2008/11/19/tana_ramsay_the_softspoken_chef.html

Jones, L. (2011). *We're as swell as Nigella.* Retrieved from: http://www.dailymail. co.uk/femail/article-1088094/Were-swell-Nigella-What-happened-asked-writers-try-magic-dress.html

Khokhar, A. (2011). *Lose weight? I'd end up looking ten years older, claims Nigella.* Retrieved from: http://www.dailymail.co.uk/tvshowbiz/article-1380528/ Nigella-Lawson-Lose-weight-Id-end-looking-10-years-older.html

Knapp, C. (2003). *Appetites: Why women want.* New York: Counterpoint.

Lawson, N. (2006). *Feast: Food that celebrates life.* London: Chatto & Windus.

Lawson, J. (2011). Food legacies: Playing the culinary feminine. *Women and Performance: A Journal of Feminist Theory, 21*(3), 337–366.

Lifestyle Food. (2011). *Poh Ling Yeow: Celebrity chef.* Retrieved from: http:// www.lifestylefood.com.au/chefs/pohlingyeow/

Ling-Yeow, P. (2010). *Poh's kitchen: My cooking adventures.* Pymble: Harper Collins Publishers.

Littler, J. (2013). The rise of the 'yummy mummy': Popular conservatism and the neoliberal maternal in contemporary British culture. *Communication, Culture and Critique, 6*(2), 227–243.

Magee, R. M. (2007). Food puritanism and food pornography: The gourmet semiotics of Martha and Nigella. *Americana, 5*(2), n.p.

McLean, S. (2012). *MasterChef star Julie Goodwin slams weight claims made by Sunday Telegraph columnist Ros Reines.* Retrieved from: http://www. dailytelegraph.com.au/masterchef-star-julie-goodwin-slams-weight-claims-made-by-sunday-telegraph-columnist-ros-reines/story-e6freuy9–122623939129 1?nk=bb2079dca1a45135ab8902432f303f13$itm=newscomau%7Centertainme nt%7Cncam-story-body-link%7C2%7Chttp%3A%2F%2Fwww.dailytelegraph. com.au%2Fnews%2Fmasterchef-star-julie-goodwin-slams-weight-claims-made-by-sunday-telegraph-columnist-ros-reines%2Fstory-e6freuy9–1226239391291%7 Cstory%7C 'Overweight'%20star%20serves%20critic%20a%20large%20portion &itmt=1411298455503

McLean, A. (2013). The intersection of gender and food studies. In K. Albala (Ed.), *Routledge international handbook of food studies.* Abingdon: Routledge.

McRobbie, A. (2006). Yummy mummies leave a bad taste for young women: The cult of celebrity motherhood is deterring couples from having children early. *We need to rethink the nanny culture.* Retrieved from: http://ww3.fl.ul.pt/ pessoais/alvaro_pina/estudos_culturais/angela_mcrobbie.pdf

Mitchell, C. M. (2010). The rhetoric of celebrity cookbooks. *The Journal of Popular Culture, 43*(3), 524–539.

Montemurro, B., & Siefken, J. M. (2012). MILFS and matrons: Images and realities of mothers' sexuality. *Sexuality and Culture, 16*(4), 366–388.

Murray, S. (2008). *The 'fat' female body*. Great Britain: Palgrave Macmillan.

Neuhaus, J. (1999). The way to a man's heart: Gender roles, domestic ideology, and cookbooks in the 1950s. *Journal of Social History, 32*(3), 529–555.

Neuhaus, J. (2003). *Manly meals and moms home cooking: Cookbooks and gender in modern America*. Baltimore: John Hopkins University Press.

Nilsson, G. (2013). Balls enough: Manliness and legitimated violence in Hell's kitchen. *Gender, Work and Organisation, 20*(6), 647–663.

Oakley, A. (1976). *Housewife*. Harmondsworth: Penguin.

Popa, T. (2012). Eating disorders in a hyper-consumerist and post-feminist context. *Scientific Journal of Humanistic Studies, 4*(7), 162–166.

PR Newswire. (2012). *Nigella Lawson shows how smaller portions can lead to weight loss*. Retrieved from: http://www.wiredprnews.com/2012/10/12/nigella-lawson-shows-how-smaller-portions-can-lead-to-weight-loss_2012101230840.html

Ramsay, T. (2009). *Tana Ramsay's real family food*. Hammersmith, London: Harper Collins Publishers.

Ramsay, T. (2010). *Tana's kitchen secrets*. Great Britain: Mitchell Beazley.

Scholes, L. (2011). A slave to the stove? The TV celebrity chef abandons the kitchen: Lifestyle TV, domesticity and gender. *Critical Quarterly, 53*(3), 44–59.

Seale, K. (2012). MasterChef's amateur makeover. *Media International Australia, Incorporating Culture & Policy, 143*, 28–35.

Shapiro-Sanders, L. (2009). Consuming Nigella. In S. Gilles & J. Hollows (Eds.), *Feminism, domesticity and popular culture*. New York: Routledge.

Sobal, J. (2005). Men, meat, and marriage: Models of masculinity. *Food and Foodways: Explorations in the History and Culture of Human Nourishment., 13*(1–2), 135–158.

Supski, S. (2006). 'It was another skin': The kitchen as home for Australian post-war immigrant women. *Gender, Place and Culture, 13*(2), 133–141.

Sydney Morning Herald. (2009, July 19). *Julie Goodwin beats Poh to MasterChef final*. Retrieved from: http://www.smh.com.au/articles/2009/07/19/1247941826808.html

Townsville Bulletin. (2009). Comfort food warms a nation's heart. *Townsville Bulletin*, p. 42.

Tyrangiel, J. (2003). Excess is hardly enough. *Time, 161*(21), 8–9.

West, I. (2007). Performing resistance in/from the kitchen: The practice of maternal pacifist politics in la WISP's cookbooks. *Women's Studies in Communication, 30*(3), 358–383.

Whiting, F. (2012). *Is Nigella's new look as delicious*. Retrieved from: http://www.couriermail.com.au/news/new-look-nigella-could-sell/news-story/8316f331c3b56321171b0b5e0df82d07

Wolf, N. (1990). *The beauty myth: How images of beauty are used against women*. London: Vintage.

CHAPTER 6

Flavours of Feminism: Iconic Feminist Voices and Body-Policing Narratives

Best-selling diet books and contemporary cookbooks are littered with feminist references that position their depictions of food and eating as emancipatory and countercultural, despite their reliance on cultural narratives that encourage women—either implicitly or explicitly—to constantly be aware of the weight and shape of their bodies. Indeed, one of the key features of iconic feminist texts, and the reason I have chosen to analyse them in this book, is for their contemporary methods of consciousness-raising and, more specifically, for their ability to reach large female audiences, especially in the context of food- and eating-related discourses. Feminist consciousness-raising allows one to change one's interpretation of the world and, as such, to influence others through forms of self-empowerment. Some writers suggest that this is one of the benefits of consciousness-raising in a contemporary feminist context; raising one's awareness does not require in-depth group participation but, rather, can be practised individually from the confines of the home (Sowards and Renegar 2004; Vanderford 2009). How effective this approach is, however, in comparison to traditional consciousness-raising practices, is contestable. As explained earlier in the book, the development of a feminist identity, which is often prompted by feminist influences in mainstream cultural sources (e.g., Hinds and Stacey 2001), has been considered one of the primary deterrents of disordered eating behaviour in women (Orbach 2006). Despite the promise of reducing eating disorder symptoms in women, however, a large body of the psychological literature has indicated that a

© The Author(s) 2017
N. Jovanovski, *Digesting Femininities*,
DOI 10.1007/978-3-319-58925-1_6

feminist identity is not a solid construct when it comes to preventing body dissatisfaction and eating-related psychopathology. Rather than attributing the problem to cultural discourses such as the media, writers such as Green et al. (2008) argue that this effect may have something to do with the state of feminist discourses themselves and, indeed, in the process of contemporary feminist consciousness-raising itself. In this chapter, I will argue that iconic feminist voices discussing women's relationships with food and their bodies both politicise women's uncomfortable relationships with food and their bodies, and simultaneously defang the potency of their feminist politics by suggesting individual solutions, many of which contain traces of body-policing narratives.

Specifically, this chapter will examine how iconic feminist writers, such as Susie Orbach (2006) and Naomi Wolf (1990), discuss women's relationships with food and eating. The food femininities they adopt (i.e., the feminist self-help and the liberal-feminist) will be closely examined for their reinforcement of gender narratives that contain body-policing messages. Through the second-wave feminist mantra, 'the personal is political,' the different sections of this chapter will be divided into two parts: the 'political' and the 'personal.' It is my contention in this chapter that Orbach (2006) and Wolf's (1990) influential feminist texts begin with analyses of the politicisation of women's eating behaviour but fundamentally resort to individualising the problem when looking for a solution. Unlike diet books and cookbooks, which have been explicitly studied for their reinforcement of (often) problematic gender norms, iconic feminist texts have not yet been given the same level of attention. Rather, influential feminist voices, such as that of Susie Orbach (2006), have been labelled as beneficial to women's personal and political well-being and instrumental in challenging cultural institutions that shape women's relationships with food and their bodies (Bordo 2004). Additionally, in light of the best-selling diet books and popular cookbooks studied, iconic feminist texts are less obvious sources of data. As such, I argue that they promote problematic messages surrounding food and eating in tacit, rather than obvious, ways. It is also important to note that while I provide a critique of iconic feminist voices on women's relationships with food and their bodies, I am not dismissing the significance of their ideas and positive influence over women's lives. Rather, I am arguing that their narratives contain problematic messages that can, and should, be challenged and added to by future generations of feminist writers.

DEFINING 'FEMINIST ICON'

Examining feminist icons and their perspectives on women's relationships with food is important, as they influence cultural understandings of disorder and, concurrently, the way women view their own relationships with food and their bodies. As Bordo (2004) explains in *Unbearable Weight*, iconic feminist writers on women's eating behaviour have been responsible for encouraging women to politicise their disordered eating patterns rather than perceive them as shameful, personal activities. Some writers, such as Orbach (2006) and Wolf (1990), have become iconic in mainstream cultural discourses due to the novelty and political potency of their arguments and, simultaneously, the marketability of their public persona. Despite being known for their significance to the feminist movement, however, Orbach (2006) and Wolf (1990) constitute a certain type of feminist figure, one that is more public and accessible to mainstream audiences than other feminist sources. One of the reasons why their feminist messages have gained mainstream cultural success has something to do with their involvement in popular cultural discussions about food, beauty and the female body.

As Showalter (2001) explains in her article for the *Guardian*, the feminist icon has become less about protest and activism in the contemporary feminist arena, and more about mainstream cultural appeal. Rather than dismissing contemporary feminist icons as politically diluted, overpublicised versions of traditional feminist figures, Showalter (2001, n.p.) explains:

> I believe that feminist icons still exist and that we still need them. But in the age of communication and modern media, our feminist icons are likely to be successful women raised to celebrity status by the power of publicity.

The status of the iconic feminist figure, one reinforced by "the power of publicity," is also one that must uphold a certain level of emotional restraint that is different from their often angry, and sometimes militant, second-wave feminist counterparts. According to Showalter (2001), contemporary feminist icons are less likely to "succumb to despair" like previous generations of iconic women (i.e., Sylvia Plath) and, thus, more likely to present themselves as "resilient and determined to survive adversity and betrayal" (Showalter 2001, n.p.). This message of empowerment is one that defines contemporary depictions of the feminist icon in the Western media and is bolstered by third-wave feminist notions on the difference between what it means to be a powerful feminist and one that supposedly over-identifies with her victimhood (e.g., Wolf 1993).

In their article on the changing polemics of feminist identity throughout the decades, however, Love and Helmbrecht (2007) provide a critique of this third-wave feminist notion of empowerment (i.e., a facet of power feminism) through their examination of contemporary feminist icons, such as the famous pop singers Pink and Britney Spears. They argue that by relying on a rhetoric of individualism, mainstream feminist figures within popular culture reinforce messages that both espouse feminist values (e.g., empowerment) and, paradoxically, rely on antiquated stereotypes of femininity to further their careers (e.g., objectification). As Love and Helmbrecht (2007) further explain, iconic feminist figures that gain mainstream cultural appeal also tend to conform, at least somewhat, to oppressive patriarchal standards, which is why these types of "feminists and feminist statements ... sell" (p. 51). Speaking in reference to how women gain visibility in mainstream cultural discourses, they argue that:

> When women or anyone else is "othered" in Western culture ... [they] are given visibility. This visibility is often accompanied by surveillance, voyeurism, and the desire to possess another (pp. 41–42).

Thus, when a woman achieves the title of feminist icon, she is allowed mainstream cultural visibility through her implicit (and sometimes explicit) allegiance with patriarchal cultural practices (e.g., self-surveillance). In this chapter, both Susie Orbach's (2006) work in *Fat is a Feminist Issue* and Naomi Wolf's (1990) work in *The Beauty Myth* will be positioned as iconic feminist texts that situate women's relationships with food and their bodies in both political (i.e., situated within patriarchal institutions) and personal (i.e., situated within the self) terms. While both women will be shown to reproduce body-policing narratives in their books, however, it must be stated that their reinforcement of body-policing attitudes occurs at an implicit, and less obvious, level than the best-selling diet books and cookbooks analysed in this book.

The popularity of *Fat is a Feminist Issue* and *The Beauty Myth* rests, in part, on the dominant and iconic personalities of their authors. During the late 1970s, Susie Orbach rose to feminist fame with her first edition of *Fat is a Feminist Issue*, which was touted as a refreshing and politically potent alternative to existing psychological texts that painted women's disordered relationships with food as individual problems (Bordo 2004). Since its original popularity, *Fat is a Feminist Issue* has been republished to include both a 'how to' guide to the political messages of the first edition and an introduction into how the book still applies in the twenty-first century (Orbach 2006). Similarly, Naomi Wolf's *The Beauty Myth* has also been labelled as a significant feminist text, which rests, in part, upon Wolf's (1990) charismatic public persona, her now famous argument with Camille Paglia and the media's obsession with her conventional attractiveness. While both writers come from different political periods and approach women's relationships with food from two different feminist perspectives, their work carries a type of cultural significance that other feminist texts do not so readily possess. Hinds and Stacey (2001) refer to the importance of their work (and their public personae) as a significant, culturally influential phenomenon. They state:

> The iconic figure is the one that accrues such a powerful set of associations as to be immediately recognisable, as to produce a visceral reaction, and as to condense a complex history of contested meanings in one gesture or sentence ... such a figure serves as a cultural loadstone, producing a magnetic force which generates an endless capacity for further signification (p. 156).

As such, Orbach (2006) and Wolf's (1990) texts will be analysed to emphasise how influential voices in feminism paint a body-policing narrative surrounding women's relationships with food and their bodies, both implicitly and explicitly. Despite being used as important political seeds of knowledge for women, especially women who have been psychopathologised, both texts will also be emphasised for their problematic reliance on individualistic solutions. As such, the two sections (i.e., Orbach's Feminist Self-Help Food Femininities and Wolf's Liberal-Feminist Food Femininities) will contain both the political facets of their analyses and an example of how they individualise solutions, implicitly reinforcing body-policing narratives aimed at (largely) heterosexual, female audiences.

ORBACH'S FEMINIST SELF-HELP FOOD FEMININITIES IN *FAT IS A FEMINIST ISSUE*

Susie Orbach's (2006) *Fat is a Feminist Issue* is considered an iconic feminist text that politicises women's personal relationships with food and their bodies. According to Bordo (2004), it is among one of the first of its genre and has been an influential part of psychotherapeutic understandings of women's eating behaviour. Throughout *Fat is a Feminist Issue*, Orbach (2006) discusses the phenomenon of 'compulsive eating' symptoms in women by situating them within six major points: "eating when you are not physically hungry"; "feeling out of control around food, submerged by either dieting or gorging"; "spending a good deal of time thinking and worrying about food and fatness"; "scouring the latest diet for vital information"; "feeling awful about yourself as someone who is out of control" and "feeling awful about your body" (pp. 9–10). Each of these points signifies what psychologists would traditionally refer to as women's psychopathological relationships with food and their bodies.

In Orbach's (2006) account of compulsive eating, however, the emphasis is not so much on the individual, but more so on the harmful gender norms that surround the individual. One harmful gender norm that Orbach (2006) discusses is the notion of body policing, which is encouraged through the unwanted sexualisation of women in patriarchal culture. While Orbach (2006) politicises the origins of body policing, she also inadvertently strengthens their existence by conflating compulsive eating with 'fat,' inadvertently psychopathologising the 'fat' female body. Using both feminist and self-help perspectives in relation to women's relationships with food and their bodies, Orbach (2006) tacitly reinforces body consciousness in her readers through both her lipoliterate reading of 'fat' and her individualistic solutions to women's politically motivated problems with food. In this section of the chapter, I will show how Orbach (2006) both politicises and individualises women's body-conscious relationships with food through the promotion of feminist self-help versions of food femininity.

'Fat' as a Resistance to Ideal Femininity

In the spring of 1978, Susie Orbach (2006) wrote the first edition of *Fat is a Feminist Issue*, with a novel feminist take on women's compulsive eating behaviour. Rather than attributing binge eating in women to individual patterns of dysfunction (i.e., biological, genetic, neuropsychological factors), Orbach (2006) was one of the first to acknowledge that culture played a part in the development of disordered eating in women and, more specifically, to their over-adherence to harmful norms of femininity. In the introductory section of *Fat is a Feminist Issue*, Orbach (2006) examined compulsive eating in women through a feminist lens that associated women's personal relationships with food and their bodies with the influence of harmful cultural messages (i.e., the political). Specifically, she viewed compulsive eating and women's 'fat' as tacit acts of resistance against rigid cultural proscriptions of femininity:

> The fact that compulsive eating is over-whelmingly a woman's problem suggests that it has something to do with the experiences of being female in our society. Feminism argues that being fat represents an attempt to break free from society's sex stereotypes (pp. 14–15).

Orbach (2006) is clear when she argues that compulsive eating and the development of a 'fat' female body are symptoms of a culture that prioritises harmful sex role stereotypes in women (i.e., the thin-ideal). This excerpt shows that she employs a feminist perspective in relation to compulsive eating that outwardly politicises the way gender norms function to oppress women, both culturally and physically (through a shield of 'fat'). She also engages with the sentiments expressed by radical feminists who claim that sexual objectification is essentially harmful to women (e.g., Dworkin 1974; Jeffreys 2005; MacKinnon 1989) and adds disordered eating behaviour to the list of possible detrimental outcomes. Evidence of this is shown in the following quotes, where she refers to women's physical appearance as being both a dominant part of their social capital and, paradoxically, a way to be controlled:

> The relegation of women to the social roles of wife and mother has several significant consequences that contribute to the problem of fat. First, in order to become a wife and mother, a woman has to have a man. Getting a man is presented as an almost unattainable and yet essential goal. To get a man, a woman has to learn to regard herself as an item, a commodity, a sex object. *Much of her experience and identity depends on how she and others see her* (p. 16; italics added).

> Since women are taught to see themselves from the outside as candidates for men, they become prey to the huge fashion and diet industries that first set up the ideal image and then exhort women to meet them. The message is loud and clear – the woman's body is not her own (p. 17).

Orbach's (2006) second-wave feminist influences are made abundantly clear in her identification of body consciousness as a social phenomenon rooted in 'femininity.' According to Orbach (2006) and other feminists writing on the harms of objectification (Bartky 1990; Dworkin 1974;

Jeffreys 2005; MacKinnon 1989), to be quintessentially female in a patriarchal cultural landscape is to internalise the notion that one is "an item, a commodity, a sex object" (Orbach 2006, p. 16) and that one's body is "not her own" (p. 17).

There is also a significant body of psychological literature that has also supported the idea that objectification is harmful (de Vries and Peter 2013; Fredrickson and Roberts 1997; Fredrickson et al. 1998; McKinley and Hyde 1996; Tiggemann 2013). According to researchers Fredrickson and Roberts (1997) and McKinley and Hyde (1996), women who are objectified internalise unwanted sexualisation by viewing themselves from an outsider's perspective, which can be referred to as self-objectification (Fredrickson and Roberts 1997) or objectified body-consciousness, respectively (McKinley and Hyde 1996). This process of persistent self-monitoring has been shown in the psychological literature to be associated with severe psychopathological conditions, such as major depression, self-harm and various eating disorders (Calogero et al. 2005; Harper and Tiggemann 2008; Swami et al. 2010). Through the lens of sexual objectification, Orbach (2006) encourages her female readers to conform to a feminist perspective that identifies, questions and critiques harmful cultural practices that allude to thinness as an ideal state of femininity. She continues by using the image of a thin, and relatively weak, woman as a reason why women turn to compulsive eating behaviours and subsequent weight gain. Speaking in relation to how women get taken seriously in the workplace, Orbach (2006) states:

> It is unusual for women to be accepted for their competence in this sphere. When they lose weight, that is, begin to look like a perfect female, they find themselves being treated frivolously by their male colleagues. When women are thin, they are treated frivolously: thin-sexy-incompetent worker (pp. 21–22).

By discussing thinness as a potential precursor to unwanted sexual attention, Orbach (2006) presents the 'fat' female body as a resistant alternative. In a sense, Orbach (2006) emphasises how patriarchal institutions both prioritise and victimise the 'thin' woman and, in doing so, depict women's compulsive relationships with food as a form of self-protection, where the incidence of sexual objectification decreases when the body is shielded by layers of 'fat.' This juxtaposition of the thin and the 'fat' body serves as a major argument in Orbach's (2006) critical understanding of compulsive eating behaviour in women, one that has shaped generations of feminist, sociological and psychological writers in their identification of gender as a harmful cultural phenomenon (Bartky 1990; Bordo 2004). By focusing on the thin body as being at risk of sexual objectification, however, the notion that 'fat' is somehow both protective, but more so counterproductive, is a potentially harmful way to stereotype those considered 'fat.' Some have argued that this type of stereotyping leads to the unnecessary pathologising of the 'fat' female body (Murray 2008; Young 2005).

Pathologising the 'Fat' Female Body

Orbach's (2006) understanding that compulsive eating is driven by restrictive feminine norms has been seen as a powerful feminist analysis that acknowledges women's personal relationships with food and their bodies as residing within a sexist, cultural context (Bordo 2004). Yet her reluctance to see the 'fat' female body as anything other than a form of psychopathological resistance to rigid gender norms can be seen as a harmful and inaccurate portrayal. Indeed, it can be argued that Orbach's psychopathological reading of 'fatness' signifies a tacit reinforcement of body consciousness in women whose bodies do not fit socially proscribed understandings of health and beauty.

Murray (2008) uses the example of lipoliteracy, or the superficial reading of body weight, as an indicator of overall well-being, to signify how Western health discourses conflate pathology with body 'fat.' She explains that, "the negative constructions of 'fat' female embodiment that are articulated by our popular and medical 'lipoliteracies', are productive of 'obesity' rather than descriptive of it" (p. 14). From this perspective, Orbach's (2006) conflation of 'fat' and psychopathology can be seen as a reproduction of body-policing gender narratives aimed at women, rather than just a description of them. Orbach (2006) conveys a lipoliterate reading of women's 'fat' and, in doing so, shifts attention away from a critique of compulsive eating and onto the appearance of women's bodies as indicators of distress. In the following excerpts, Orbach (2006) describes 'fatness' as a result of culturally driven forms of psychopathology:

> Fat is a symbolic rejection of the limitations of women's role, an adaptation that many women use in the burdensome attempt to pursue their individual lives within the proscriptions of their social function (p. 22).

Fat is a response to the many oppressive manifestations of a sexist culture. Fat is a way of saying "no" to powerlessness and self-denial, to a limiting sexual expression which demands that females look and act in a certain way, and to an image of womanhood that defines a specific social role (p. 29).

Fat is an adaptation to the oppression of women and, as such, it may be an unsatisfying personal solution to an ineffectual political attack (p. 30).

Despite her conflation of women's 'fat' bodies with their resistance to oppressive culturally motivated feminine norms, the underlying theme in Orbach's writing is the notion that 'fat' exists as a result of maladaptive coping mechanisms relating to food. Indeed, the assumption that compulsive eating leads to overweight and obesity has been examined and subsequently debunked in much of the psychological literature on binge-eating disorders. While some sources suggest that there is a direct link between repeated binge eating and weight gain (de Zwaan 2001; Schag et al. 2013), other studies indicate that even women who appear within the healthy confines of the body mass index suffer from compulsive eating behaviours (Grilo et al. 1994). As such, the size and shape of the body may not be a reliable source of information about a person's healthy or unhealthy eating habits, and the notion that one can read the 'fat' body as an indicator of psychopathology is, thus, not entirely supported in the academic literature (Murray 2008). From this perspective, it can be seen that Orbach (2006) uses the symbol of the 'fat' female body as a way to pathologise women's relationships with food. Rather than focusing strictly on women's culturally motivated compulsive eating behaviours, Orbach (2006) moves into discourses that pathologise and asexualise the appearance of the 'fat' female body.

These and similar sentiments have led to the development of fat-acceptance movements throughout Canada and the United States, and other countercultural projects vocal in criticising the moralising of 'fat' bodies (Kirkland 2008; Murray 2008). According to Murray (2008), fat-acceptance movements (or size-acceptance movements) have employed the same "rhetoric of pride movements of the past" (p. 106) and focused their efforts on empowering people considered overweight or obese, criticising discourses that describe 'fat' as a form of pathology or moral affront. A central tenet of fat-acceptance movements is the resignification of 'fat' from a culturally loaded object carrying negative connotations, to a positive part of the body. As explained by Murray (2008), "size acceptance is not a unified or singular political movement" (p. 106), but, rather, is a project that is made up of multiple movements, such as the National Association to Advance Fat Acceptance (NAAFA as cited in Kirkland 2008) and the fat grrl movement (Shantz 2005). These social movements, both mainstream and countercultural, explicitly reject the notion that 'fat' is a state of psychopathology or aesthetic affront, and contradict claims made by writers such as Orbach (2006) that 'fat' is any more an indication of psychopathology than hair or eye colour is.

Body Policing and the Asexual 'Fat' Woman

One of the key arguments that Orbach (2006) makes in *Fat is a Feminist Issue* is the notion that the 'fat' female body signifies an erasure of 'femininity' and, by default, of sexual attractiveness. She states that:

> Many women [feel] a sense of relief at not having to conceive of themselves as sexual. Fatness took them out of the category of woman and put them into the androgynous state of "big girl" (p. 43).

In this excerpt, Orbach's (2006) assertion that 'fatness' equates to asexuality or androgyny can be perceived as a tacit reinforcement of body-policing gender narratives. Unsurprisingly, the cultural discourse surrounding Orbach's (2006) assumption that the 'fat' female body is, automatically, an asexual one, is one that has been challenged by various countercultural movements devoted to fat politics (Shantz 2005). As explained by Shantz (2005) in his piece on the feminist politics of 'fat,' the fat grrl movement, which originated in the United States in the mid-1990s, combined the politics of 'fat' feminism, radical democracy and anarchism to challenge caricatures of femininity that rigidly proscribed to thinness. Rather than conceptualising 'fat' as a form of psychopathology or moral affront, Shantz (2005) describes the 'fat grrl' movement as a progressive way of empowering women, politicising the inequality experienced by those considered 'fat' and moving away from discourses that problematise 'fatness,' such as medical and psychological research.

Challenging the labels ascribed to 'fat' by traditionally patriarchal institutions such as the media and the medical profession, fat grrls participate in activities that have been traditionally reserved for thin (and thus, conventionally sexually attractive) women. Activities such as "radical cheerleading [and] burlesque shows" (Shantz 2005, p. 102) have been, according to Shantz, among some of the activities that 'fat grrls' engage in to push the boundaries of ideal femininity. Through a playful engagement with activities traditionally designated to thin women, members of the fat grrl movement attempt to resignify their 'fat' with a "sense of humour [and] open defiance" (p. 103). Other writers, such as Murray (2008), have also discussed the transformative promise of fat-acceptance movements in resignifying 'fat' as a positive marker of femininity.

In *The 'Fat' Female Body*, Murray (2008) explains how seductive some fat-acceptance messages can seem to women who have grown up identifying 'fat' (and their bodies) with negative and asexual connotations. She states:

> Fat pride [is] envisaged ... [as] an attractive "exit" to "fat" girls who have been told certain interactions, performances and practices are off-limits: for example, fat pride organisations hold events such as Fat Lingerie Parties, Fat Pool Parties, Fat Fashion Parades. Here, boxes of size 26 g-strings are ripped open with glee; lacy negligees guaranteed to slide effortlessly over ample hips are offered up, bellies hang over new bikini bottoms with impunity. In short, "fat" girls are offered the chance to take up the position of privilege denied to them as a result of the pathologising, hegemonic constructions of identity and difference, which cast them into the domain of abjection (Murray 2008, p. 107).

From a fat-acceptance perspective, the resignification and sexualisation of the 'fat' female body serves as a useful counter-discourse that situates women's traditionally asexual 'fat' bodies into a cultural landscape that acknowledges them as sexual beings. These countercultural acts can be seen, on the surface, as a way of breaking Orbach's (2006) theory that 'fat' equals psychopathology, where the rejection of mainstream, idealised versions of femininity opens up space for women to express sexual agency in their newly signified 'fat' bodies. Some writers, however, have been rightfully sceptical of this solution. Murray (2008) identifies fat-acceptance projects as being problematic for the way in which they rely on the individual to resignify a culturally stigmatised object. Nevertheless, Murray (2008) makes an important point when she emphasises that if it were not for writers such as Orbach (2006) who pathologise the 'fat' female body to begin with, that countercultural movements such as the fat-acceptance movement would not have originated. She states:

> Orbach's thesis has not simply instituted a trouble-free course of action for fat politics, but ... it has also, more significantly, established an ontological legacy that continues to haunt attempts to reinscribe the "fat" female body (Murray 2008, p. 95).

By promoting 'fat' as a symbol of psychological instability and oppression, Orbach (2006) implicitly reinforces that those who have a 'fat' body should be conscious about it. Her feminist perspective, then, serves the dual function of both empowering women through a critical reading of oppressive gender norms, and inadvertently shaming women by suggesting that their 'fat' bodies are as a result of psychopathology. Her solution to curb compulsive eating behaviour in women, and, therefore, the contours of their 'fat' bodies, rests upon a narrative of self-change that is similar to Murray's (2008) criticisms of the fat-acceptance movements. One of the dominant ways that she encourages self-change in women is through a feminist self-help version of food femininity, one that is encouraged in solitary consciousness-raising practices and participation in introspective self-help activities.

Fat Is a Feminist Issue as a Consciousness-Raising Tool

Orbach's feminist perspective on food and eating takes on a self-help focus in her discussion of, and participation in, consciousness-raising practices. As explained earlier in the book, cultural changes from 1975 onwards marked a transformation in feminist consciousness-raising practices, where the use of feminist and self-help books replaced communal practices involving story-telling and group sharing (Sowards and Renegar 2004; Vanderford 2009). According to Hazleden (2011), many feminist writers over the years have employed "a confessional tone" (p. 274) in their narratives through the use of personal parables, as ways for their readers to relate and to create a surrogate consciousness-raising experience, without connecting with other women in the same physical space. Sowards and Renegar (2004) argue that this literary device included women who were isolated from greater political projects. The solitary act of reading of self-help books, thus, served the dual function of exposing women to a critical awareness of gender inequality and providing them with tools for personal change without the need for greater political involvement. Early in the introductory section of *Fat is a Feminist Issue*, Orbach (2006) positions herself within a second-wave feminist framework when she discusses her own participation in consciousness-raising practices. She describes her personal experiences of compulsive eating and her involvement in feminist self-help groups as catalysts towards critical reflection and recovery from compulsive eating and a reliance on 'fat' to protect her. Discussing this process, Orbach (2006) states:

> We had taken the formula of a women's group and one by one we shared how we felt about our bodies, being attractive, food, eating, thinness, fatness and clothes. We detailed our previous diet histories and traded horror stories of doctors, psychiatrists, diet organisations, health farms and fasting (p. 7).

Rather than approaching the subject from a psychotherapeutic perspective, which is where her expertise lies, Orbach (2006) introduces compulsive eating to her readers from a feminist consciousness-raising perspective. Although she refers to her meetings as being similar to "a woman's group" (p. 7) rather than constituting a women's group per se, some writers, such as Riessman (1990), have suggested that contemporary self-help groups were created out of consciousness-raising practices. Despite lacking an explicit reference to feminist consciousness-raising practices, Orbach (2006) alludes to feminist sharing through her own experiences of attending self-help groups. The personalisation of her story situates the *Fat is a Feminist Issue* narrative in slightly autobiographical terms, where the reader vicariously experiences Orbach's (2006) consciousness-raising experiences through the privacy of a book. The once political act of sitting together with like-minded women is transformed in Orbach's (2006) book into an isolated practice where the individual woman empowers herself with learning about certain types of knowledge. Evidence of Orbach's (2006) own introspective learning processes is shown in *Fat is a Feminist Issue* as a way to mirror changes in her readers:

> Slowly and unsurely we stopped dieting. Nothing terrible happened. My world did not collapse. Carol raised the central question; maybe we did not want to be thin. I dismissed that out of hand. Of course I wanted to be thin, I would be ... The dots turned out to hold the answer. Who I would be thin was different from who *I* was. I decided I did not want to be thin, there was not much in it. You were more hassled by men, you became a sex object. No, I definitely did not want to be thin ... I developed a new political reason for not being thin – I was not going to be like the fashion magazines wanted me to be; I was a Jewish beatnik and I would be *zaftig* [sic] ... Why was I afraid of being thin? (p. 8).

Orbach (2006) gives her female readers an introspective look into her own thought processes during her recovery from compulsive eating and, perhaps most obviously, begins to allude to the notion of self-reflection as a viable form of action. At this stage of the discussion, Orbach (2006) shifts her focus from a feminist perspective to a feminist self-help one.

Unsurprisingly, some writers (e.g., Riessman et al. 1992; Schrager 1993) express scepticism over the ability of self-help to achieve political change. In their article on the politicising of the self-help movement, Riessman colleagues (1992) argue that self-help and consciousness-raising have various factors in common, but that self-help requires no need for political engagement. Schrager (1993), too, emphasises that self-help stems from consciousness-raising practices, but argues that the link between feminist theory and self-help practices may not be a viable method of accomplishing political change. When considering Orbach's (2006) main arguments from this perspective, the discussion of consciousness-raising in a self-help format can be understood as a way of advocating for consciousness-raising by proxy, a solitary act of political awareness that ultimately relies on the individual to change their cognitions and subsequent behaviours around food and their bodies.

The Unhappy Marriage of Feminism and Self-Help

Orbach's (2006) feminist perspective has been criticised by some writers for its emphasis on 'fat' as a form of psychopathology (e.g., Murray 2008). It has also, however, been criticised for its inclusion of self-help discourses to address what she otherwise illustrates as a deeply ingrained political issue. Orbach's understanding of the 'fat' female body (and compulsive eating), or her self-help version of food femininity, is one of the dominant ways that she tacitly reinforces body-policing narratives to women.

The term self-help is described by writers such as Greenhill et al. (2009) as a method of self-improvement and education that has a wide variety of mediums, ranging from "books, workshops, media presentations and support groups" (p. 623). According to Hazleden (2011), women constitute the vast majority of self-help consumers, which indicates that 'self-help' is, in fact, a contemporary, gendered phenomenon. Indeed, Hazleden (2011) adds that the inclusion of feminist theories to self-help narratives has marked what has seemed to be a contradictory move on the part of feminist writers. On the one hand, she argues that "feminism has been largely formed against expertise" (p. 272), and on the other, she explains that feminism "has equally embraced expertise, employed it, and created it" (p. 272). This complex balancing act between the critique of political ideologies and the transformation of the self have been a guiding factor in Orbach's (2006) construction of a feminist self-help version of food femininity.

Indeed, Orbach's (2006) book can be conceived of as a contradictory feminist text, one that both resists mainstream psychopathological discourses on women's disordered eating behaviours and simultaneously uses them to further pathologise the 'fat' female body. Rather than presenting Orbach's (2006) book as a seminal 'feminist' text, some writers, such as Fikkan and Rothblum (2012), explain that *Fat is a Feminist Issue* is, first and foremost, a self-help manual and perhaps the best known self-help text of its genre. Perhaps most importantly, Orbach's (2006) positioning within the self-help genre changes the way her feminist message is read. Rather than critiquing patriarchal structures that oppress women's relationships with food and their bodies, Orbach (2006) awkwardly joins the ranks of other figures within psychotherapy through her dissemination of self-help advice. In the second half of *Fat is a Feminist Issue*, Orbach (2006) explains why she decided to focus her sights on an increasingly self-therapeutic perspective:

> Since *Fat is a Feminist Issue* was published in the spring of 1978. I have received hundreds of letters from individual women about their eating problems. Many of these letters made it clear to me that women needed more detailed guidelines on how to translate the ideas in *Fat is a Feminist Issue* into practice (p. 185).

> Fat is a Feminist Issue II will spell out in more detail the kinds of practical interventions that can be helpful in working on a compulsive eating problem (p. 187).

Recognising a demand in therapeutic advice-giving, Orbach (2006) provides the reader with a template for how to control one's eating behaviour (and unspoken, one's body weight). Despite its demand and her willingness to assist women, some writers have located problems with feminist texts that employ a self-help focus (Riessman et al. 1992; Schrager 1993). The phenomenon of feminist self-help texts has been discussed critically by Schrager (1993) in the context of changing feminist discourses. Schrager (1993) refers to feminist self-help texts as discourses that borrow from feminism "even as they work against feminism's fundamental tenets" (p. 176). Psychoanalytic or psychotherapeutic interventions are often argued to be counter-intuitive to feminist streams of thought because they neglect to locate women's personal problems with food and eating as politically situated problems. In reference to discourses, such as Orbach's (2006), that frame political inequalities in terms of individual problems, Schrager (1993) argues that:

Far from representing an alternative to traditionally psychotherapeutic discourses that are structured around women's disempowerment, the goal of the contemporary women's self-help narrative ... is to produce a female subject better suited to inhabiting a gender-asymmetrical society than to challenging its political and social basis (n.p.).

While it can be argued that Orbach (2006) does provide her readers with a comprehensive analysis of patriarchal structures that lead to the objectification and weight-related scrutiny of women, she does not call for women to *act* politically. Rather, she assists them to focus introspectively and to learn to challenge their relationships with food. The following excerpt provides an example of Orbach's (2006) self-help encouragement, which draws strongly from psychotherapeutic interventions:

> Remember back to the most recent time this week that you either ate more than you were wanting or that you were drawn to eating and started to eat but knew you weren't hungry ... Were you on your own or with others, in your kitchen or in a public place? ... Draw the scene vividly in your mind's eye as you can, so that it's as though you were observing a film of yourself in the situation ... And now I'd like you to replay the incident slowly, frame by frame ... Start by focusing on what was happening just before you ate when you weren't really hungry ... Does the scene feel familiar? ... Is this the time you usually overeat? ... Is this one of those persistently difficult times you have around food? ... Had you prepared to eat or did you just sort of stumble into the refrigerator or candy store or whatever? ... Now that you've set the scene, focus on the emotional state just before you ate ... How were you feeling? ... Can you give your feelings a name? ... Let whatever feelings you were having then come to the surface now ... (pp. 336–337).

Unlike critical feminist discourses that situate change within the rupturing of political institutions, *Fat is a Feminist Issue* focuses on change from within an individual. Orbach (2006) views feminist empowerment as a practice that first involves the changing consciousness of the woman, and implicitly fails to provide an explanation of how political equalities affecting women's body-conscious relationships with food will be faced. This is not dissimilar to other psychological interventions that use mindfulness-based or cognitive-behavioural techniques focusing on the amelioration or management of the symptom but not on the underlying problem (e.g., Bush et al. 2014); however, in the context of a politically charged feminist debate, Orbach's (2006) feminist self-help version of food femininity takes away from women more than it gives. Riessman colleagues (1992) describe texts that focus on self-help as "diversion[s] from social change" (n.p). Rather than presenting self-help texts as apolitical statements, though, Riessman colleagues (1992) argue that they can be conceived of as a first step in the political engagement of the individual.

Other writers have shared more individualistic views on the efficacy of self-help texts. In their qualitative study uncovering the popularity of self-help texts among women, Bruneau et al. (2010) found that self-help authors rely on a "revisioning of self" (p. 225). They explained that:

> Revisioning the self can be thought of as a process that an individual goes through when considering questions such as, "Who do I want to be?" and "How will I become this person that I want to be?" (p. 226).

Taking in this perspective, Orbach's (2006) feminist self-help promotion of food femininity in *Fat is a Feminist Issue* encourages women to subscribe to two contradictory messages. On the one hand, she encourages women to reflect critically upon the sexualisation and cultural scrutiny of their bodies and how this correlates to disordered eating behaviours, and, on the other hand, she relies on their own individual efforts to change these behaviours and, more implicitly, to lose weight and their supposedly defensive 'fat' bodies. Orbach's (2006) feminist self-help version of food femininity unintentionally reinforces body-policing narratives to women through a reliance on self-transformation, which ultimately involves psychopathologising of the 'fat' body. In a similar sense, Naomi Wolf's (1990) *The Beauty Myth* also relies on a narrative of individualism that can be perceived as unintentionally strengthening narratives of body policing in relation to food and eating.

WOLF'S LIBERAL-FEMINIST FOOD FEMININITIES IN *THE BEAUTY MYTH*

Naomi Wolf's (1990) liberal-feminist promotion of food femininity in *The Beauty Myth* signifies both a politicisation of women's beauty practices, such as dieting, and a personalisation of the solution. In ways that are distinct from Orbach's (2006) feminist self-help position in *Fat is a Feminist Issue,* Wolf (1990) focuses on the thin female body and how beauty practices, such as dieting, are used by male-dominated cultures to psychologically enslave women. Through a system that favours beauty over feminist gain, Wolf (1990) demonstrates how both the political (i.e., patriarchal institutions) and the personal (i.e., self-starvation) play a part in explaining women's conflicted relationships with food and their bodies. In critiquing *The Beauty Myth*, I will demonstrate how Wolf's (1990) liberal-feminist reinforcement of food femininity ultimately individualises women's experiences with policing their bodies in relation to food and, as such, inadvertently reinforces body-surveillance narratives through the third-wave feminist use of the term choice. However, before I start this section, an examination of Wolf's (1990) second-wave feminist influences will be discussed to show how she initially politicises women's disordered eating behaviours, and even problematises some beauty practices, such as dieting, by arguing that women experience a limited range of choices.

Wolf's Second-Wave Feminist Influences

Like Orbach (2006), Wolf's (1990) understanding that women's conformity to beauty practices, such as dieting, reside within a patriarchal social order rests heavily upon her second-wave, and particularly radical, feminist influences and their criticisms of gender (e.g., Dworkin 1974). During the 1970s, some feminist writers with radical politics conceptualised beauty as yet another symptom of a cultural disease that created and stringently reinforced gender hierarchies. A critical feature of this radical feminist thought was the notion that gender, the socially constructed norms that dictate appearance and behaviour, created divisions between the sexes that positioned women as subordinate and men as dominant. As explained by Jeffreys (2005) in *Beauty and Misogyny*, patriarchal cultures have long relied on an "eroticised power difference" (p. 24) between men and women, where someone ultimately has to "play the girl" (p. 24) and, thus, be the subordinate one. Playing the girl, or being feminine as many others have described it, is enacted and reinforced through a myriad of social practices, most of which require some level of harm to women and personal sacrifice. Beauty practices, according to writers such as Dworkin (1974), Jeffreys (2005) and Bordo (2004), are among some of the ways that women are controlled and subordinated in patriarchal cultures. Dworkin (1974) and Jeffreys (2005), for example, argue that male-supremacist cultural norms are behind the perpetuation of beauty ideals, such as thinness, and that they rely on the notion of 'gender' to achieve discrimination between the sexes. Writers such as Bartky (1990) and Bordo (2004), however, add a post-structural perspective to their analyses and conclude that a panoptic social gaze teaches women to internalise their objectification and, thus, engage in harmful beauty practices. In these examples, all of the writers, despite their philosophically divergent perspectives, have conceived of beauty as a reinforcement of harmful gender norms that ultimately affect women as a class.

Wolf (1990), by contrast, uses second-wave feminist arguments as the basis for her thesis, but takes her critique of beauty one step further by arguing that the normative reliance on feminine practices, such as dieting and women's general lack of comfort around food, rests upon a cultural reaction against gains made by the first- and second-wave feminist movements of yesteryear. She refers to this aestheticised backlash against feminism as 'the beauty myth.' In the introductory section eponymously titled 'The Beauty Myth,' Wolf (1990) explains both what the 'beauty myth' is and why she believes it originated:

> We are in the midst of a violent backlash against feminism that uses images of female beauty as a political weapon against women's advancement; the beauty myth (p. 10).

The notion that female beauty can be used as a "political weapon" (p. 10) against feminist progress is an original angle that Wolf (1990) presents, drawing upon radical understandings that beauty is both harmful and political (Dworkin 1974; Jeffreys 2005) and bringing the reader back to the contemporary cultural landscape that sees feminism as a dying social movement (Faludi 1993). Central to Wolf's (1990) thesis that beauty is used to harm women's advancement is the notion that beauty itself is, and has been, a brand of political sedative. She traces this idea historically through a comparison of the cultural status of women and the beauty practices that were prevalent in the era and explains that "every generation since about 1830 has had to fight its version of the beauty myth" (p. 11). The following quotes exemplify how Wolf (1990) claims the beauty myth has coincided with a feminist backlash:

> The more legal and material hindrances women have broken through, the more strictly and heavily and cruelly images of female beauty have come to weigh upon us (p. 10).

> Beauty is a currency system like the gold standard. Like any economy, it is determined by politics and in the modern age in the West it is the last, best belief system that keeps male dominance in tact (p. 12).

Wolf's (1990) critical engagement with women's historical subordination, as well as men's simultaneously felt dominance, situates her voice within the framework of a feminist perspective, one that explicitly politicises women's inequalities and locates "male dominance" (p. 12) as a critical factor behind women's reliance on 'beauty' and dieting as arbiters of cultural success. Like other feminist writers who came before her (e.g., Bartky 1990; Orbach 1993), Wolf (1990) problematises dieting as a primary symptom of women's subordinated and politically sedated lives. Rather than focusing on the individual woman, which is what psychological discourses have done for decades (Bordo 2004; Grogan 2008), Wolf (1990) focuses on how cultural institutions encourage and reinforce thinness in women as a disciplinary mechanism:

> A cultural fixation on female thinness is not an obsession about female beauty but an obsession about female obedience (p. 187).

> Dieting is the most potent political sedative in women's history; a quietly mad population is a tractable one (p. 187).

Wolf's (1990) focus on the cultural "fixation" and "obsession" (p. 187) with the emaciated and seemingly controlled female body is in stark contrast to the way women's disordered relationships with food are typically presented. Her repositioning of disorder as a symptom of culture rather than the individual woman has been a common feature of revolutionary feminist writing with a second-wave flavour (Bartky 1990; Bordo 2004; Orbach 2006). Indeed, Wolf (1990) goes as far as to say that "women must claim [eating disorders] as political damage done to us" (p. 208). This emphasis on the political origins of women's personal psychopathologies gives Wolf's (1990) work more of a radical feminist flavour. She conveys a perspective that aligns firmly with radical feminist sentiments on beauty, and gives the impression that her solutions to the problem will be political, too. She does so through the juxtapositioning of the Ugly Feminist stereotype with the figuration of the Iron Maiden, and through her criticism of choice as a depoliticised concept:

> The caricature of the Ugly Feminist was resurrected to dog the steps of the women's movement (p. 19).

> The original Iron Maiden was a medieval German instrument of torture, a body-shaped casket painted with the limbs and features of a lovely, smiling young woman. The unlucky victim was slowly enclosed inside her; the

lid fell shut to immobilise the victim, who died either of starvation or, less cruelly, of the metal spikes embedded in her interior. The modern hallucination in which women are trapped *or trap themselves* is similarly rigid, cruel, and euphemistically painted. Contemporary culture directs attention to imagery of the Iron Maiden, while censoring women's faces and bodies (p. 17; italics added).

Our culture gives a young woman only two dreams to which to imagine her body, like a coin with two faces: one pornographic, the other anorexic; the first for nighttime [sic], the second for day – the one, supposedly, for men and the other for women. *She does not have the choice to refuse to toss it – not, yet, to demand a better dream.* The anorexic body is sexually safer to inhabit than the pornographic (p. 199; italics added).

The function of these caricatures of femininity, one that conforms (Iron Maiden) and the other that resists (Ugly Feminist), is to emphasise how feminist activism has been reduced to women's physical appearances. The figurative example of the Iron Maiden is one of the key images that Wolf (1990) uses throughout *The Beauty Myth*, where women are perceived to be enslaved in their own bodies in a culture that judges their worth according to their appearance and their choice of food. Her assertion that women's "choices" are actually just part of a rigid Madonna–Whore binary, where the emaciated body of anorexia is a perceived solution, resonates with previous feminist analyses on the topic (e.g., Orbach 1993). Indeed, throughout her chapter entitled 'Hunger,' Wolf (1990) describes dieting as one of the primary mechanisms through which women's subordination takes shape. She argues:

The world is not coming to an end because the cherished child in five who "chooses" to diet slowly is a girl. And she is merely doing too well what she is expected to do very well in the best of times (p. 181).

If food is honour; if dieting is semistarvation; if women have to lose 23 percent of their body weight to fit the Iron Maiden and chronic psychological disruption sets in at a body weight loss of 25 percent; if semistarvation is physically and psychologically debilitating, and female strength, sexuality, and self-respect pose the threats explored earlier against the vested interests of society ... then we can understand why the Iron Maiden is so thin. The thin "ideal" is not beautiful aesthetically; she is beautiful politically. *The compulsion to imitate her is not something trivial that women choose freely to do to ourselves. It is something serious being done to us to safeguard political power.* Seen in this light, it is inconceivable that women would not have to be compelled to grow thin at this point in our history (p. 196; italics included).

One factor that resonates in the aforementioned excerpts is the notion that Wolf (1990) actively politicises the notion of choice as an answer to why women engage in dieting behaviours. Indeed, she presents a some-what radicalised understanding of choice by positioning it within a broader political framework, and understanding that choices are constrained by the prevailing sociocultural climate. It is not Wolf's (1990) politicisation of dieting and the emaciated Western ideal of beauty, however, that are perceived to be problematic. It is her reliance on an individualistic solution to women's dissatisfaction with their bodies that causes concern in this analysis. Wolf's (1990) liberal-feminist version of food femininity, predicated upon a depoliticised notion of choice and personal responsibility, removes the radical sting out of her analysis and, as she states in reference to dieting as a political solution, "take[s] the teeth out of [the] revolution" (p. 188).

A Liberal-Feminist Food Femininity

According to Groenhout (2002), liberal feminism has been described as a combination of liberal political theory and feminist analysis, a study of the "rights, autonomy and reason" (p. 51) of the individual woman. While the blending of liberal and feminist politics can be perceived as progressive step for women in the twenty-first century, some feminist writers, especially those with radical politics, have been vocal about their distrust of individualistic perspectives in feminist theory and activism (Groenhout 2002; e.g., Jeffreys 2005; MacKinnon 1989). Groenhout (2002) explains that the staunch liberal tradition of fostering rationality in the individual has been one of the dominant criticisms launched against liberal feminist writings by radical feminists. In her piece *Toward a Feminist Theory of the State*, radical feminist legal scholar Catharine MacKinnon (1989) discusses the notion of rationality in liberal feminist politics as being built on a framework of cultural and institutional sexism. Central to MacKinnon's (1989) argument is the understanding that rationality could only be conceived of within the context of male supremacy and, thus, any rational conclusion made by women within this landscape was based on their cultural objectification. As explained by Groenhout (2002), MacKinnon's (1989) radical feminist perspective explicitly problematises liberal feminist notions of rationality and choice:

> If rationality/objectivity is inherently connected to the objectification of women, then the "rationality" of women becomes problematic. On this view, women must either deny their nature as women (become honorary

men) and objectify other women in order to be rational, or they must accept their status as objectified (not objectifiers) and so be incapable of rationality (Groenhout 2002, p. 52).

From MacKinnon's (1989) perspective, the notion that women can use their rationality to make informed decisions about their beauty practices, such as dieting and other forms of food restriction, comes from a cultural landscape that provides women with limited choices to begin with. Under this system, women either become complicit to their objectification (i.e., develop body-policing attitudes) or become an objectifier. In *The Beauty Myth*, Wolf (1990) calls on the rationality of the female reader through the implicit encouragement of a liberal-feminist version of food feminin-ity and, in some ways, fits between being both the objectified and the objectifier. In the concluding chapter of *The Beauty Myth* entitled 'Beyond the Beauty Myth,' Wolf (1990) explains how a change in media images addressing thinness is not enough to curb the problem:

> While we cannot directly affect the images, we can drain them of their power. We can turn away from them, look directly at one another, and find alternative images of beauty in a female subculture ... We can lift ourselves and other women out of the myth – but only if we are willing to seek out and support and really look at the alternatives (p. 277).

Wolf's (1990) suggestion that women can "turn away" (p. 277) from harmful cultural images is contradictory to the more radical feminist angle of the critique she presents, initially where her key argument is centred around the pervasiveness of the beauty myth and its harmful grip on women's lives. The implication that women who are taught to be body conscious should merely "find alternative images" (p. 277) of feminin-ity is simplistic and contradictory, as the basis of her book demonstrates how difficult it is for women to avoid the stronghold of the beauty myth. Wolf's (1990) liberal-feminist version of food femininity in relation to women's bodies can be seen as a fitting example of MacKinnon's (1989) assertion that liberal feminist rationality is implicitly couched within male-centred politics that espouse objectification. Rather than challenging these politics, Wolf (1990) places ultimate trust in women's rationality to change their anxious relationships with food and their bodies, and, in doing so, normalises body policing in women through an over-reliance on individual, as opposed to political and institutional, solutions.

The notion that liberal-feminist politics fall short of providing women with the adequate tools for emancipation is not new (e.g., MacKinnon 1989; Jeffreys 2005). Referring to the tensions between liberal politics and feminist analysis, Groenhout (2002) asserts that, "if liberalism, viewed accurately, is simply male dominance writ large, feminist liberalism is an oxymoron, which makes those who defend it perhaps just morons" (pp. 61–62). Wolf's (1990) liberal-feminist food femininity, from Groenhout's (2002) perspective, is an oxymoron; it suggests that culture is responsible for disseminating the beauty myth and yet relies on the individual to find the solution. This train of thought is also evident in her use of the term choice to describe women's engagement with alternative forms of beauty:

> Women will be free of the beauty myth when we can choose to use our faces and clothes and bodies as simply one form of self-expression out of a full range of others. We can dress up for our pleasure, but we must speak up for our rights (pp. 273–274).

Wolf's (1990) liberal-feminist use of the term choice is somewhat idealistic, as the concept of choice can only ever be couched within pre-existent cultural scripts of ideal femininity and, indeed, in harmful gender stereotypes to begin with (Jeffreys 2005; Lazar 2009). Given that Wolf (1990) herself argues that cultural standards of beauty are predicated upon the ideology that women are "worth less" (p. 18), it is surprising that she relies on the individual woman to choose to "feel worth more" (p. 18), especially after she critiques dieting as emanating from a lack of choice. Wolf's (1990) decontextualised use of the term choice in reference to beauty practices can be seen as an implicit reinforcement of body-policing cultural narratives, as it idealistically resituates responsibility into the hands of individual women rather than within the political structures that shape them.

One of the major criticisms levelled against Wolf's (1990) proclamations of choice come from radical feminist scholar Sheila Jeffreys (2005). In her book *Beauty and Misogyny*, Jeffreys (2005) refers to Wolf's (1990) assumption that women have the power to 'choose' their beauty practices, as erroneous and ill-conceived. According to Jeffreys (2005), "the absence of any alternative culture within which women can identify a different way to be a woman enforces oppressive practices" (pp. 7–8). When women are confronted with a cultural landscape that psychologically and physically inflicts beauty practices onto them, and they participate in these practices from fear of social stigma and ostracism, then their actions cannot be conceived of as mere choices. As such, Wolf's (1990) depiction of choice inadvertently strengthens the shame that women already feel about their body consciousness and their lack of control over it.

The contemporary notion that women freely choose to engage in beauty practices such as dieting is painted by second-wave feminist writers, such as Jeffreys (2005) and Bordo (2004), as an implicit failure to acknowledge how gender norms operate to oppress women and to situate them within the social hierarchy as the denigrated other. Wolf (1990), however, presents an alternative depiction of women's choices to engage in beauty regimens when she almost apologetically states:

> I am not attacking anything that makes women feel good; only what makes us feel bad in the first place. We all like to be desirable and feel beautiful (p. 271).

Wolf's (1990) announcement that she is not "attacking [what] makes women feel good" (p. 271) is a powerful statement, one that inadvertently reflects how liberal-feminists hesitate to politicise women's engagement with beauty practices. Rather than continuing to view dieting and beauty practices as harmful gender norms, Wolf (1990) reverts to individualistic thinking in an attempt to avoid alienating her young (and new generation of) readers. While this angle may seem beneficial in a contemporary feminist landscape, it can also be perceived as problematic. Jeffreys (2005) discusses how harmful beauty practices, and specifically in relation to dieting behaviours, position women's choices from a depoliticised perspective, one that ultimately places responsibility into the hands of the individual woman. That is, Jeffreys (2005) argues that regardless of whether or not a woman chooses beauty practices that give her pleasure, "choice is no defense" (p. 27) for engaging in cultural practices rooted in women's oppression.

Engaging in beauty practices that "feel good" (p. 271) has also been problematised in the psychological and sociological literature. Some psychological studies have pointed to the danger of relying on women's enjoyment of dieting practices as an indicator of psychological well-being. In their study on women's positive experiences of restrictive eating, Serpell, Treasure, Teasdale and Sullivan (1999) found that in their sample of 18 clinically diagnosed participants, anorexic symptomatology was viewed as holding both personal and social benefits. Among some of these benefits, women reportedly gained enjoyment from their restrictive eating behaviour, as it gave them a sense of control (e.g., "I really need [anorexia] to provide me with direction in everything I do"; p. 180), made them feel more attractive (e.g., "When I'm out socialising, I feel more men are interested in me and I feel as though this has a lot to do with [anorexia]"; p. 180) and permitted them to behave in a more extroverted way (e.g., "Often when In company, [anorexia] make[s] me more extroverted than I used to be"; p. 180). The researchers argued that the positive aspects of eating disorders, which are largely overlooked in mainstream discussions of psychopathology, carry clues into the culturally seductive nature of starvation in women, something which Wolf (1990) overlooks in her encouragement of women's engagement with beauty practices that make them "feel good" (p. 271).

Another factor that Wolf (1990) surprisingly overlooks is how women are encouraged to view beauty practices as positive, and even feminist, experiences in popular cultural discourses. In her article on the marketing of beauty practices and the post-feminist lifestyle, Lazar (2009) analyses the content of beauty advertisements found in increasingly Westernised countries such as Singapore. Examining discourses on the basis of their objectifying messages, Lazar (2009) identifies that part of the seduction of engaging in beauty practices is the social and cultural promise it offers women: acceptance through a facade of feminist values. She argues that engaging in beauty practices (which typically include dieting) has been constructed in contemporary beauty advertising as "women's right to be beautiful" (p. 38), and, as such, reflects how beauty advertisers have appropriated feminist terminology to supposedly curb women's body consciousness. From Lazar's (2009) perspective, Wolf's (1990) encouragement of Western beauty practices that make women "feel good" (p. 271) decontextualises how women are taught to value themselves in the first place. Her liberal-feminist promotion of food femininity is, thus, one that simultaneously denounces dieting but hesitates to politicise beauty practices in general.

The Feminist Third-Wave: A New Way to See

One of the solutions that Wolf (1990) poses in the concluding chapter of *The Beauty Myth* is the application of feminist theories to a younger generation. She does this by proposing a new wave of feminist activism, which she refers to as the 'third-wave':

> The beauty myth can be defeated for good only through an electric resurgence of the woman-centered political activism of the seventies – a feminist third wave – updated to take on the new issues of the nineties. In this decade, for young women in particular, some of the enemies are quieter and cleverer and harder to grasp (p. 281).

Wolf's (1990) suggestion that a feminist third-wave is needed to counter-act the "harder to grasp" (p. 281) enemy is distinct from feminist narratives that use second-wave politics to address women's issues (e.g., Bartky 1990; Bordo 2004). While writers using a second-wave feminist lens view the panoptic gaze over women as an institutional problem (i.e., patriarchy, sexism, etc.; Bartky 1990; Bordo 2004), third-wave feminist politics favour the choices of the individual in tackling such political issues.

The politics of the third wave, which were only in their infancy when Wolf (1990) wrote *The Beauty Myth*, have been said to reflect changes in women's lived experiences that acknowledge and favour personal choices over political critiques. Wolf (1990) has been cited as one of the major proponents of third-wave feminist thought, which has included liberal-feminist, post-feminist, post-modern and post-structural conceptions of femininity (Nguyen 2013). Vu (2011) describes the feminist third-wave as a "valoris[ation] of personal narratives" (p. 874) and, as such, a change from second-wave feminist politics espousing consciousness raising and sisterhood. From the context of Wolf's (1990) proposal—that a new wave of feminism is needed to tackle panoptic cultural forces—a feminist third wave promises to address the issue of beauty practices from a perspective that favours the individual preferences of women.

While the politics of the third wave, which include post-structural and post-modern theories, have been beneficial in understanding the "quieter and cleverer and harder to grasp" (p. 281) enemies that Wolf (1990) speaks of, some writers, such as Nguyen (2013), have made reference to third-wave politics as having succumbed to "postfeminist seductions" (p. 157). Nguyen (2013) argues that the third-wave feminist emphasis on empowerment in what she labels as 'girl culture' signified a change in the way that women approached their victimhood, which Wolf (1993) referred to as either victim feminism (i.e., second-wave feminist politics) or power feminism (i.e., her proposed third-wave feminist politics). Nguyen (2013) explains that "power feminism, or girlie feminism, envisages not women combating institutional sexism, but girls experimenting with personal choices in a perpetual state of youth and innocence" (p. 156). From Wolf's (1990) perspective, contemporary feminist writers and activists need to acknowledge institutional sexism but act according to their own individual agency. As such, her advice to women reflects a third-wave, even post-feminist, flavour that emphasises individual choices rather than political upheaval. Referenced throughout the book, Wolf (1990) describes the third-wave movement in terms of a change in how one sees oneself:

If we are to free ourselves from the dead weight that has once again been made out of femaleness; it is not ballots or lobbyists, or placards that women will need first; it is a new way to see (p. 19).

The next phase of our movement forward as individual women, as women together, and as tenants of our bodies and this planet, depends on what we decide to see when we look in the mirror. What *will* we see? (p. 291; original italics).

Unlike the vigour of second-wave feminist activism, a movement which aimed to facilitate change through group involvement and a politicisation of the personal, Wolf's (1990) depiction of "a new way to see" (p. 19) seems less about sisterhood and more about individual development and transformation. Indeed, when contrasted against radical feminist challenges to beauty, Wolf's (1990) liberal-feminist construction of food femininity seems to fall short. Rather than asking women "what *will* we see?" (p. 291; original italics), radical feminists created challenges to ideal femininity by *showing* women ways to resist harmful beauty practices.

One example of second-wave feminist activism that emphasises resistance and contrasts against Wolf's (1990) "new way to see" (p. 291) was the birth of the freedom trash can. In her article on the development of feminist politics, Dow (2003) examined cultural myths that have been harmful to the feminist movement and, among them, discussed the origins of the freedom trash can. At the 1968 *Miss America Pageant*, a group of second-wave feminists conducted a protest, challenging the rigid constructions of femininity and the cultural objectification of women. Throwing what they called their "instruments of torture" (p. 131), such as "girdles, high heels, cosmetics, eyelash curlers, wigs, issues of *Cosmopolitan, Playboy* and *Ladies Home Journal*" (p. 131; original italics) into a regular trash can (which they called the freedom trash can), the women then lit a match as a symbol of feminist resistance. The famous act, according to Dow (2003), was a public way of denouncing the sexual objectification of women and signalled a movement that was explicitly focused on the critical reading of beauty practices. Yet, in the days following the Miss America Pageant, feminist activists were ridiculed and labelled by the popular press as hysterical bra-burners, a label that has since stuck, despite its factual inaccuracies.[1] According to Dow (2003), the consequences of displaying a feminist stance during the second-wave movement particularly challenging beauty, was a testament to how difficult it was to call oneself a feminist. Wolf's (1990) liberal-feminist position on beauty and, implicitly, women's relationships with food, however, downplays the importance of refusing culturally proscribed feminine norms and, in doing so, waters down her analysis of beauty. She states, rather idealistically:

> In a world in which women have real choice, the choices we make about our appearance will be taken at last for what they really are: no big deal (p. 273).

The assertion that beauty practices will become "no big deal" (p. 273) is a clear example where Wolf (1990) conveys distance from more radical feminist politics through a liberal-feminist position. In an attempt to shy away from the oppressive caricature of the 'Ugly Feminist,' or the 'bra-burner' of the past, Wolf (1990) proclaims that women will still be willing to engage in beauty practices in a culture that is critical of objectification and control. Addressing claims made by Wolf (1990) that beauty practices will become "no big deal" once sexual equality has been achieved, Jeffreys (2005) poses the question: why would any women want to continue engaging in harmful beauty practices after the revolution has happened? Indeed, Wolf's (1990) failure to identify that beauty practices, except for dieting, are oppressive *feminine* practices shows crucial gaps in her argument, gaps that tacitly normalise the notion of body consciousness in women and ignore that, like dieting, body-policing attitudes are not empowering or freely chosen. In contrast to radical feminist protests against objectification, Wolf's (1990) assertion that beauty practices can be resignified into positive feminist actions can be perceived as a strengthening of the cultural *status quo*. From a radical feminist perspective, Wolf's (1990) appropriation of a liberal-feminist construction of food femininity in regards to beauty can be seen as a figurative act of rummaging through the freedom trash rather than threatening to set it on fire. Indeed, her preference for some beauty practices as opposed to others (e.g., dieting) presents a confusing feminist narrative, one that both politicises the notion of choice and personalises the narrative to suit current aesthetic ideals. These contradictory messages about food, beauty and women's bodies only serve to add to the confusion that women already feel about their right, as women, to enjoy food and live their lives free of objectification.

As shown throughout this chapter, both Orbach (2006) and Wolf (1990) find distinct ways of reinforcing body-policing narratives to their female readers through various, individualising versions of food femininity. While Orbach (2006) comes from a primarily psychotherapeutic position (albeit, informed by feminism), her reliance on self-help is similar to the individualism found in Wolf's (1990) liberal-feminist depiction of food femininity. Both iconic feminist writers rely on rhetoric of individuality, where the empowerment of the individual takes precedence over the dismantling of oppressive gender norms. As contemporary consciousness-raising texts, both *Fat is a Feminist Issue* and *The Beauty Myth* convey feminist perspectives that cater to individualist solutions. While this may be viewed as being in line with contemporary consciousness-raising practices that are experienced in isolation (e.g., through reading), what the popularity of these texts shows is how the voices of the iconic feminist authors could only politicise the topic to a certain extent. Indeed, as Jeffreys (2005) explains in reference to *The Beauty Myth*, the radical sting of Wolf's (1990) feminist analysis tapered as she published more books, indicating that the pressure of conforming to mainstream cultural discourses involves a mixture of political debate and a reliance on the patriarchal dictates of how entitled a woman is to critique sexist ideologies (Love and Helmbrecht 2007). The same can be said for Orbach's (2006) text, which initially politicises the origins of compulsive eating in women and then pathologises 'fat' and provides self-help-styled solutions to curb the problem.

While the examination of iconic feminist texts yielded results similar to the analysis of cookbooks and diet books, the acknowledgement that the three genres share similarities is important when trying to determine what is behind the reinforcement and normalisation of body-policing narratives of food and eating that target female, largely heterosexual, audiences. An examination of diet books, cookbooks and iconic feminist texts as food and eating-related discourses will, thus, be examined in the next chapter to contextualise both how and what gendered processes are behind the reinforcement of body-policing narratives to women. Additionally, throughout Chap. 7, narratives of body policing identified in the contemporary food discourses analysed in this book will be positioned in terms of the prevailing cultural malaise that surrounds women's relationships with food and their bodies, namely, through the identification and discussion of a bulimic or pathogenic cultural consciousness (Bordo 2004; Popa 2012).

Note

1. According to Dow (2003), no item of clothing/literature was burnt during the Miss America protest.

REFERENCES

Bartky, S. L. (1990). *Femininity and domination: Studies in the phenomenology of oppression.* New York: Routledge/Taylor & Francis Group.

Bordo, S. (2004). *Unbearable weight: Feminism, Western culture, and the body.* Berkeley: University of California Press.

Bruneau, L., Bubenzer, D. L., & McGlothlin, J. M. (2010). Revisioning the self: A phenomenological investigation into self-help reading. *The Journal of Humanistic Counselling, Education and Development, 49*(2), 217–230.

Bush, H. E., Rossy, L., Mintz, L. B., & Schopp, L. (2014). Eat for life: A work site feasibility study of a novel mindfulness-based intuitive eating intervention. *American Journal of Health Promotion, 28*(6), 380–389.

Calogero, R. M., Davis, W. N., & Thompson, J. K. (2005). The role of self-objectification in the experience of women with eating disorders. *Sex Roles, 52*(1–2), 43–50.

de Vries, D. A., & Peter, J. (2013). Women on display: The effect of portraying the self online on women's self-objectification. *Computers in Human Behaviour, 29*(4), 1483–1489.

de Zwaan, M. (2001). Binge eating disorder and obesity. *International Journal of Obesity and Related Metabolic Disorders: Journal of the International Association for the Study of Obesity, 25*(1), 51–55.

Dow, B. J. (2003). Feminism, Miss America, and media mythology. *Rhetoric and Public Affairs, 6*(1), 127–149.

Dworkin, A. (1974). *Woman hating: A radical look at sexuality.* New York: E. P. Dutton.

Fikkan, J. L., & Rothblum, E. D. (2012). Is fat a feminist issue? Exploring the gendered nature of weight bias. *Sex Roles, 66*(9–10), 575–592.

Faludi, S. (1993). *Backlash: The undeclared war against women.* London: Vintage.

Fredrickson, B. L., & Roberts, T.-A. (1997). Objectification theory. *Psychology of Women Quarterly, 21*(2), 173–207.

Fredrickson, B. L., Roberts, T.-A., Noll, S. M., Quinn, D. M., & Twenge, J. M. (1998). That swimsuit becomes you: Sex differences in self-objectification, restrained eating, and math performance. *Journal of Personality and Social Psychology, 75*(1), 269–284.

Green, M. A., Riopel, C. M., Skaggs, A. K., & Scott, N. A. (2008). Feminist identity as a predictor of eating disorder diagnostic status. *Journal of Clinical Psychology, 64*(6), 777–788.

Greenhill, P., Vaughn, T. A., & Locke, L. (2009). *Encyclopedia of women's folklore and folklife.* Westport: Greenwood Press.

Grilo, C. M., Shiffman, S., & Carter-Campbell, J. T. (1994). Binge eating antecedents in normal-weight nonpurging females: Is there consistency? *International Journal of Eating Disorders, 16*(3), 239–249.

Groenhout, R. E. (2002). Essentialist challenges to liberal feminism. *Social Theory and Practice, 28*(1), 51–75.

Grogan, S. (2008). *Body image: Understanding body dissatisfaction in men, women, and children.* New York: Routledge.

Harper, B., & Tiggemann, M. (2008). The effect of thin ideal media images on women's self-objectification, mood, and body image. *Sex Roles, 58,* 649–657.

Hazleden, R. (2011). Dragon-slayers and jealous rats: The gendered self in contemporary self-help manuals. *Cultural Studies Review, 17*(1), 270–295.

Hinds, H., & Stacey, J. (2001). Imaging feminism, imaging femininity: The bra-burner, Diana, and the woman who kills. *Feminist Media Studies, 1*(2), 153–177.

Jeffreys, S. (2005). *Beauty and misogyny: Harmful cultural practices in the west.* East Sussex: Routledge.

Kirkland, A. (2008). Think of the hippopotamus: Rights consciousness in the fat acceptance movement. *Law & Society Review, 42*(2), 397–432.

Lazar, M. M. (2009). Entitled to consume: Postfeminist femininity and a culture of post-critique. *Discourse and Communication, 3*(4), 371–400.

Love, M. A., & Helmbrecht, B. M. (2007). Teaching the conflicts: (Re)engaging students with feminism in a postfeminist world. *Feminist Teacher, 18*(1), 41–58.

MacKinnon, C. A. (1989). *Toward a feminist theory of the state.* Cambridge, MA: Harvard University Press.

McKinley, N. M., & Hyde, J. S. (1996). The objectified body consciousness scale development and validation. *Psychology of Women Quarterly, 20*(2), 181–215.

Murray, S. (2008). *The 'fat' female body.* Great Britain: Palgrave Macmillan.

Nguyen, T. (2013). From slutwalks to suicidegirls: Feminist resistance in the third wave and postfeminist era. *Women's Studies Quarterly, 41*(3/4), 157–172.

Orbach, S. (1993). *Hunger strike: The anorectic's struggle as a metaphor for our age.* London: Karnac.

Orbach, S. (2006). *Fat is a feminist issue.* London: Arrow Books.

Popa, T. (2012). Eating disorders in a hyper-consumerist and post-feminist context. *Scientific Journal of Humanistic Studies, 4*(7), 162–166.

Riessman, F. (1990). Restructuring help: A human services paradigm for the 1990s. *American Journal of Community Psychology, 18*(2), 221–230.

Riessman, F., Bay, T., & Madara, E. J. (1992). The politics of self-help. *Social Policy, 23*(2), 28–38.

Schag, K., Schonleber, J., Teufel, M., Zipfel, S., & Giel, K. E. (2013). Food-related impulsivity in obesity and binge-eating disorder – A systematic review. *Obesity Reviews: An Official Journal of the International Association for the Study of Obesity, 14*(6), 477–495.

Schrager, C. D. (1993). Questioning the promise of self-help: A reading of women who love too much. *Feminist Studies, 19*(1), 177–192.

Serpell, L., Treasure, J., Teasdale, J., & Sullivan, V. (1999). Anorexia nervosa: Friend or foe? *International Journal of Eating Disorders, 25*(2), 177–186.

Shantz, J. (2005). Fat! … So? The fat grrl revolution. *Feminist Media Studies, 5*(1), 102–104.

Showalter, E. (2001). *In search of heroines.* Retrieved from: http://www.theguardian.com/world/2001/jun/14/gender.uk

Sowards, S. K., & Renegar, V. R. (2004). The rhetorical functions of consciousness-raising in third wave feminism. *Communication Studies, 55*(4), 535–552.

Swami, V., Coles, R., Wyrozumska, K., Wilson, E., Salem, N., & Furnham, A. (2010). Oppressive beliefs at play: Associations among beauty ideals and practices and individual differences in sexism, objectification of others, and media exposure. *Psychology of Women Quarterly, 34*(3), 365–379.

Tiggemann, M. (2013). Objectification theory: Of relevance for eating disorder researchers and clinicians. *Clinical Psychologist, 17*(2), 35–45.

Vanderford, A. (2009). Consciousness raising. In P. Greenhill, T. A. Vaughn, & L. Locke (Eds.), *Encyclopedia of women's folklore and folklife.* Westport: Greenwood Press.

Vu, S.-L. (2011). Reclaiming the personal: Personal narratives of third-wave feminists. *Women's Studies, 40*, 873–889.

Wolf, N. (1990). *The beauty myth: How images of beauty are used against women.* London: Vintage.

Wolf, N. (1993). *Fire with fire: The new female power and how it will change the 21st century.* London: Chatto & Windus.

Young, M. (2005). One size fits all: Disrupting the commercialised, pathologised, fat female form. *Feminist Media Studies, 5*(2), 249–252.

CHAPTER 7

Unveiling a Pathogenic Food Consciousness: Gender, Patriarchy and the Neoliberal Subject

I have dedicated the last few chapters to looking at the way in which diet books, cookbooks and iconic feminist texts, when combined, operate as overarching food discourses that perpetuate body-policing narratives. In this chapter, I look into the pathogenic culture behind gendered food discourses and uncover consumerist and patriarchal messages that perpetuate women's dissatisfaction with, and surveillance over, their bodies (Bordo 2004; Popa 2012; Malson 2009). I also address why the patriarchal social order *needs* body-policing attitudes to permeate gendered discourses on food and eating. I question the purpose of multiple food femininities, with a specific focus on the way women are encouraged to eat themselves into feminine subjectivities that either glamourise or normalise an anxious surveillance over the weight and shape of their bodies. Additionally, I use my analysis to question the appeal of gendered food discourses by identifying the resistant messages they espouse, and how their subversion of oppressive food narratives actually feeds into patriarchal constructions of gender. In essence, in this chapter, I ask *why* body-policing narratives are subsumed within gendered discourses on food and eating, and *how* they function to inflict harm on women in implicit and more explicit ways. Before a discussion of why patriarchy needs body-policing narratives in discourses on food and eating, it is important to establish resonances and tensions between the three genres analysed and, specifically, to understand the cultural consciousness that these narratives are subsumed within.

© The Author(s) 2017
N. Jovanovski, *Digesting Femininities*,
DOI 10.1007/978-3-319-58925-1_7

In keeping with the notion that body-policing attitudes are symptoms of a pathogenic culture (e.g., Malson 2009), analysis of diet books, cookbooks and iconic feminist texts reveals that casting surveillance over, and being dissatisfied with, one's body plays a central role in gendered discourses food and eating aimed at women. As explained in detail in Chap. 2, body-policing attitudes, also referred to in the feminist literature as self-objectification (Fredrickson and Roberts 1997), objectified body-consciousness and self-surveillance (Bartky 1990) play a harmful role in reinforcing women's dissatisfaction with their bodies (Rodin et al. 1984), in many cases, leading to women's conflicted relationships with food and eating (Bartky 1990; Bordo 2004; Orbach 2006; Grogan 2008; Wolf 1990). Traditionally, the psychological literature has chosen to focus on the role of the individual woman in the development of body surveillance, body dissatisfaction and eating disorders, minimising the role that culture plays in disseminating messages associated with body consciousness. In this book, rather than focusing on the individual, emphasis is placed on the symptomatic culture that promotes women's anxieties surrounding food and their bodies, and how this harmful narrative is reinforced and normalised in popular cultural discourses that focus on food and eating. One of the most important ways that this is identified is through the "diagnosis" of the culture behind food discourses, referred to here as a pathogenic or bulimic cultural consciousness (i.e., one that simultaneously emphasises narratives of consumption/hedonism/entitlement and narratives of restraint/guilt/psychopathology through body-policing narratives). Women are surrounded by a bulimic cultural consciousness when they consume food and eating-related discourses, a cultural consciousness that, on the one hand, encourages them to binge on versions of femininity that promote consumption, and on the other, asks them to purge themselves of their perceived flaws and gustatory sinfulness. Mirroring the individual psychopathology of bulimia nervosa, I argue here that popular food and eating-related discourses reinforce a confusing culture of both excess and restraint among women that inevitably drives a body-policing narrative.

IDENTIFYING A BULIMIC CULTURAL CONSCIOUSNESS

In this book, contemporary best-selling diet books, cookbooks and iconic feminist texts are shown to perpetuate messages of body anxiety directed towards women. While each genre presents a seemingly distinct set of food femininities for women to choose from and aspire to, all three genres promote messages painting women's relationships with food from a self-conscious, body-policing perspective. One of the ways they achieve this is through the lens of individualism and, indeed, by promoting an anxious set of femininities for women to aspire to in a culture that values notions of choice, agency and empowerment (Popa 2012). Perhaps unsurprisingly, all three genres are interconnected through their perpetuation of messages that combined notions of excess and restraint. I refer to their contradictory messages about food and eating as restrained hedonism, or, as Popa (2012) briefly suggests, as evidence of a "bulimic" (p. 162) cultural attitude towards women's food consumption. While both Popa (2012) and Bordo (2004) have previously referenced the notion of a bulimic cultural consciousness of food and eating, I expand on their references and examine more thoroughly the way the gendered food discourses perpetuate a cultural food consciousness based on bingeing and purging. The diet books, cookbooks and iconic feminist texts analysed all contribute to this pathogenic cultural consciousness, encouraging women to consume food (and desire) through the pathological lens of restraint and body surveillance.

The binge–purge cycle of popular food discourses is centred on the conflict between consumption and self-discipline (Brown et al. 2008). Some of the diet books, cookbooks and iconic feminist texts that I analysed contain mixed narratives of hedonism and restraint. In their best-selling diet books *Skinny Bitch* (2005) and *Skinny Bitch in the Kitch* (2007), for example, fashion executive Rory Freedman and former model and nutritionist Kim Barnouin rely on a post-feminist version of food femininity, which is bolstered by a narrative of celebration and fun, and simultaneously coupled with a punitive and sarcastic counter-narrative that encourages women to restrict their food intake. In the introductory paragraph of *Skinny Bitch in the Kitch* (2007), Freedman and Barnouin exaggerate their love of food and create what is initially perceived as a conducive environment for women to explore their gustatory pleasures. Their repeated, emphatic references to loving food (e.g., "We're total pigs and eating is, without a doubt, our favourite thing to do. We love eating so much it makes us mad. We have almost a violent passion for food"; 2007, p. 11), coupled with their reinforcement of a post-feminist caricature of ideal femininity characterised by thongs and *Charlie's Angels*, centre their narrative on food and eating strictly in terms of consumption. Indeed, the authors even go so far as to label women who do not enjoy food as being somehow strange, arguing that food is better than sex. Through their exaggerated love of food and their reinforcement of consumerist values, however, they also pose a strong counter-narrative that shames women for their ingestion of certain types of food. In Chap. 4, I identify that the authors use non-human referents to shame their female audience into consuming foods that they consider to be unethical or unhealthy, branding women fat, pigs, cows and pussies for succumbing to their so-called unacceptable food choices. This confusing message, of both hedonism and restraint, plays a consistent and dominant role in the diet books examined, where women are encouraged to binge on the message of consumerism, but purge due to a constant reminder that their bodies are abject and food choices are unethical.

Strong evidence of restrained hedonism, and a bulimic cultural consciousness, is also found in the contemporary cookbooks examined. Nigella's *Feast* (2006) and Poh's *Poh's Kitchen: My Cooking Adventures* are two texts that contained particularly strong narratives of consumption and guilt, demonstrating a cultural binge–purge cycle that constructs women's relationships with food as an almost expected, and normative, struggle between desire and restraint. In *Feast* (2006), for example, Nigella asserts her gustatory hedonism by using academic sources to reinforce the importance of feasting, positioning herself among the "joyful French" (2006, p. 263) and emphasising her appreciation of food and eating through sensuality and seduction (Magee 2007). With less sexualised overtones, in *Poh's Kitchen: My Cooking Adventures* (2010), Poh argues that enjoying food and being occasionally sinful prevent her from wallowing in excess, focusing paradoxically on both consumption and restraint. While these texts appear to reinforce an almost hedonistic encouragement of food in women, however, what lies implicitly in these narratives is the notion of restraint, which is primarily expressed through the medium of control. Both Nigella and Poh fall prey to, and implicitly perpetuate, this bulimic cultural narrative of consumption by encouraging a hedonistic enjoyment of food and, simultaneously, a fear of its potentially destructive potential to the weight and shape of their bodies.

Even in discourses that politicise and problematise mainstream narratives of food and eating, such as the iconic feminist texts that purport to challenge these narratives, there is still an overarching conflict between the notions of restraint versus consumption. Despite their deconstruction and politicisation of disordered eating behaviours, and their encouragement of women to adopt a counter-cultural feminist sense of entitlement over food, the iconic feminist writers analysed in this book also reveal underlying messages that encourage women to control the weight, shape and the general appearance of their bodies. In *Fat is a Feminist Issue* (2006), for example, feminist psychotherapist Susie Orbach devotes much of her attention to the political origins of why women binge, constructing what she argues to be excess body fat as a maladaptive symbol of emotional protection. Instead of focusing on the cultural perceptions that surround the 'fat' female body, and how these perceptions tie into consumerist culture and its unhealthy reinforcement of food femininities, Orbach centres attention to how this 'fat' protective body should be controlled and made healthy, a task that is presented as an individualistic, self-help achievement. Without explicitly wanting to, Orbach (2006) proffers a narrative of both consumption and restraint, giving women the impression that their desires and actions are valued and, at the same time, unintentionally pathologising them for the appearance of their bodies. This "lipoliterate" or weight-oriented depiction of the female body is one dominant way that the iconic feminist texts studied in this book propagate a bulimic cultural consciousness among women.

Another way that the bulimic cultural consciousness permeates iconic feminist texts is through the individualistic lens of liberal-feminist ideologies. In Naomi Wolf's *The Beauty Myth* (1990), the notion of dieting is initially problematised and positioned in reference to women's cultural subordination. Wolf (1990) presents a somewhat radical argument when she asserts that dieting behaviours are a contemporary method of stifling women's social, occupational and political involvement, a reinvigorated version of the feminine mystique, and calls for women to be critical of dieting practices and organisations. However, through the introduction of a liberal-feminist perspective, Wolf (1990) also positions other body-policing practices, such as the use of cosmetics, as potentially empowering experiences for women. On the one hand, her radical critique of dieting encourages women to embrace food and eating, and yet, on the other, her calls for a feminist third wave that takes pleasure in the surveillance and modification of the body depoliticises—and defangs—her initial message.

When combined, all three genres produce a confusing set of narratives for women to relate to, encouraging them to simultaneously consume (food, versions of femininity) and purge (restrict food, rejecting certain messages about food and femininity). Indeed, many seem to repackage body-policing narratives as ways to manifest this bulimic lifestyle. Some feminist writers, such as Bordo (1997), Malson (2009) and Popa (2012), make mention of the restrained hedonism found in popular cultural discourses as symptoms of a pathogenic or bulimic culture; however, they do not elaborate by tying certain discourses to the promotion of a disordered cultural consciousness. One factor that they do promote, however, is that women's individual psychopathologies in relation to food and their bodies are reflective of the culture from which they reside, and not a part of their intrapsychic conflicts, an argument that resonates throughout this book. Writers on food and feminism have attempted to understand the cultural anxiety surrounding women's relationships with food and their bodies, and emphasised consumerist culture and ethics as being a key part of this destructive culture of bingeing and purging (Bordo 2004; Jackson 2010; Popa 2012).

In her article linking consumer culture with the development of eating disorders, feminist writer Teodora Popa (2012) cites eminent sociologist Gilles Lipovetsky and his work on feasting in both ancient and contemporary Western cultures. She argues that, based on Lipovetsky's sociological observations, ancient Dionysian expressions of culinary hedonism involved a sense of "abundance ... [and] collective[ly] celebrating the passage from one season to the other" (p. 163). In stark contrast, when Lipovetsky analysed the current trends in culinary hedonism, he discovered a loss of "self-control" and "a time of guilt and pathology" (p. 163). Attempting to explain why contemporary depictions of culinary hedonism ultimately rely on narratives of guilt and restraint, Popa (2012) argues that the rise in consumer culture has strengthened women's already flourishing anxieties about food and their bodies. She states that:

> Rich contemporary societies have reached a point of endemic excessiveness, of "addiction to growth" and of "anesthetising" consumerism, because of a corollary of factors: ... the increasing feeling of insecurity and control, the development of a hyper-individualism, the unreachable standards of beauty and the abundance of options of the consumer (p. 163).

In this chapter, the application of Popa's (2012) concept of a bulimic food culture, thus, emphasises the notion of consumerism, especially in reference to consuming gender, as a harmful and confusing cultural narrative. In the context of this book, Popa's research positions the body-policing messages found in popular food discourses in terms of consumerist and patriarchal ideologies that increase women's reliance on their individual choices. Indeed, this notion of 'hyper-individualism' is also one that has been explored further by food theorist Peter Jackson (2010). In his article entitled 'Food Stories: Consumption in the Age of Anxiety,

Jackson (2010) identifies a similar cultural pattern of events that leads to people's conflicted relationships with food. Specifically, he argues that the intensification of consumer culture has given people an abundance of food options to choose from, which has led to an increase in individual responsibility and paranoia about making the 'right' food options and decisions. Jackson (2010) explains that even if the individuals themselves are not personally affected by this anxiety, the food culture surrounding the individual is permeated with this anxious consciousness in an unavoidable, yet all-encompassing, way. He explains that:

> In examining anxieties about food, we need to attend to ... the nature of anxiety as a social condition ... Anxiety might then be defined as a social field that can be occupied by many different social actors, including those who are caught up in discourses of anxiety even if they are not themselves anxious (p. 154).

Indeed, when taking Jackson's (2010) perspective on the social nature of food anxiety into account, it can be argued that the food discourses that I have analysed represent an important part of that anxiety, namely, that many food discourses both promise to ease, and (sometimes inadvertently) exacerbate, women's anxieties around food and eating. Supporting Jackson's (2010) perspective, I argue that gender plays a key operative role in mediating this consumer anxiety, strengthening the bulimic cultural consciousness that encourages women to consume and purge themselves of their consumption at the same time. As explained more thoroughly in Chap. 3, when analysing gendered discourses from a feminist perspective, it is imperative to acknowledge the harmful role patriarchy plays in normalising and instantiating harmful messages. As Rundstrom-Williams (2012) explains, "through examining language and uncovering a discourse, one can also identify an ideology" (p. 10). I argue that the ideology operating behind this bulimic cultural consciousness is a patriarchal one.

THE ROLE OF PATRIARCHY IN THE BULIMIC CULTURAL CONSCIOUSNESS

Patriarchy plays a key role in sustaining gender norms that instantiate and normalise body-policing attitudes among women. According to Lazar (2004), "patriarchy as an ideological system ... interacts in complex ways with ... corporations and consumerist ideologies" (pp. 141–142). As such, patriarchy and consumerist ideologies can be seen as interconnected driving forces behind gendered discourses on food and eating. Feminist writers have been instrumental in identifying patriarchy as the governing force behind the bulimic culture of consumption and restraint (Bordo 1997, 2004; Popa 2012), with Popa (2012) explaining that it plays a dominant role in providing women with seemingly distinct and multiple choices. In her chapter for *Food and* Culture, feminist writer Susan Bordo (1997) identifies cultural discourses as psychopathological, rather than focusing on the individual. Like Popa (2012) and Jackson (2010), Bordo (1997, 2004) attributes the pathogenic or bulimic cultural consciousness to a rise in consumerist culture and an endless array of food choices, but adds the role of patriarchy in her analysis by focusing specifically on the way gender is constructed for women. Speaking in reference to the comparison between psychopathology and culture, Bordo (1997) states:

> Psychopathologies that develop within a culture, far from being anomalies or aberrations [are] … characteristic expressions of that culture; … indeed, [they are] the crystallisation of much of what is wrong with it (p. 229).

Bordo (1997) explains that the notion of "crystallisation" (p. 229) refers to the pernicious role of patriarchal messages that construct women's relationships with food and their bodies in terms of lack and dysfunction. She argues that patriarchal social structures play a seminal role in reinforcing gender norms that position women as active, yet implicitly vulnerable, consumers, as characters that "consume endlessly, to capitulate to temptation, and desire" (Brown et al. 2008, p. 93) and, simultaneously, restrict and control these urges. In her article 'We Feed off the other: Master Bulimic Narrative as Cultural Materialisation,' Julie Ann Scott (2013) also argues that patriarchy works in tandem with consumerism (and capitalism) to sustain a bulimic cultural consciousness. Comparing the individual presentation of bulimia with the cultural reinforcement of its symptoms, she explains that:

> Through acknowledging the bulimic's struggle as the visceral materialisation of a shared cultural conundrum we are able to not only empathise … but also better understand the binge and purge cycle we collectively share with her (p. 26).

While demonstrating that the individual woman is influenced by the collective cultural consciousness that surrounds her, Scott (2013) also alludes to the importance of how food femininities, and femininities more generally, are constructed in contemporary Western culture. One point that she argues eloquently is that the patriarchal construction of a bulimic culture, involving both consumption and restraint, sets women up to relate to a profoundly unfeminine version of food femininity. Speaking in reference to the individual woman, Scott (2013) states that:

> The secret performance of bingeing on excessive amounts of food and then purging food from the body is a grotesque display of out of control ... "unfeminine femininity" is central to the spectacle of this familiar mental illness of culture (p. 30).

To Scott (2013), the bulimic narrative of femininity, one that reinforces "capitalist indulgence" simultaneously with a sense of "puritan[ical] self-restraint" (p. 24), sets up a gendered food discourse that leaves women feeling as if they are constantly in a state of capitulating to feminine ideals rather than achieving them. In other words, the food discourses themselves construct a gendered narrative that encourages women to consume certain food femininities that will, ultimately, leave them feeling grotesque and unfeminine.

Understanding why contemporary food discourses mirror these bulimic narratives involves an examination of how femininities are reinforced and why body-policing attitudes are used to reinforce them. That is, identification of patriarchy as a key reinforcer of a bulimic cultural consciousness around food and the body makes it important to question why it *needs* body-policing narratives to inform women's relationships with food and eating. I argue that there are two dominant reasons behind the patriarchal construction of body-policing narratives in discourses on food and eating. Firstly, encouraging women to police their bodies increases their aesthetic palatability and reconfigures body surveillance as a normative and even empowering practice of self-management. Secondly, to be aesthetically palatable, one must consume gender and its attendant limitations, and be made to feel like this consumption was freely chosen and was even an empowering or subversive experience.

AESTHETIC PALATABILITY

Part of being female and socialised to comply to the aesthetic demands of femininity, involves appealing to, and internalising, the heterosexual male gaze. According to some feminist theorists, to conform to the male gaze, the female body must be in a constant state of improvement, and subject to a range of cosmetic, dietary and beauty procedures that colonise virtually every part of the body (Dworkin 1974). Feminist writers have long associated women's body-policing practices as evidence of their subordinated social status and endemic victimisation. In her radical feminist text *Beauty and Misogyny* (2005), Jeffreys argues that under a patriarchal system the female body becomes a "thing" designed to sexually titillate and be used for decorative purposes. As a result, women learn to "thingify" themselves to cope with the ongoing demands of patriarchal culture (Jeffreys 2005, p. 8). Tending to one's aesthetic palatability is, thus, intimately related to seeing one's body as a site of anxiety and constant surveillance (Bartky 1990; Bordo 2004). The body-policing messages embedded in popular food discourses are, thus, part of the patriarchal social structure that encourages women to monitor (and enjoy the monitoring) their bodies through the consumption and preparation of food.

From some feminist perspectives, when women strive to become aesthetically palatable, in a traditional feminist sense, they become victims of the male gaze (Bartky 1990). Both the radical and post-structuralist feminist literature frame the objectification and scrutiny of the female body as a sign of oppression, governed by a male-supremacist (Dworkin 1974; Jeffreys 2005) or patriarchal social structure (Bartky 1990; Bordo 2004). When internalised, women are said to take on a panoptic surveillance over their bodies, scrutinising the way they look in an effort to conform to pre-existent social norms, a behaviour that has been linked to a number of psychological disorders, including disorders of food and eating (Kroon and Perez 2013; Harper and Tiggemann 2008; Monro and Huon 2006; Morry and Staska 2001). Wolf (1990) argues that the surveillance women impose over their bodies, governed by an oppressive patriarchal consciousness, stifles their social, cultural and political potency. Specifically, in *The Beauty Myth* she explains that:

> A cultural fixation on female thinness is not an obsession about female beauty but an obsession about female obedience (p. 187).

In many ways, this body of feminist literature argues that body-policing practices are designed by patriarchy to keep women fixated on their bodies and away from broader social, cultural and political issues. Despite feminist criticisms pointing to the social harms of body-surveillance attitudes, however, this book identifies that the presence of body-policing attitudes is not only normalised but also considered an accepted part of contemporary Western women's lives. In the food discourses analysed in this book, for example, body-policing attitudes were sometimes seen as a positive addition to women's lives. They were re-signified to be feminist and empowering (e.g., diet books), normalised by being cast in a humorous light (e.g., cookbooks), considered part of the treatment process of disordered eating (e.g., Orbach 2006) and implicated to the disavowal of patriarchal culture (e.g., Wolf 1990). Body-policing attitudes are, thus, only problematised when they are not motivated by the woman's own choices. The implications for encouraging women to choose to objectify themselves are potentially harmful and far-reaching.

In the diet books analysed, Freedman and Barnouin (2005, 2007) and Bridges (2010, 2011) rely on what appears to be an empowering subversion of objectification, or what Rosalind Gill (2007) refers to as the post-feminist shift towards sexual subjectification. In *Skinny Bitch* (2005) and *Skinny Bitch in the Kitch* (2007), for example, Freedman and Barnouin draw a distinction between body-policing practices that are driven by self-loathing and body-policing practices that are driven by empowerment, beautification and sexuality. In their initial description of the skinny bitch lifestyle, the authors ask their readers if they are "sick and tired" of the "self-loathing" (p. 10) that accompanies living in a 'fat' body, and, as a perceived solution, offer women a post-feminist caricature of femininity that "empower[s] [them] to become a skinny bitch" (p. 10). Presenting women with a hyper-sexualised, thong-wearing, Charlie's Angeles stereotype of femininity is, thus, considered a welcome alternative. As such, Freedman and Barnouin do not eliminate the necessity of body policing but, rather, repackage it to become more palatable in a contemporary cultural setting.

Similarly, in *Losing the Last Five Kilos* (2011), celebrity fitness trainer Michelle Bridges implicitly delineates between self-objectification and self-subjectification when she asks her readers to replace their immature relationships with their bodies (i.e., worrying about one's body without actively changing one's lifestyle), with the controlled and empowered one that she touts in the *Losing the Last Five Kilos* diet. Reinforcing a liberal-individualist food femininity, Bridges draws comparisons between negative body-consciousness and positive body-consciousness, arguing that a loss of control over one's body and eating behaviour leads to a loss of control in other areas of life. In an interview with Danielle Teutsch (2012) for the *Sydney Morning Herald*, Bridges even refers to her own growth and maturity in terms of body consciousness when she describes herself transforming from a self-conscious young girl to the confident, body-monitoring woman that she is today. By encouraging women to closely monitor their food intake and body weight, Bridges reconceptualises body-policing narratives as sources of female empowerment and well-being (Dubriwny 2012).

What is evident in both Freedman and Barnouin's (2005) and Bridges' (2011) texts are that body-policing practices have become re-signified or given a culturally acceptable makeover, rather than being abolished entirely. As Gill (2003) explains in her article on post-feminist objectification narratives, the shift from sexual objectification to subjectification in contemporary Western discourses is part of an ongoing effort to legitimise keeping surveillance over women's bodies. Gill (2003) argues that shifting one's thinking from objectification to subjectification practices requires a shift "from an external male gaze to a self-policing narcissistic gaze" (Gill 2003, p. 104). While the messages themselves are no different from previous accounts of objectification, such as those discussed in Bartky's (1990) and Dworkin's (1974) feminist texts, women are encouraged in dietary discourses to enjoy the objectification of their bodies.

Similarly, cookbooks written by female food celebrities also include the normalisation and even glamourisation of body-policing narratives. Rather than positioning body-surveillance practices as empowering additions to women's lives, as is the dominant theme in the diet books analysed, most of the female food celebrities I analysed in this book justify their self-surveillance practices through a tongue-in-cheek attempt at humour. In *Tana Ramsay's Real Family Food* (2009) and *Tana's Kitchen Secrets* (2010), for example, Tana repeatedly alludes to her "naughty" desire for certain foods, using infantilised, cheeky tones to express her hedonistic appreciation for food (Littler 2013). When she is shown not infantilising her desire to eat, she is described running a "half-marathon" in order to earn the pleasure. Tana's hedonistic relationship with food is, thus, predicated upon a playful sense of guilt in relation to pleasure, a guilt that translates to her relationship with her body. Throughout *Poh's Kitchen: My Cooking Adventures* (2010), Poh too uses similar infantilised and judgemental terms when she calls her indulgence in certain food as 'sinful' and "naughty" (p. 20). In doing so, she brings attention back to the body in an implicit way, jokingly expressing the tensions involved in enjoying food as a woman. Indeed, this casual, tongue-in-cheek approach to communicating is not new. In her article on popular discourses and advice-giving, Winch (2011) identifies that contemporary conduct books aimed at women contain a humorous, tongue-in-cheek element that trivialises important, and often harmful, concerns that women face. In this book, the body-policing attitudes expressed in cookbooks appear to give women permission to feel anxious about their bodies, but also to accept body-policing attitudes as a standard part of their lives, thereby normalising it.

Even in the iconic feminist texts, which aim to subvert dominant cultural narratives about women and oppression, such as Orbach's *Fat is a Feminist Issue* (2006) and Wolf's *The Beauty Myth* (1990), body-policing narratives are reinforced through the authors' depoliticisation of the solutions they offered women. Without explicitly reinforcing the aesthetic palatability of their female readers, the authors implicitly construct a narrative of body anxiety when they rely on the individual woman, and her body, to change. Despite playing a part in both of the texts analysed, body-policing narratives are expressed quite differently. In *Fat is a Feminist Issue* (2006), for example, feminist psychotherapist Susie Orbach constructs a rich, feminist narrative that initially politicises women's problematic relationships with food and their bodies, associating body-policing narratives with patriarchal oppression and surveillance over women's bodies. However, through her feminist self-help position, she offers a solution to women's pathological relationships with food that involves modifying their bodies (i.e., questioning why they inhabit a 'fat' body) to match their mental health. Throughout *Fat is a Feminist Issue* (2006), she inadvertently pathologises the 'fat' female body when she alludes to women's recovery from disordered eating. Wolf (1990), too, initially perceives body-policing narratives as being problematic, calling the idealised Western beauty dictates found in magazines and diet books as contributing to women's psychological experiences of being trapped in the contemporary armour of the Iron Maiden. She removes the sting of her feminist critique, however, when she encourages women to take pleasure in beauty practices, arguing that, if these practices are not influenced by patriarchy, they can be empowering facets of women's lives. Although expressed differently, both feminist sources rely on an implicit narrative of body consciousness, with Orbach (2006) pathologising the 'fat' female body (and therefore, implicitly reinforcing a narrative of body-surveillance), and Wolf (1990) critically rejecting some beauty practices (e.g., dieting) while, confusingly, valorising others that are associated with body-monitoring attitudes and practices (e.g., the use of cosmetics).

Given that all three food and eating-related genres analysed yield a range of body-policing attitudes, from being empowering, humorous and a facet of one's well-being, it can be said that these narratives are being used in a way that appeals to women and masks their oppressive connotations. The aesthetic palatability of women is, thus, intimately tied to women's choice to be empowered and is no longer considered as explicitly harmful as previous feminist research would suggest (e.g., Bartky 1990; Dworkin 1974; Jeffreys 2005; MacKinnon 1989). Indeed, the general shift from objectification to subjectification attitudes suggests that a cultural shift has occurred that presents body-policing attitudes as empowering and agentic; it has become even more complicated to identify women's oppression precisely because it is masked as "no big deal" and tied so intimately to their identification with food.

A Smorgasbord of Food Femininities

Another reason why patriarchy *needs* the existence of body-policing narratives is to reinforce femininity in all its oppressive, contemporary guises (Popa 2012). Femininity, while touted as a potentially liberating source of identity for women in these texts, is viewed in this book as an oppressive factor, perpetuating women's dissatisfaction with, and surveillance over, their bodies through the medium of food (and eating). In *Carnal Appetites: Food/Sex/Identities* (2000), Elspeth Probyn discusses the importance of food as an arbiter of cultural messages, arguing that the mere act of eating conveys a number of factors related to race, class, gender and sexuality. Rather than merely viewing food as an object that works in conjunction with culture to construct meaning, Probyn (2008) argues that it is useful to perceive "food as a way of eating into gender" (p. 123). When popular food discourses convey gender, they do so by encouraging women to consume certain versions of gender through the medium of food.

The veritable smorgasbord of choices presented to women in food discourses indicates that food is used as a way of eating into certain versions of gender and, indeed, into femininities, encouraging women to view their bodies as being in a perpetual state of monitoring and improvement. According to Popa (2012), the multiple femininities that manifest in contemporary Western culture reflect the consumerist emphasis on choice and personal responsibility that are responsible for women's anxious relationships with food and their bodies. Rather than celebrating women's seemingly endless array of choices, however, Popa (2012) indicates that it is useful to understand how these perceived choices construct women's pathological relationships with food.

Indeed, throughout the food discourses I focused on in this book, eating is presented as a way of consuming both an entitled and inherently guilt-ridden version of femininity. In diet books, women are encouraged to adopt an entitled attitude to food and eating through a self-subjectifying, empowering food femininity, and yet, at the same time, implicitly encouraged to stringently monitor their food intake. The popular cookbooks analysed follow a similar trajectory. While women are encouraged to consume a maternal food femininity that subverts traditional, other-oriented stereotypes, they are also constructed as guilt-ridden, and ashamed when taking pleasure from food themselves. Even in iconic feminist texts, the entitlement to consume is politicised but ultimately dependent upon the need to control one's body shape and weight, cast as a way of empowering women into good health (e.g., Orbach 2006) and self-expression (e.g., Wolf 1990). Indeed, the notion that women are active, agentic subjects, eating themselves into multiple and often 'empowered' femininities is a problematic one. However, it is also one that aims to entice women through a range of what may initially appear to be resistant food femininities.

Resistant Food Femininities

Popular discourses on food and eating take place within a structure that reinforces the surveillance of women's bodies through a thin veneer of empowerment, the consumption of multiple femininities and a bulimic relationship to food and eating. However, despite knowing that food discourses reinforce harmful messages about women's relationships with food and their bodies, this does not explain why the messages and versions of food femininity available to women in these texts are so popular. It can be argued that the reason why these texts are so fashionable, and palatable, is due to some resistant message they espouse, offering women versions of gender that on the surface may seem culturally subversive. It can be seen that women consume diet books, cookbooks and ionic feminist texts, and their attendant food femininities, in a way that suggests they are subversive, and as if they have something new and perhaps forbidden to offer them. The supposedly subversive femininities promoted in popular food discourses are referred to in this chapter as resistant femininities, hybrid femininities (Rundstrom-Williams 2012) and power femininities

(Lazar 2004). All three terms relate to some aspect of resistance that is reinforced in through women's gendered relationships with food.

To provide some context into how diet books, cookbooks and iconic feminist texts maintain their popularity and reinforce harmful body-policing narratives, an understanding of the narratives of resistance (or ways to relate to food that subvert 'traditional' feminine stereotypes) they offer women is essential. In her book *Empowered Femininity: The Textual Construction of Femininity in Women's Magazines*, Rundstrom-Williams (2012) explains that, "sometimes language can cue more than one ideology, which leads to competing and potentially contradictory discourses or identities" (p. 9). Specifically, she outlines two types of femininities that intersect to create a hybrid version, namely, through a combination of the traditional and the resistant. Versions of femininity that are promoted in diet books, cookbooks and iconic feminist texts pose a resistance to traditional food femininities that are associated with oppression and women's subordination. As such, they appear, on one level, to be subversive.

According to Rundstrom-Williams (2012, p. 12), traditional femininity refers to the "stereotypical characteristics or traits of women which frame them as communal but less powerful," which is typically characterised by "being understanding, compassionate, affectionate, kind, helpful, warm, tactful, sensitive to others' feelings, sociable, concerned with equity, and able to devote oneself to others." Although traditional femininity is, arguably, the most normative type of femininity, it continues to inform contemporary women's relationships with food and their bodies. From a food-related perspective, traditional femininities are gendered ways of being that rely on an other-oriented, caretaking and selfless representation of women's relationships with food and eating (Greer 1999; Neuhaus 1999). As such, traditional food femininities in a contemporary cultural context are often viewed with derision, influenced by the critiques generated during the second-wave feminist movement (e.g., Friedan 1963; Oakley 1976).

At the opposite end of the spectrum, infiltrating many of the food discourses examined in this book, is the 'resistant' version of food femininity. Resistant femininity, according to Rundstrom-Williams (2012), is a way of rebelling against traditional and often oppressive conceptions of how to be female. The "strong, assertive, hierarchical, and agentive" (p. 17) characteristics of 'resistant femininity,' which are often expressed through the use of "direct language, curs[ing] [and] interrupt[ing]" (p. 201), demonstrate what Coates (1999) refers to as backstage talk, a type of communication that transcends traditional feminine norms and branches into modes of communication that mirror gossip, cursing and so on. In backstage talk, "women flout stereotypes such as being nice, being a good wife and mother, and being concerned with appearance" (p. 18). According to Coates (1999), "backstage interaction fulfils a vital need in women's lives to talk about behaving badly, whether this means recounting incidents where we behaved badly, or whether it means fantasizing about such behaviour, or whether it means discussing and celebrating the unconventional behaviour of other women" (p. 77). As such, women are said to relish in stereotypes of resistant femininity, a theme that is strongly reflected in the versions of food femininity conveyed by authors of popular food discourses.

The multiple versions of food femininity conveyed in popular food discourses seem to offer the reader an opportunity to engage somewhat rebelliously in backstage talk regarding food and gender. At the same time, however, they also implicitly rely on traditional depictions of food femininity, which involve body consciousness and restrictive eating to convey their message. In the diet books I analysed, for example, Freedman and Barnouin (2005, 2007) and Bridges (2010, 2011) promote gendered relationships with food that, on the surface, appear to challenge the oppressive stereotypes that are typically designated to dieting women (e.g., Bartky 1990; Bordo 2004; Orbach 2006; Wolf 1990). In *Skinny Bitch* (2005), for example, Freedman and Barnouin repeatedly make reference to the vegan, skinny bitch lifestyle in a way that emphasises its agentic, strength-inducing qualities, rather than women's vulnerability. They use coarse language to relate to their readers (e.g., "don't be a pussy") and present a tongue-in-cheek expression of dieting that encourages women to empower themselves through adopting a vegan lifestyle, a typical feature of post-feminist conduct books (Winch 2011). The Hollywood appeal of the *Skinny Bitch* diet is testament to its resistant, yet deeply traditional, take on food and gender, one that both adheres to and resists dominant representations of femininity.

Similarly, in *Losing the Last Five Kilos* (2011), Bridges, too, relies on a narrative of tough love and coarse language to offer women a resistant expression of food femininity. Her much-emphasised phrase, "just fucking do it!" emblazoned on her caps and T-shirts, emphasises the extent to which she adheres to casual, girl power notions of female empowerment. Rather than associating dieting from an oppressive, culturally subordinated perspective, Bridges relies on confession and consistency to empower women into achieving healthier (and lighter) bodies. While the traditional (and harmful) preoccupation with monitoring the female body remains ever-present in both the *Skinny Bitch* series and in Bridges' texts, the food femininities offered to women resonate with themes of resistance.

Cookbooks, too, contain narratives that blend both traditional and resistant food femininities to appeal to their largely female audiences. Nigella's *Feast* (2006) and Poh's *Poh's Kitchen: My Kitchen Adventures* (2010) contain mixed narratives of both traditionalism and resistance in their maternal and hedonistic versions of food femininity. Throughout *Feast* (2006), Nigella plays on her trademark hedonistic persona by emphasising the importance of her own culinary desires. Deconstructing the much maligned caricature of the happy housewife found in second-wave feminist texts (e.g., Friedan 1963; Oakley 1976), she outwardly expresses the drudgery involved in feeding her children (e.g., calling her children "instinctive ingrates," p. 240) and casts her own desires for food and eating at the forefront of *Feast* in a playful and somewhat sensual way (e.g., "its melting squidginess tends to fall darkly to my white sheets," p. 272). Similarly, Poh also resists traditional aspects of culinary femininity when she disengages from the domestic kitchen and is shown associating with professional and internationally renowned chefs. Although she references her maternal influences as significant, she nevertheless resists these narratives by reinforcing her own desire for the taste and pleasures of food and eating. As Magee (2007) explains, such writers construct their relationships with food as rebellious in an effort to encourage women (and men) to voyeuristically gaze into their lives and, perhaps, adopt elements of it at the same time.

Rather expectedly, iconic feminist texts are resistant mostly in their promotion of a feminist standpoint. Orbach's seminal text *Fat is a Feminist Issue* (2006) and Wolf's groundbreaking book *The Beauty Myth* (1990) both resist dominant (and traditional) representations of women's disordered relationships with food and their bodies. Through a politicisation of women's disordered symptoms (including body dissatisfaction, body-policing attitudes and disordered eating behaviour), the authors demonstrate and promote what seems to be a resistant narrative for women to conform to. According to Bordo (2004), the novelty of Orbach's work is a testament to her resistance towards patriarchal constructs of food and eating for women. Indeed, Orbach constructs a deeply politicised version of food femininity by drawing links between patriarchal oppression and women's fluctuating body weight and shape and disordered relationships with food. Likewise, Wolf (1990), too, provides women with what appears to be an emancipatory feminist discourse that favours feminist analysis above patriarchal dictates of beauty, but criticises and politicises those associated with dieting. She attempts to merge feminist debate with contemporary notions of ideal femininity, an effort that has been contentious to some feminist writers (e.g., Jeffreys 2005), but, nevertheless, offers women a sense of resistance to these harmful gender norms.

While traditional stereotypes associated with selflessness, motherhood and sexuality were resisted, curiously, harmful stereotypes associated with body-policing attitudes were not. One notable exception, and perhaps the most traditional representation of food femininity in my analysis, is Julie and the maternal and hedonistic food femininities she expresses in her cookbook *The Heart of the Home* (2011). While Julie constructs her relationship with food in terms of a traditional (and traditionally subordinated) maternal version of food femininity, colonised by the male gaze of her husband and sons, the scrutiny and surveillance over her body were not present in her cookbook. In fact, Julie subverts the stereotypes depicted in Nigella's food narratives by relying on a traditional, other-oriented relationship with feeding, but with an unashamedly hedonistic relationship with food itself. The notion that the same discourse (e.g., cookbooks) can generate multiple and often conflicting cultural narratives is not unusual. As Rundstrom-Williams (2012) explains, certain genres can offer women multiple femininities, sometimes seemingly with the same text. Although the messages conflict, they contribute to an overarching or global discourse on food and eating. This was evident in all of the texts I analysed, where the female authors both complied to and subverted these traditional caricatures of femininity.

Before celebrating the resistant food femininities uncovered in popular food discourses, however, it is important to recognise that discourses are implicitly couched within an oppressive patriarchal system that glamourises gender differences and, subsequently, women's subordination. Indeed, the resistant food femininities depicted in diet books, cookbooks and iconic feminist texts can only resist so much of the patriarchal structure of society that surrounds them before they succumb to harmful gender messages, such as normalising women's surveillance over their bodies. As Rundstrom-Williams (2012) explains in reference to resistant femininities, "the femininities available to women are not limitless; there are constraints and parameters to the identities women can enact in order to be seen as feminine" (p. 11). As such, it is important to acknowledge the ways in which they subordinate women through these messages of resistance.

In her article 'Pro-Anorexia and Binge Drinking: Conformity to Damaging Ideals or New, Resistant Femininities?,' Day (2009) asserts that resistant femininities pertaining to food and eating often mirror features of hegemonic masculinity and, thus, cannot be held entirely as subversive counter-narratives. Studying the gendered subjectivities available in 'pro-ana' and 'pro-mia' online communities, where women share their experiences of eating disorders and tips on how to continue them, Day (2009) found that narratives of resistance were not dissimilar to the patriarchal constraints on women that feminist writers discuss.[1] Indeed, Day (2009) states that:

> It is sometimes tempting to celebrate such resistance as a signalling of women's power, as this avoids falling back on problematic, determinist accounts of women as passively inscribed by oppressive discourses. However, notions of resistance … must be treated with caution … [While] women do demonstrate agency in terms of how competing discourses and the identities that these constitute are taken up, negotiated, and resisted, the options available are not limitless and a rejection of traditional notions of femininity can sometimes entail a fall back on traditional masculine values instead (p. 246).

As Day (2009) explains, femininities that appear to be outwardly resistant are not always subversive. Indeed, as I show in this chapter, the resistant voices found in diet books, cookbooks and iconic feminist texts resist one part of women's subordination, but often reinforce another. Understanding the way these discourses instantiate and normalise body-policing attitudes and, indeed, how patriarchal social structures gain power through women's body-policing practices, is of central importance. Despite showing elements of 'resistance,' the food femininities conveyed in these texts still reinforce a harmful cultural narrative that perpetuates a bulimic cultural consciousness among women, which simultaneously encourages indulgence and restraint.

Ultimately, all three food and eating-related genres produced a range of femininities that reflect a form of bulimic cultural consciousness. Driven by both patriarchal and consumerist ideologies, it has been shown that readers are discursively encouraged to binge on consumerist ethics and versions of femininity, and purge themselves of their guilt by monitoring and policing their bodies. The importance of body-policing narratives to the patriarchal social structure was also discussed, and was shown to be related to women's continued subordinated social status. By encouraging women to remain aesthetically palatable to the male gaze, the responsibility has shifted to the individual woman in attaining this feminine ideal. Additionally, the food femininities identified, despite their resistant undertones, revealed confusing messages that cast women as both traditionally body conscious and yet resistant against traditionalism. It is important to scrutinise the why and how of popular discourses to generate an emancipatory social discourse, or, as Lazar (2004) explains, for feminist researchers to be "critically reflexive of [their] own theoretical positions and practices lest these inadvertently contribute to the perpetuation, rather than the elimination, of hierarchical differential and exclusionary treatment of women" (p. 153). Indeed, the analysis presented in this chapter aimed to raise awareness on how food is used against women and how it is, in so many facets of life, inextricably connected to their dissatisfaction with and surveillance over their bodies. By identifying this pathogenic or 'bulimic' cultural consciousness, it is hoped that others may create a radical counter-narrative in its place.

NOTE

1. Pro-ana, or 'pro-anorexia', and pro-mia, or pro-bulimia, refer to online communities where women share tips and tricks regarding how to continue their disordered eating behaviours (Day 2009).

REFERENCES

Bartky, S. L. (1990). *Femininity and domination: Studies in the phenomenology of oppression.* New York: Routledge/Taylor & Francis Group.

Bordo, S. (1997). Anorexia nervosa: Psychopathology as the crystallisation of culture. In C. Counihan & P. Van Esterik (Eds.), *Food and culture.* New York: Routledge.

Bordo, S. (2004). *Unbearable weight: Feminism, Western culture, and the body.* Berkeley: University of California Press.

Bridges, M. (2010). *Crunch time cookbook: 100 knockout recipes for rapid weight loss.* Camberwell: Penguin Books.

Bridges, M. (2011). *Losing the last 5 kilos: Your kick-arse guide to looking and feeling fantastic.* Camberwell: Penguin Books.

Brown, C. G., Weber, S., & Ali, S. (2008). Women's body talk: A feminist narrative approach. *Journal of Systemic Therapies, 27*(2), 92–104.

Coates, J. (1999). Women behaving badly: Female speakers backstage. *Journal of Sociolinguistics, 3*(1), 65–80.

Day, C. (2009). Does my bum look big in this? Reconsidering anorexia nervosa within the culture context of 20th century Australia. *Surveillance and Society*, *6*(2), n.p.

Dubriwny, T. N. (2012). *The vulnerable empowered woman: Feminism, postfeminism, and women's health*. Piscataway: Rutgers University Press.

Dworkin, A. (1974). *Woman hating: A radical look at sexuality*. New York: E. P. Dutton.

Fredrickson, B. L., & Roberts, T.-A. (1997). Objectification theory. *Psychology of Women Quarterly*, *21*(2), 173–207.

Freedman, R., & Barnouin, K. (2005). *Skinny bitch: A no-nonsense, tough-love guide for savvy girls who want to stop eating crap and start looking fabulous!* Philadelphia: Running Press.

Freedman, R., & Barnouin, K. (2007). *Skinny bitch in the kitch: Kick-ass recipes for hungry girls who want to stop cooking crap (and start looking hot!)*. Philadelphia: Running Press.

Friedan, B. (1963). *The feminine mystique*. Harmondsworth, Middlesex: Penguin Books.

Gill, R. (2003). From sexual objectification to sexual subjectification: The resexualisation of women's bodies in the media. *Feminist Media Studies*, *3*(1), 100–106.

Gill, R. (2007). Postfeminist media culture: Elements of a sensibility. *European Journal of Cultural Studies*, *10*(2), 147–166.

Goodwin, J. (2011). *The heart of the home*. North Sydney: Random House.

Greer, G. (1999). *The whole woman*. London: Doubleday.

Grogan, S. (2008). *Body image: Understanding body dissatisfaction in men, women, and children*. New York: Routledge.

Harper, B., & Tiggemann, M. (2008). The effect of thin ideal media images on women's self-objectification, mood, and body image. *Sex Roles*, *58*, 649–657.

Jackson, P. (2010). Food stories: Consumption in an age of anxiety. *Cultural Geographies*, *17*(2), 147–165.

Jeffreys, S. (2005). *Beauty and misogyny: Harmful cultural practices in the west*. East Sussex: Routledge.

Kroon, V. D. A. M., & Perez, M. (2013). Exploring the integration of thin-ideal internalisation and self-objectification in the prevention of eating disorders. *Body Image*, *10*(1), 16–25.

Lawson, N. (2006). *Feast: Food that celebrates life*. London: Chatto & Windus.

Lazar, M. (2004). *Feminist critical discourse analysis: Gender, power and ideology in discourse*. New York: Palgrave Macmillan.

Ling-Yeow, P. (2010). *Poh's kitchen: My cooking adventures*. Pymble: Harper Collins Publishers.

Littler, J. (2013). The rise of the 'yummy mummy': Popular conservatism and the neoliberal maternal in contemporary British culture. *Communication, Culture and Critique*, *6*(2), 227–243.

MacKinnon, C. (1989). *Towards a feminist theory of the state*. Cambridge, MA: Harvard University Press.

Magee, R. M. (2007). Food puritanism and food pornography: The gourmet semiotics of Martha and Nigella. *Americana, 5*(2), n.p.

Malson, H. (2009). Appearing to disappear: Postmodern femininities and self-starved subjectivities. In H. Malson & M. Burns (Eds.), *Critical feminist approaches to eating dis/orders*. London: Routledge/Taylor and Francis Group.

Monro, F. J., & Huon, G. F. (2006). Media-portrayed idealised images, self-objectification, and eating behaviour. *Eating Behaviours, 7*, 375–383.

Morry, M. M., & Staska, S. L. (2001). Magazine exposure: Internalisation, self-objectification, eating attitudes, and body satisfaction in male and female university students. *Canadian Journal of Behavioural Science, 33*(4), 269–279.

Neuhaus, J. (1999). The way to a man's heart: Gender roles, domestic ideology, and cookbooks in the 1950s. *Journal of Social History, 32*(3), 529–555.

Oakley, A. (1976). *Housewife*. Harmondsworth, Middlesex: Penguin.

Orbach, S. (2006). *Fat is a feminist issue*. London: Arrow Books.

Popa, T. (2012). Eating disorders in a hyper-consumerist and post-feminist context. *Scientific Journal of Humanistic Studies, 4*(7), 162–166.

Probyn, E. (2000). *Carnal appetites: FoodSexIdentities*. London: Routledge.

Probyn, E. (2008). IV. Silences behind the mantra: Critiquing feminist fat. *Feminism and Psychology, 18*(3), 401–404.

Ramsay, T. (2009). *Tana Ramsay's real family food*. London: Harper Collins Publishers.

Ramsay, T. (2010). *Tana's kitchen secrets*. Great Britain: Mitchell Beazley.

Rodin, J., Silberstein, L., & Striegel-Moore, R. (1984). Women and weight: A normative discontent. *Nebraska Symposium on Motivation, 32*, 267–307.

Rundstrom-Williams, T. (2012). *Empowered femininity: The textual construction of femininity in women's fitness magazines*. Newcastle upon Tyne: Cambridge Scholars Pub.

Scott, J. A. (2013). We feed off the other: Master bulimic narrative as cultural materialisation. *American Communication Journal, 15*(3), 24–39.

Teutsch, D. (2012). *The naked truth*. Retrieved from: http://www.smh.com.au/lifestyle/the-naked-truth-20120807-23rz5.html

Winch, A. (2011). 'Your new smart-mouthed girlfriends': Postfeminist conduct books. *Journal of Gender Studies, 20*(4), 359–370.

Wolf, N. (1990). *The beauty myth: How images of beauty are used against women*. London: Vintage.

CHAPTER 8

Hold the Femininities: Ordering a Radical Feminist Food Consciousness

In this book, I set out to illustrate how gendered discourses on food and eating instantiate and normalise harmful body-policing narratives aimed at women. Specifically, I focused on the expression of food femininities, or the gendered ways that women are socialised to relate to food, in best-selling diet books, popular cookbooks and iconic feminist texts, and how these versions of femininity all rely on an underlying or implicit narrative of body consciousness. In contrast to the existing academic tradition, I focused my attention on discourses pertaining to food and eating, rather than on fashion and beauty discourses, to show how food, and the act of eating itself, are significant cultural objects and practices in their own right (Probyn 2000). Rather than focusing on symptoms that manifest within the individual woman, I acknowledged that narratives promoting body policing are part of a pathogenic culture that in certain circumstances praises women's consumption of food but, simultaneously, encourages them to purge themselves of it through various body-monitoring practices. The paradoxical reinforcement of both consumption (i.e., through hedonism) and restraint (i.e., through body-policing attitudes) in the food discourses studied was labelled as a pathogenic or 'bulimic' cultural consciousness, perpetuating a cultural discourse that encourages women to feel anxious about food and their bodies.

In making the argument that food discourses contain gender narratives that promote body-policing practices in women, it was necessary to reconsider the body-centric and individualistic perspectives currently

© The Author(s) 2017

N. Jovanovski, *Digesting Femininities*,

DOI 10.1007/978-3-319-58925-1_8

dominating the feminist and psychological literature (see Chap. 2). The body-centric perspective in feminism and psychology, attributing body-policing attitudes and behaviours to the pernicious impact of fashion and beauty discourses, has become a popular way of understanding women's body image and disordered eating patterns over the last four decades (Calogero et al. 2005; Grabe et al. 2008; Harper and Tiggemann 2008; Kroon and Perez 2013). Much of the writing on fashion and beauty discourses has implicated images of skinny models to women's body dissatisfaction, self-surveillance and disordered eating behaviour, arguing that a diversification of body shapes in the media will prompt a positive change in women's eating behaviour and sense of self (see Chap. 2). While these initiatives have been somewhat successful through their mainstream exposure in advertising and the media, such as *Dove's* Campaign for Real Beauty, their longitudinal success has been less clear (Murray 2013; Tiggemann et al. 2013). Indeed, some have even argued that drawing further attention to women's bodies may have a paradoxical, and indeed harmful, effect of women's health and well-being (Papies and Nicolaije 2012). To counteract the body-centrism currently pervading feminist discourses, I set out to understand the importance of food in constructions of women's body consciousness.

Turning attention to food discourses was a vital step in this feminist research project. Rather than focusing on how the female body is depicted in the media, and how symptoms of eating disorders manifest in the individual, in this book, the main prerogative was on a diagnosis of food and eating-related discourses and their perpetuation of body-policing narratives. As discussed at length in Chap. 3, the need to focus attention on diet books, cookbooks and iconic feminist texts was important as it cast these seemingly innocuous discourses as resonant and potentially harmful gender narratives. The so-called diagnosis of food culture, through an examination of diet books, cookbooks and iconic feminist texts, was, thus, identified as being of primary importance, where the focus was on critically analysing the cultural discourses surrounding food and eating, rather than on the individual woman.

An analysis of best-selling diet books, known traditionally for their harmful body-policing narratives (e.g., Spitzack 1987), uncovered both post-feminist and liberal-individualist versions of food femininity that reinforced self-surveillance and body surveillance as facets of female empowerment rather than oppression. Freedman and Barnouin's diet books *Skinny Bitch* (2005) and *Skinny Bitch in the Kitch* (2008) generated a post-feminist position that reinforced body-policing attitudes through their repeated aspirational focus on being skinny. Rather than constructing a diet that outwardly restricts women from enjoying food, the authors depicted the skinny bitch lifestyle in a relatively glamourous way, reconfiguring attitudes and behaviours that have typically been designated to women's subordination and oppression (i.e., such as self-objectification) into self-empowering, self-subjectifying narratives. Their promotion of a vegan diet, where the ethical treatment of animals overrides the dangers of objectifying women, was further evidence that women's perceptions of their bodies were sacrificed for the greater good of others (in this case, animals). In a similar sense, celebrity fitness trainer Michelle Bridges' diet books *Losing the Last Five Kilos* (2011) and *Crunch Time Cookbook* (2010) promoted a liberal-individualist position, where individualistic narratives of self-empowerment through the catchphrase "just fucking do it" encouraged women to confess their dietary sins and maintain a panoptic surveillance over their bodies and their eating habits. Rather than reflecting elements of subordination and oppression, Bridges was shown using her liberal-individualist version of food femininity to emphasise women's empowerment as individuals, transforming the insecurities typically associated with policing one's body into facets of strength, agency and technologies of the self. An analysis of the diet genre, thus, uncovered body-policing narratives associated with food and eating that were reinforced to women through the lens of empowerment and self-subjectification.

An examination of contemporary cookbooks also found that body-policing narratives were part of women's culinary relationships with food and that feeling conscious of one's body (and body weight) was part of the norm in these discourses. Four female food celebrities were examined for the gendered messages they conveyed (e.g., Tana, Nigella, Julie and Poh), with all four sources demonstrating some element of the maternal and hedonistic in their food narratives. The maternal food femininity was colonised by the male gaze and, in some instances, resisted. Both Tana and Julie presented more traditional versions of food femininity that relied on other-oriented, care-driven relationships with food. Nigella and Poh, however, demonstrated elements of resistance by framing their maternal depictions with food in terms of responsibility and professionalism. Nigella, for example, outwardly and unashamedly emphasised the drudgery involved in cooking for her children, while Poh branched out of the domestic kitchen and interacted with professional chefs. However, it was only when hedonism was expressed that resistance to gender norms surrounding food preparation was depicted, and 'traditional' narratives were lost. While all four food celebrities expressed their love of food, and the enjoyment they receive from eating, Tana, Nigella and Poh's narratives all revealed an underlying body-policing message. All three writers masked their body-policing attitudes in a tongue-in-cheek attempt at humour, laughing off their anxious relationships with food to being "naughty" and "sinful." The evidence sourced from cookbooks indicated that, despite their resistance of traditional, other-oriented stereotypes of food femininity, body-policing attitudes were part of a normative culture of women's relationships with food. Like diet books, cookbooks also contributed to reinforcing a culture of body consciousness in women.

In contrast to the largely commercialised angle of best-selling diet books and popular cookbooks, it was interesting to find that even iconic feminist texts, which are known for their political potency and subversive cultural status, also reinforced gendered positions that focused extensively on the responsibilities of individual women rather than subverting cultural messages about food and the body in a political way. In implicit and unintentional ways, both Susie Orbach and Naomi Wolf conveyed versions of food femininity that focused strongly on individual responsibility and agency. Despite both writers providing a strong political rationale behind women's 'disordered' relationships with food and their bodies, they ultimately reinforced an individualistic gender narrative that placed primary responsibility in the hands of women. Orbach outwardly politicised women's struggles with food and eating in *Fat is a Feminist Issue*, linking their disordered eating patterns to the patriarchal subordination of women in general. Specifically, her framing of the 'fat' female body as an inherently disordered body reinforced her feminist-psychotherapeutic position. However, in doing so, Orbach (2006) implicitly constructed a gendered narrative that made women feel even more aware of their bodies and eating behaviour, a phenomenon that has been associated with an increase in eating disorder symptoms among women (Diest and Perez 2013; Harper and Tiggemann 2008; Monro and Huon 2006; Morry and Staska 2001). In a distinct yet similar sense, Wolf's much publicised book *The Beauty Myth* (1991) was shown to rely on narratives of individualism, which ultimately cast women as free agents to choose traditionally oppressive beautification practices that have been associated with body-policing attitudes (Dworkin 1974; Jeffreys 2005). Like Orbach (2006), Wolf (1990) explicitly outlines the patriarchal confines surrounding women's relationships with food, and calls for the Iron Maiden caricature of contemporary Western femininity to be challenged. Her liberal feminist version of food femininity, however, minimised the significance of her political critique of patriarchy by suggesting that women can 'choose' beauty practices—other than dieting—without the influence of patriarchy. Indeed, it can be seen that the evidence taken from iconic feminist texts demonstrated that body-policing attitudes are a deeply ingrained, normative part of women's relationships with food and eating, even when the discourse is subversive.

The underlying narrative of both consumption and restraint (i.e., through body-policing attitudes) found in the food and eating-related discourses analysed was referred to in this book as pathogenic (Malson 2009) or constituting a bulimic cultural consciousness (Bordo 2004; Popa 2012). All three genres contributed to instantiating and normalising body-policing attitudes through a (seemingly) wide range of food femininities. These food femininities, although variable and—on the surface— distinct, reflected similarities that indicated they were part of a broader narrative of food and gender; indeed, that they were identified as a part of a patriarchal social structure that relies on body consciousness to perpetuate gender hierarchies. Upon 'diagnosing' popular food and eating-related discourses as bulimic through critical analysis, it was crucial to establish why patriarchal social structures need body-policing attitudes and multiple food femininities to maintain power imbalances between the sexes. Building upon some of the previous feminist literature on the topic, it was found that body-policing narratives oppress women through a thin veneer of self-empowerment. Indeed, it was argued that in contemporary diet books, cookbooks and iconic feminist texts, body-policing attitudes were transformed into empowering, subversive and supposedly feminist subjectivities that masked the dangers and political reinforcement of body consciousness. The multiplicity of food femininities was also part of this oppressive patriarchal social structure. Rather than perceiving the food femininities on offer as providing women with a smorgasbord of choices, it was argued in this book that they reinforced a system of restrained consumption. Even when the food femininities appeared to resist, or subvert, traditionally oppressive food femininities, they were still couched within the strict confines of gender. The answer, then, was not to invent counter-femininities, but to question gender every time it appears, and to offer women something new.

RADICALISING OUR TASTE BUDS: IMAGINING A GENDERLESS FOOD CULTURE

As I have shown so far, a variety of cultural messages about food and eating work to (re)produce gender narratives that frame women's relationships with their bodies in terms of surveillance and control, a notion that is reinforced through women's consumption of gendered messages about food and eating. These food femininities conflictingly promote both notions of consumption and restraint. In this book, I referred to this phenomenon as a pathogenic or bulimic cultural consciousness (Bordo 1997; Malson 2009; Popa 2012). Upon discovering the link between food discourses and body-policing narratives, I, like many other feminist researchers before me, was left questioning whether women could truly be emancipated from the gendered, pathogenic food consciousness of contemporary Western culture. I began wondering if, indeed, it was practical and conceivable to promote a food discourse aimed at women that was not gendered and, subsequently, contained body-policing sentiments. I wondered if radicalising the taste buds was even possible in a cultural backdrop that gendered virtually everything in its reach.

I recognised that imagining a discourse on food and eating that appealed to women *without* the inclusion (and intrusion) of gender was a difficult task, but also the logical next step. As Elspeth Probyn (2000) argues in *Carnal Appetites: Food/Sex/Identities*, food is an arbiter of many cultural messages, among which are themes of gender, race and class. Indeed, as I have demonstrated throughout the book, gender is consumed through food and is reinforced throughout popular discourses in the form of normative, yet harmful, messages of body consciousness. I began asking myself if it was possible for women to consume cultural messages about eating that focused on a more subversive, genderless consciousness, one that encouraged a feminist cultural consciousness rather than a conflicting, self-policing and patriarchal one. I wondered if there was a way to transform the cultural messages surrounding food and eating, where women were encouraged to consume a visceral, embodied, empowering and nourishing message about food, without the bitter aftertaste of gender and its rigid proscriptions of what being a woman should mean. Specifically, I wondered if popular food discourses could ever be utilised in a way that simply promoted genderless and politically engaging messages.

Like myself, other feminists, in a more general sense, have wished to challenge (e.g., Bartky 1990; Bordo 2004; Orbach 2006; Wolf 1990), and even eliminate (e.g., Dworkin 1974; Jeffreys 2005; MacKinnon 1989), the harmful effects of gender on women's lives. Over the last four decades, psychological and feminist writers in particular have tried to imagine a world where women related to food and their bodies without consuming the pathological dictates of contemporary Western culture (e.g., Bordo 2005; Orbach 2006, 2010; Wolf 1990). As I discussed more comprehensively in Chap. 6, iconic feminist writers Susie Orbach and Naomi Wolf were among the first to outwardly politicise eating and body-policing attitudes by associating them with women's subordinated cultural status under patriarchy (Bordo 2004). Their influence on contemporary Western culture and, indeed, in psychological interventions pertaining to women's disordered relationships with food and their bodies is acknowledged as iconic by other feminist writers such as Bordo (2004). While raising awareness through therapy has been a positive inclusion to the highly individualistic, clinical focus of traditional psychological scholarship, a major limitation of the feminist approach is that it does not focus enough on changing the broader sociocultural and political antecedents of women's body-policing attitudes. What results from these interventions is an individualisation of the solution when the problem is becoming increasingly more culturally embedded. As Lazar (2004) explains in her article on Feminist Critical Discourse Analysis, while feminists and scholars are relying increasingly on liberal reformist ideological positions to enact change, a radical and emancipatory social perspective is needed instead. This became a challenge in the present book.

Given that eating disorders continue to rise despite the introduction of feminist perspectives in psychology, and that food and eating-related entertainment continue to dominate the media and appeal to Western audiences, it seems that now is the time to challenge harmful gendered narratives about food and eating and whether they are, indeed, necessary in popular discourses aimed at women. As I have shown throughout the book, the culture surrounding women's relationships with food and their bodies is a pathogenic one, so any solutions aimed at changing this pathogenic cultural consciousness must revolve around changing and challenging culture rather than the individual. Loosely based on Elspeth Probyn's (2000) assertion that identities are consumed through our interactions with food, and that we eat ourselves into social existence, one potential answer to the current problem is to create a subversive, collective and radical feminist consciousness around food and eating. In other words, the answer may lie in encouraging women to consume a subversive feminist consciousness that politicises solutions rather than individualises them. Taking examples from early second-wave feminist sources may be useful. One example is the Boston Women's Health Book Collective and their first edition of *Our Bodies Ourselves* (1973), where women were actively encouraged to relate to food and exercise that emphasise strengthening their bodies and improving their well-being, rather than focusing on their appearance and the stereotypes associated with their eating behaviour. At the same time, the discourses embedded in *Our Bodies Ourselves* encouraged collective action and consciousness-raising, which fundamentally challenged women's dependence on traditional expertise. The development and reinforcement of a feminist food consciousness, a process of radicalising our taste buds, would be in stark contrast to the neoliberal food femininities that have been problematised in this book.

Creating a radical feminist food consciousness for a contemporary and increasingly liberal feminist Western culture would not be without its difficulties. Indeed, fostering and producing a mainstream discourse on food and eating that encourages women to consume a subversive feminist consciousness does not conform to contemporary notions of ideal femininity and narratives of empowerment. The reinforcement of a genderless consciousness may be seen as a utopian, if not archaic, vision of feminist emancipation (Lazar 2004). As Rundstrom Williams (2012) explains, reinforcing a subversive feminist consciousness in a contemporary Western context has its risks:

> Women must be careful to not appear too capable; showing vulnerability keeps women aligned as peers and friends... while women's exposure to feminist discourses leads them to try to resist dominant patriarchal discourses, not caring about appearance and being strong too closely approaches masculinity and may lead the women to feel they are not feminine if they enact them (p. 16).

Applied to the context of food and eating, the reinforcement of a feminist food consciousness might, thus, be seen as a reinforcement of social exclusion and ostracism. Indeed, this appears to have happened in some of the popular discourses analysed in this book. When feminist sentiments are expressed, they are emphasised in the context of women's sexualisation (e.g., Bridges 2011; Freedman and Barnouin 2005, 2007; Lawson 2006) or their individual responsibility to eat and remain aesthetically palatable (Orbach 2006; Wolf 1990). Women's relationships with food, thus, risked being co-opted by patriarchal social structures if they become mainstream. The dismantling of structural, consumerist and patriarchal systems of food and eating is not an easy task. Indeed, it will take a change of consciousness and the strengthening of grass-roots political movements focused on the importance of food and eating.

My intention for this book is to prompt the beginning of a radical, genderless food consciousness. Rather than relying on subversive or resistant food femininities to emancipate women from harmful body-policing norms, I am identifying the need for a change in cultural consciousness, from one based on gender and patriarchal proscriptions of what being a woman means, to one imparting a feminist consciousness (i.e., a political discussion on food and eating, without individualised solutions). As Lazar (2004) and Lehtonen (2007) explain, feminist research is more than just theory; it is also about practice. Rather than simply remaining at a theoretical level, the evidence found in feminist research should be used to foster an emancipatory cultural discourse, aiming to free women from gender oppression (Lazar 2004). By identifying gender as a problem, and locating it in a multitude of seemingly conflicting narratives and guises, I have shown that the need for a feminist consciousness, and a politicisation of gendering food and eating, is needed more than ever before. After all, the goal of feminist research is to foster "radical social change" through "analytical activism" (Lazar 2004, p. 160). The findings in this book are merely one step in achieving this goal. By identifying the need for a feminist consciousness in discourses on food and eating, we have half the ingredients that we need to create radical social change.

REFERENCES

Bartky, S. L. (1990). *Femininity and domination: Studies in the phenomenology of oppression*. New York: Routledge/Taylor & Francis Group.

Bordo, S. (1997). Anorexia nervosa: Psychopathology as the crystallisation of culture. In C. Counihan & P. Van Esterik (Eds.), *Food and culture*. New York: Routledge.

Bordo, S. (2004). *Unbearable weight: Feminism, Western culture, and the body*. Berkeley: University of California Press.

Boston Women's Health Book Collective. (1973). *Our bodies, ourselves: A book by and for women*. New York: Simon and Schuster.

Bridges, M. (2010). *Crunch time cookbook: 100 knockout recipes for rapid weight loss*. Hawthorn: Penguin Books.

Bridges, M. (2011). *Losing the last 5 kilos: Your kick-arse guide to looking and feeling fantastic.* Melbourne: Penguin Books.

Calogero, R. M., Davis, W. N., & Thompson, J. K. (2005). The role of self-objectification in the experience of women with eating disorders. *Sex Roles,* *52*(1–2), 43–50.

Dworkin, A. (1974). *Woman hating: A radical look at sexuality.* New York: E. P. Dutton.

Freedman, R., & Barnouin, K. (2005). *Skinny bitch: A no-nonsense, tough-love guide for savvy girls who want to stop eating crap and start looking fabulous!* Philadelphia: Running Press.

Freedman, R., & Barnouin, K. (2007). *Skinny bitch in the kitch: Kick-ass recipes for hungry girls who want to stop cooking crap (and start looking hot!).* Philadelphia: Running Press.

Grabe, S., Ward, L. M., & Hyde, J. S. (2008). The role of the media in body image concerns among women: A meta-analysis of experimental and correlational studies. *Psychological Bulletin, 134*(3), 460–476.

Harper, B., & Tiggemann, M. (2008). The effect of thin ideal media images on women's self-objectification, mood, and body image. *Sex Roles, 58,* 649–657.

Jeffreys, S. (2005). *Beauty and misogyny: Harmful cultural practices in the west.* East Sussex: Routledge.

Kroon, V. D. A. M., & Perez, M. (2013). Exploring the integration of thin-ideal internalisation and self-objectification in the prevention of eating disorders. *Body Image, 10*(1), 16–25.

Lawson, N. (2006). *Feast: Food that celebrates life.* London: Chatto & Windus.

Lazar, M. (2004). *Feminist critical discourse analysis: Gender, power and ideology in discourse.* New York: Palgrave Macmillan.

Lehtonen, S. (2007). Feminist critical discourse analysis and children's fantasy fiction – modelling a new approach. In *Past, present, future – from Women's studies to post-gender research.* Umea. Retrieved from http://semiotics.nured.uowm.gr/pdfs/FEMINIST_CRITICAL_DISCOURSE_ANALYSIS_LEHTONEN.pdf

MacKinnon, C. A. (1989). *Toward a feminist theory of the state.* Cambridge, MA: Harvard University Press.

Malson, H. (2009). Appearing to disappear: Postmodern femininities and self-starved subjectivities. In H. Malson & M. Burns (Eds.), *Critical feminist approaches to eating dis/orders.* London: Routledge/Taylor and Francis Group.

Monro, F. J., & Huon, G. F. (2006). Media-portrayed idealised images, self-objectification, and eating behaviour. *Eating Behaviours, 7,* 375–383.

Morry, M. M., & Staska, S. L. (2001). Magazine exposure: Internalisation, self-objectification, eating attitudes, and body satisfaction in male and female university students. *Canadian Journal of Behavioural Science, 33*(4), 269–279.

Murray, D. P. (2013). Branding real social change in Dove's campaign for real beauty. *Feminist Media Studies, 13*(1), 83–101.

Orbach, S. (2006). *Fat is a feminist issue.* London: Arrow Books.

Orbach, S. (2010). *Bodies.* London: Profile Books.

Papies, E. K., & Nicolaije, K. A. H. (2012). Inspiration or deflation? Feeling similar or dissimilar to slim and plus-size models affects self-evaluation of restrained eaters. *Body Image, 9*(1), 76–85.

Popa, T. (2012). Eating disorders in a hyper-consumerist and post-feminist context. *Scientific Journal of Humanistic Studies, 4*(7), 162–166.

Probyn, E. (2000). *Carnal appetites: FoodSexIdentities.* London: Routledge.

Rundstrom-Williams, T. (2012). *Empowered femininity: The textual construction of femininity in women's fitness magazines.* Newcastle upon Tyne: Cambridge Scholars Pub.

Spitzack, C. (1987). Confession and signification: The systematic inscription of body consciousness. *Journal of Medicine and Philosophy, 12*(4), 357–369.

Tiggemann, M., Slater, A., Bury, B., Hawkins, K., & Firth, B. (2013). Disclaimer labels on fashion magazine advertisements: Effects of social comparison and body dissatisfaction. *Body Image, 10*(1), 45–53.

Wolf, N. (1990). *The beauty myth: How images of beauty are used against women.* London: Vintage.

Index[1]

[1] Note: Page numbers followed by "n" refers to notes.

© The Author(s) 2017
N. Jovanovski, *Digesting Femininities*,
DOI 10.1007/978-3-319-58925-1

Printed in Great Britain
by Amazon